Deans and Truants

Deans and Truants

Race and Realism in African American Literature

GENE ANDREW JARRETT

PENN

University of Pennsylvania Press

Philadelphia

10   9   8   7   6   5   4   3   2   1

Published by
University of Pennsylvania Press
Philadelphia, Pennsylvania 19104–4112

Library of Congress Cataloging-in-Publication Data
Jarrett, Gene Andrew, 1975–
    Deans and truants : race and realism in African American literature / Gene Andrew Jarrett.
        p. cm.
    Includes bibliographical references and index.
    ISBN-13: 978-0-8122-3973-7 (acid-free paper)
    ISBN-10: 0-8122-3973-3 (acid-free paper)
    1. American literature—African American authors—History and criticism.   2. African Americans—Intellectual life.   3. African Americans in literature.   4. African American aesthetics.   5. Race in literature.   6. Realism in literature.   I. Title.
PS153.N5J395   2006
81.9'352996073—dc22

                                                                    2006044662

For the joys of my life,
Renée and Nyla,
and in memory of an excellent scholar,
Claudia Tate (1946–2002)

Contents

The Problem of African American Literature

What is African American literature? People tend to call literary texts "African American" or "black" whenever they feature African American main characters alongside certain historical themes, cultural geographies, political discourses, or perspectives defined by race. Black literary texts are deemed "authentic" when their authors identify themselves or are identified by others as black. This definition has determined the way authors think about and write African American literature; the way publishers classify and distribute it; the way bookstores order and sell it; the way libraries catalogue and shelve it; the way readers locate and retrieve it; the way teachers, scholars, and anthologists use it; the way students learn from it—in short, the way we know it.

The implication that African American literature must be written by and about blacks neglects the history of blacks interested in reading and writing literature not "about themselves."[1] Thinkers ranging from Nobel Laureates to scholars have addressed this issue and suggested that African American literature is a problem: It requires intellectual debate on how literary portrayals or representations of the race have factored not only into the creative decisions and goals of black authors but also into the expectations and experiences of readers.[2]

Ever since the late nineteenth century, the problem of African American literature divided the American literati into two groups that are in extreme ideological disagreement. The first group, de facto deans of literary movements, wielded enough authority to dictate the critical and commercial conditions for African American literature. William Howells in the 1890s, Alain Locke in the 1920s, Richard Wright in the 1930s and 1940s, and Amiri Baraka in the 1960s and 1970s arbitrated public expectations that black authors should write authentic literature demonstrating *racial realism*, which supposedly portrayed the black race in accurate or truthful ways. Howells's minstrel realism, Locke's New Negro modernism, Wright's New Negro radicalism, and Baraka's so-called Black Aesthetic shackled the creative decisions and objectives of many black authors to "the chain of reality," as Walter Mosley once put it.[3]

Such demands for racial realism perpetuated the discrepancy between what the public expected of African American literature and what black authors intended to write or actually wrote. Frustrated by this discrepancy, certain black authors tried to break the chains of reality by writing *anomalous* fiction that resisted and sometimes critiqued the conventional restriction of authentic African American literature to racial realism. By featuring main characters who were racially white, neutral, or ambiguous and by employing genres that disrupted the mutual dependence of racial and realist ideologies, this literature undermined the principles and principals of African American literary schools. Playing truant from these schools, Paul Laurence Dunbar adopted literary naturalism, George S. Schuyler wrote science fiction, Frank Yerby embraced historical romance, and Toni Morrison incorporated postmodernism to unsettle the models of racial realism sanctioned or deemed acceptable by Howells, Locke, Wright, and Baraka.

In examining the differences between traditional and anomalous paradigms of African American literature, I am not calling for the end of African American literature as a category and institution, as problematic as it may have been and continues to be. Nor am I necessarily arguing for the inclusion of anomalous texts in the canon, or the greatest works, of African American literature, though this book could possibly begin that process. Nor am I proposing, therefore, yet another subjective set of aesthetic and racial-political standards in the name of African American canon reformation or literary-tradition rebuilding. Rather, I hope to explain why, at certain discrete but interconnected moments in history, people tended to judge a book by its author's skin. I plan to show how such judgments hinged on presumptions about race and realism. Last, I intend to illuminate the long-standing consequences of classifying, interpreting, politicizing, and assessing the aesthetic value of African American literature based on these presumptions.

Judging a Book by Its Author's Skin

What does it mean, really, to judge a book by its author's skin? Is doing so as problematic—and shallow—as judging a book by its cover? Ward Connerly thinks so. In "Where 'Separate but Equal' Still Rules," the chairman of the American Civil Rights Institute complains that books he and other black authors have written are being "racially profiled":

The shelving of their books in a special section [called "African American Interest"] deprives black authors or "race" authors of significant sales opportunities, putting them at a competitive disadvantage compared with authors whose books are not ghettoized. But the economic harm pales in contrast to the intellectual and cultural damage caused by the bookstores' version of racial profiling. They have fallen into the trap of thinking that a writer's skin color is a reliable guide to judging the contents of his or her books.[4]

By quoting Connerly at length I do not intend to endorse his related legal and political mission to enforce color-blind policies in American education and other social and cultural institutions. Nor does my reference to him at the outset of this book mean that I associate or agree with his political views, which reject the racial classifications and race-based value judgments central to affirmative action. Rather, his critique of bookstores provides a succinct and practical example of the problem with presuming human and cultural identification.

By the end of this book, it should become clear, and ironic, that we can talk about something that Connerly and Toni Morrison—the latter one of the most celebrated authors of African American literature and one of the best spokespersons for the distinctiveness of black culture—have in common: the desire for a cultural world in which race no longer matters. But it should also become clear that their common desire diverges in two political directions. Whereas Morrison would agree with Connerly's indictment of racial profiling in bookstores, she would pardon such profiling as part of their historical, political, and sophisticated obligation to preserve and appreciate black culture. By contrast, Connerly has implied, more irascibly, that the profiling is nothing more than a modern-day, superficial demonstration of liberal political correctness.

Though closer to Morrison than to Connerly on this point, I must honestly concede, as many scholars probably would, that the mode of identification of which Connerly speaks is indeed a significant problem. The tendency of bookstores to catalogue and shelve a book according to an author's skin—among other biological traits supposedly constitutive of racial identity—has frustrated countless black authors, past and present. These authors have dealt with a cultural market of publishers, editors, and general readers who, on the sole basis of the paratexts, presume what their texts will say or mean or who dictate what the texts should say or mean. By "paratext," I am referring to Gérard Genette's notion that certain exterior illustrative and linguistic codes "enable . . . a text to become a book and to be offered as such to its readers and, more generally, to the public."[5] Discrepancies can form between a book's taxonomic label in a bookstore or library and the author's own identification of the book and its locus of associations, including his or her identity. Such are the pitfalls of American culture's preoccupation with the authenticity of African American literature.

A 1996 debate between Katya Gibel Azoulay and Kwame Anthony Appiah allows a more sophisticated discussion of the above taxonomic discrepancy. Azoulay examines the subtext of Appiah's *In My Father's House* (1993), in which Appiah "dismisses the validity and viability of any notion of communities of meaning that are based on race—this he views as merely biologizing ideology." Azoulay believes that Appiah fails to account adequately for the problems of identification, including the maintenance of racism and hierarchies of power: "[T]o institute an identity is to assign a social essence (whether a title or a stigma), to impose a name and to impose a right to be as well as an obligation to be so. . . . There is thus a healthy tension between resisting the imposition of an imaginary identity (including race) and the linguistic limitations within which we can choose to rename ourselves."[6]

In response, Appiah acknowledges the perspicacity of Azoulay's critique and follows up with his own description of the "theoretical gap" in racial identification. "If we follow the badge of color," he writes, "we are thus tracing the history not only of a signifier, a label, but also a history of its effects." He goes on to say that, "[b]ecause the ascription of racial identities—the process of applying the label to people, including ourselves—is based on more than intentional identification," "there can be a gap between what a person ascriptively is and the racial identity they perform."[7]

The taxonomic gap of which Appiah speaks has major implications for readers and writers of African American literature. African American literature has undergone an evolving list of labeling in support of its taxonomic order. This list dates back to the turn of the eighteenth century and includes, without intending to be perfectly comprehensive and chronological, such terms as "Afric' literature," "Negro literature," "Aframerican literature," "colored literature," "black literature," "Afro-American literature," "AfricanAmerican literature," "African-American literature," and "African American literature." The last label, which is circulating today, indicates the terminological gravitation of the taxonomy from racial to ethnic emphasis. It captures the contemporary ethnic intersection of racialism—the doctrine of categorizing the human world according to races—and American nationalism. In general, the labels reflect specific historical contexts and ideological circumstances in the racial and nationalist classification of authors and their literary texts.

How should one define African American literature, then, while remaining mindful of the potential taxonomic gap and the dynamic nominalism that partially govern it? How does one do so without personally imposing a mythical one-drop rule on authors or their literary characters, meaning that a drop of African ancestral blood coursing through their bodies makes them black?

First of all, one must remain fully aware of the fluidity and contestability of racial identity. In the past, authors either embraced black identity or dealt with the public's thrusting it on them, and, in the latter case, they sometimes rejected it. Frank Yerby insisted during one interview: "Do not call me 'black.' That word bugs me. I have more Seminole than Negro blood in me anyway. But when have I ever been referred to as that 'American Indian author'?"[8] A more famous case of an author resisting identification with the black community is Jean Toomer. Against the wishes of publisher Horace Liveright, who advised Toomer to mention his "colored blood" in the publicity for *Cane* (1923), Toomer wrote a remarkable sentence encapsulating his racial complexity: "My racial composition and my position in the world are realities which I alone may determine."[9] The cases of Yerby, whom I discuss in Chapter 6, and Toomer force us to consider how authors interpret, comply with, or overcome the demands of the literary marketplace.

Unfortunately, the historical record of black authors interrogating the racial identities and literary expectations thrust on them has had little impact on past and present definitions of African American literature in terms of racial authenticity. Anthologies of African American literature, for example, belong to "the collective project, ongoing since the late sixties, of expanding the canon and curriculum of American literature, especially in response to the activism and scholarship of feminists and people of color."[10] Of course, the aim of these collections—to teach students about the ethnic diversity of American culture—is admirable and necessary. However, that goal presumes and promotes an "authentic" version of ethnic literature, in which literary representations of ethnicity must correlate with the ethnicity of their author(s). The cost of defying the essentialist paradigms of ethnic authenticity and realism, or the belief that these qualities are essential or required, is marginality or exclusion in the academic and cultural marketplaces.[11]

By indicting the categorization of African American literature in terms of authenticity and reality, I am not contradicting my personal and political desires to move black voices from the margin to the center of American literary studies. We have already witnessed the movement to institute African American studies as an independent program within multiethnic departments of American studies or to establish it as an independent department. Analogously, African American literary studies deserves to make a case for its own set of anthologies claiming independence from, yet acknowledging their special place within, the larger multiethnic tradition of American literature, or to make a case that it is a distinctive tradition for which American literature is not the sole default rubric. The anthologization of African American literature rightly affirms a collective resistance to co-optation or disenfranchisement by the hegemonic order of racism, particularly the belief in white supremacy that has, for over a century, rationalized the erasure of black authors from anthologies of American literature.

Nonetheless, a pattern of canonical exclusion correlates with scholarly and editorial motives that, over time, have reflected certain ideological tendencies. Anthologies, as I discuss elsewhere, are one of the most revealing markers of ideological turns in the history of literary scholarship.[12] The kinds of anthologies that appear at a particular historical moment are telling indicators of the kinds of intellectual and political activism that are seeking to redraw or reaffirm the imaginary boundaries—drawn by publishers, acquisition editors, scholarly editors, and so forth—of inclusion or exclusion. Determining who and what and why people are reading, these boundaries could correspond to a range of identifications: of ethnicity or race (as they pertain to minority authors); gender (as it pertains to women); sexuality (as it pertains to gays, lesbians, bisexuals, or transgendered persons); class (as it pertains to the proletariat); or ideology (as it pertains to communism).

The boundaries I am focusing on in this book appear within anthologies of African American literature, which not infrequently parallel boundaries within anthologies of American literature or Western literature. In these anthologies, certain black authors are excluded but not on the basis of their identity as a minority. After all, anthologies of African American literature often presume that their selected authors at the very least share the same identity. Instead, they are excluded on the basis of what their texts say and how they say it.

In recent memory, scholarly movements have worked to overcome the problems of this approach. Black feminist scholarship in the 1970s and 1980s, black queer studies in the 1990s, and scholarship on science fiction and postmodernism since the mid-1990s have diversified African American literary anthologies and, in the process, have argued for canon reformation or literary-tradition rebuilding. Now, authors and literary texts that in earlier generations would have been an afterthought influence the direction of African American literary studies. Both traditional and revisionist anthologies of African American literature, however, have kept in place something that continues to authenticate black-authored literature. By clinging to it, they have ignored the history of many black authors, some indeed canonical, who have tried to transcend or write beyond it. That thing is racial realism.

Racial Realism

My usage of "racial realism," unlike previous philosophical and legalistic uses of the term,[13] refers to the evolution of its twin doctrines, racialism and realism, over the nineteenth and twentieth centuries. The term derives from what could be called the intellectual field of "blackness studies." This field explores the historical assignation of racial essentialism and authenticity to black authorship and culture, challenges the notion of an African American literary tradition built according to racial iconography, pinpoints the ideological lines stratifying black communities, and builds new frameworks for theorizing black intellectualism and culture.[14] In this context, I shall probe the individual traits of realism and racialism that have permitted their aesthetic, political, and discursive cooperation in African American literary history.

By "realism," I mean not just what Raymond Williams calls "a pseudo-objective *version* of reality, a version that will be found to depend, finally, on a particular phase of history or on a particular set of relationships."[15] Realism also means a rearticulation of written discourse as representational, ideological, and pragmatic. Louis Montrose connects representation to ideology. "Representations of the world in written discourse," he writes, "participate in the construction of the world: they are engaged in shaping the modalities of social reality and in accommodating their writers, performers, readers, and audiences to multiple and shifting subject positions within the world that they themselves constitute and inhabit."[16] Conversely, ideology—those spoken and unspoken systems of narratives, values, beliefs, practices, and power relations peculiar to one or more social groups—determines how literary discourse "engages," "accommodates," and "shapes" the world through various formal and thematic strategies.

Amy Kaplan pushes the paradigm of the "discursive practice" of ideology to "explore the dynamic relationship between changing fictional and social forms in realistic representation." She goes on to say that, "[i]f realism is a fiction, we can root this fiction in its historical context to examine its ideological force."[17] This formulation, arriving in the late 1980s, could be called "new historicist," but that would be an oversimplification. Kaplan does not consult history merely to elucidate the formal properties of literary texts, once a putative goal of new historicism. Rather, she considers how American literary realism at the turn of the twentieth century was pragmatic, reproducing social reality as much as it allegedly reflected it.

Racial realism pertains to a long history in which authors have sought to re-create a lived or living world according to prevailing ideologies of race or racial difference. Intellectuals in the past seldom used the term to describe African American literature, though, as I note in Chapter 3, Alain Locke came closest in 1928, when he called "modernist" black authors "race-realists." Rather, they employed other words to measure the degree to which literary representations of the race gravitated toward public expectations of realism. The words included "real," "true," "authentic," "objective," "bona-fide," "genuine," "original," "creative," "curious," "novel," "spontaneous," and "vigorous."

Each of these words belongs to a discursive genealogy resembling what W. T. Lhamon Jr. calls a "lore cycle." Holding "current beliefs together in highly charged shorthand," Lhamon writes, lore expresses "a group's beliefs so that the group does not need to weigh and consider all [the] ramifications at any given moment." Lore also increases in "self-authenticating truth" as long as it is used, even if its usages differ in intention. Lore patterns "sustain complex meaning over time, but they do not enforce the past exactly. Rather the turns of a lore cycle convert the dead hands of the past into living presences that deviate from what went before." The lore cycle may explain the connection of "Jim Crow cultural codes" in nineteenth-century minstrel performances to late twentieth-century music videos by Michael Jackson, Paul McCartney, and MC Hammer.[18] A lore cycle, analogously, characterizes one of the major discursive tendencies of African American literary criticism: the definition of authentic African American literature in terms of racial realism.

Of course, one could characterize a host of American ethnic literatures in terms of racial realism, but it resonates in special political ways vis-à-vis African American literature. According to Madhu Dubey, "[p]olitical claims about African-American literature have always depended on realist aesthetics, from the documentary impulse of the slave narratives to the reflectionist principles prescribed by the cultural nationalist program. Black literature could best fulfill its political purpose of bettering the collective condition of the race by telling the truth about black experience."[19] Dubey's claims find support in John Guillory's broader proposition that literature has long imbued textual authenticity with political implications in order to concentrate, cohere, and unify communities, nations, ethnicities, races, and classes. The "sense of representation, the representation of groups by texts," he writes, "lies at a curious tangent to the concept of political representation, with which it seems to have been confused."[20]

Another confusion occurs between two kinds of politics: the sort used in "the politics of culture" (a.k.a. cultural politics), and the sort in "the culture of politics" (political culture). The first kind refers to the way people acquire, understand, and apply power in their relationships with one another; power relations underwrite the formation of identifiable patterns of human values, discourses, attitudes, actions, or artifacts. The second kind of politics emphasizes the way these very cultural patterns inform the institutions, organizations, and interest groups of public policy and governmental activity. Across history, black cultural expressions of racial realism have consistently mediated and encouraged this relationship between cultural politics and political culture in the name of "racial progress." Black authors who wrote texts undercutting this relationship by avoiding or complicating racial realism suffered public criticism for shirking the political responsibilities inevitably bestowed on them as identifiable members of the black race.

What exactly does it mean to undermine or avoid racial realism? Indeed, to conceive of racial realism is also to imply a generic opposite. Some scholars I have encountered over the years have called the opposite "white," as in "African American white-life literature," "African American literature about white people," "white African American literature," or even "white black literature." Others have identified the nature, purpose, or implications of such literature with historical black figures or with their ideologies, particularly those classified as "assimilationist" or as "selling out" their racial souls to the American cultural mainstream. Hence I have heard such terms as "assimilationist literature" and even "the Booker T. Washingtons of African American literature." These scholarly characterizations uncritically equate the ostensible absence of blacks in literature with the presence of whites. They also associate this absence with the code words that have historically denoted black ideological affiliation with self-serving and racist white political interests. The terminology says more about its users than it does about the literature itself; it raises more problems than it solves.

Certain literary examples can reveal the conceptual limitations of this terminology. Frank Yerby's first published novel, *The Foxes of Harrow* (1946), focuses not merely on a white man but on an Irishman trying to secure cultural citizenship in antebellum Louisiana. And Toni Morrison disrupts racial codes in her only short story, "Recitatif" (1983), at a moment when readers and writers were expecting her, as they were expecting other black women writers, to paint the lives and struggles of black society and its women in a particular way. Calling *The Foxes of Harrow* or "Recitatif" "white" is as reductive as calling African American literature "black." One would be hard-pressed to find anyone calling Anglo-American literature with black main characters—Harriet Beecher Stowe's *Uncle Tom's Cabin* (1852), Mark Twain's *Adventures of Huckleberry Finn* (1884), Willa Cather's *Sapphira and the Slave Girl* (1940), or William Styron's *The Confessions of Nat Turner* (1967)—"black texts." What, then, is the benefit in uttering the converse? Just as blackness needs a substitute concept that more accurately captures the lore cycle of racial realism in African American literary history, whiteness also needs a substitute concept that provides enough discursive latitude for talking about how and why certain texts by black writers have avoided or complicated racial realism.

This is not to say that the representational category of whiteness is completely inapplicable or worthless. The field of whiteness studies has correctly refuted the notion that whiteness is a "raceless subjectivity," as Peter Mac-Laren puts it, or an "invisible norm for how dominant culture measures its own civility."[21] Whiteness is, instead, a construct whose racial politics become visible when examined in terms of the enormous impact of Anglo-Saxon diasporas on mostly Western conceptions and articulations of race, culture, nation, universality, and normativity.[22] Scholars in the past decade have appropriated and modified these ideas to interpret the aesthetics, typology, ethnology, and psychology of whiteness in African American literature.[23]

This scholarship facilitates my study of George S. Schuyler's *Black No More* (1931) in Chapter 4. Science fiction enabled Schuyler to interrogate the normative fixity of whiteness as Anglo-Saxon, socioeconomically privileged, and politically powerful by writing a story in which racial indeterminacy becomes the norm. Examining the implications, in the novel and for the world at large, of science's succeeding in "racially" transforming blacks into whites requires the critical sophistication that whiteness studies encourages and enhances. Beyond this paradigm, however, Schuyler's interrogation of whiteness operates within an iconoclastic critique of the cultural norms of the Harlem Renaissance and the racialism of its main arbiter, Alain Locke. Determining precisely how this larger critique bears on the narrative strategies of *Black No More* demands theorizing literature as an agency of counternormativity. The terminology capturing this agency is "anomaly."

Anomalies

An anomaly belongs to a taxonomy, which classifies things in established categories. Taxonomy characterizes the theoretical function of anthologies, discussed earlier, to legitimate or delegitimate texts based on their "value." In two senses, anomalies threaten taxonomies because they contest the very principles used to classify and value texts. According to Bruce Lincoln,

(1) an anomaly is any entity that defies the rules of an operative taxonomy or (2) an anomaly is any entity, the existence of which an operative taxonomy is incapable of acknowledging. In the first case the taxonomy is taken to be normative and the anomaly deviant. In the second the anomaly is judged legitimate; the taxonomy, inadequate, distorting, and exclusionary. Under the terms of both definitions, however, it is possible to see how an anomaly may both pose danger to and be exposed to danger from the taxonomic order in which it is anomalous, just as deviants are considered outlaws when the legitimacy of legal systems is affirmed, but rebels when such systems are judged illegitimate.[24]

Anomalies tend to be unclassifiable or ill-classified, unappreciated or underappreciated, nonexistent or misrepresented, precisely because taxonomic rules often fail to account for them and because we tend to privilege these rules in establishing norms. From the viewpoint of anomalies, such rules are unfair. From the perspective of those who make the rules, on the other hand, anomalies are problems because they threaten the privilege and legitimacy of the taxonomy. From this distinction I will begin to explain why anomalies are central to the problem of African American literature, just as they are central to the problem of taxonomies.

The distinction between anomalous African American literature and African American literature featuring white characters advances what Shelly Fisher Fishkin calls "transgressive" African American literature. Transgressive texts "violate" critical and commercial norms demanding that "black fiction writers . . . focus on African-American life in the United States as seen through the eyes of black characters" and that "black novelists . . . focus on issues of race and racism." Racialist approaches to African American literature often assert at least three things: Blacks possess the utmost experiential authority in talking about African America; their literature serves as an authoritative expression of their views on race and racism; and the persons, places, and things imagined in this literature automatically earn racially authentic status. For Fishkin, African American literature's disruption of such long-standing connections of race to realism tends to be, "as often as not, ignored"—that is, "out of print and out of favor."[25]

Yet what do we make of how Toni Morrison's 1998 novel, *Paradise*, defies the conventional readings of American literature by complicating *both* blackness and whiteness in literary characterization? Morrison has explained the nature of racial ambiguity in *Paradise*, in which, just as in "Recitatif," she refuses to specify the racial identities of the main characters: "The tradition in writing is that if you don't mention a character's race, he's white. Any deviation from that, you have to say. What I wanted to do was not to erase race, but force readers either to care about it or see if it disturbs them that they don't know."[26] The character is white not because of the presence of a racial marker but because of its absence.

In literary history, the lack of racial information—or the underdetermination of race—has been just as conventional in defining whiteness as the excess of racial information—or the overdetermination of race—has been in defining blackness. Readers, it is also true, have not infrequently projected their vision of universal humanity as white humanity. Despite this interpretive tendency, however, we must remain open-minded and consider that racially unmarked or ambiguous characters in African American literature are not always or necessarily white. The authors could also be subscribing to a critical universalism in which black racial subjectivity—or the perspective shaped by the experience of self-identifying or being identified as black—subtly inflects their portrayals of human beings. In this situation, the literary characters and the readers' racial identification of them can easily devolve into miscommunication if the reader is not attuned to such inflections.

If we remain mindful, then, of the potential disagreement between the intentions of an author and the impressions of her or his reader, we can examine not only Morrison's "Recitatif" and *Paradise* but also Paul Laurence Dunbar's first novel, *The Uncalled*, whose protagonist is not definitively black or white. We must interpret the novel in terms that extend beyond the racial identities of characters. We must think about how Dunbar is "transgressing" or "violating" the norms of genre, which here comprise certain historically relative principles of literary form, style, or intention. When Dunbar wrote *The Uncalled* without the conventional—that is, minstrel—stereotypes of blacks, he was experimenting with other kinds of identification, such as cultural regionalism and socioeconomic class, while adopting literary naturalism to convey human difference and a profoundly spiritual story.

The anomalies of African American literature, moreover, possess specific and special meaning. Claudia Tate's *Psychoanalysis and Black Novels* defines novels "indisputably marginal in African-American literary history" as anomalies, "primarily because they resist, to varying degrees, the race and gender paradigms that we spontaneously impose on black textuality."[27] Tate's rhetorical, semantic, and conceptual contexts for traditional and anomalous African American literatures resemble my own, leading to our general agreement on which texts belong to these two main categories. The similarity between the opening question of her book ("What constitutes a black literary text in the United States?") and mine ("What is African American literature?") symbolizes our mutual concern with how race and aesthetics influence the creative strategies and goals of black authors, and how they factor into the cultural and academic evaluation of literary texts.[28]

Tate's work and mine differ in terms of methodology, however, and thus in terms of our theses and conclusions about anomalous texts. In *Psychoanalysis and Black Novels* Tate argues that psychoanalysis, especially Freudian, Lacanian, and object-relations models, enables her to show that "the racial protocol for African American canon formation has marginalized desire as a critical category of black textuality by demanding stories about racial politics."[29] Desire—not merely "sexual longings but all kinds of wanting, wishing, yearning, longing, and striving"—has been repressed in political readings of African American literature because "it engenders in us what I suspect to be vague feelings of emotional discomfort—anxiety, shame, and/or guilt."[30] Tate's paradigm for anomalies pivots on what is more or less a "suspicion" about the relationship between the emotions and the scholarly conduct of African Americanists, who represent her primary audience and presumably the "us" mentioned above.[31]

Psychological and emotional impressions such as Tate's suspicion and her audience's "vague feelings" are ultimately subjective and transitory. Without substantial and credible evidence, the existence of these impressions can never really be detailed and proven. Tate does not specifically elaborate on who has experienced such "vague feelings of emotional discomfort," though she provides plenty of anecdotes to explain the long-standing disagreement between proponents of psychoanalytic theory and scholars of African American literature.[32] Such an unstable theoretical foundation prompts us to doubt the stability of the other methodological scaffolds in *Psychoanalysis and Black Novels*, especially as she designed them to support her interpretations of anomalous texts.

Furthermore, Tate's translation of thematic, stylistic, and rhetorical codes into the respective discourses of conscious, preconscious, and unconscious desire refers to contemporary psychoanalytic analogies between the novel and the human psyche. As one reviewer has noted, Tate's attempts to examine the "personified linguistic structures" of the novel tend to contradict her more credible efforts—traceable to a previous book about desire, *Domestic Allegories of Political Desire: The Black Heroine's Text at the Turn of the Century* (1992)—to imagine "the authors she writes about as real people exercising due control over the products of their imagination." In the case of the authors examined in *Psychoanalysis and Black Novels*, these are also "real people" who are "working out personal traumas in stories about imaginary people who themselves are working out various neuroses."[33] The methodological confusion between psychoanalysis and psychology overcomplicates Tate's readings of the anomalous texts. What is more, it constrains the ideological connection of these texts to their historical contexts of imagination, production, and reception. Limning this latter connection constitutes the alternative approach of my book.

A Theory of African American Literary History

In this book I present a theory of African American literary history. I argue that de facto deans presided over literary schools of racial realism—which were the basis of literary movements—from which certain black authors played truant by avoiding this genre. The anomalous quality of the texts written by truants reflected their existence in a field of power relations in which they competed with deans for the authority to determine what their texts should say or mean. Anomalous texts ultimately demonstrated the extent to which certain black authors were conscious of and resistant to the dominant forms of aesthetic philosophy and cultural-political power during their historical moment.

The texts and contexts of racial realism led to diverse forms of African American literature and therefore evolved as black writers responded to various historical circumstances. The biases of William Howells, Alain Locke, Richard Wright, and Amiri Baraka, however, especially limited the nature, range, and effect of African American literature. Their authority was hegemonic—powerful, persuasive, and pervasive. True, their authority was disputed in several intellectual circles, and several of their literary contemporaries were influential. However, the deans I focus on were believed by most readers and writers of the era to be the leaders of schools or movements. The authority of deans did not require continual argumentation or justification; people simply accepted it as a given. Various local and international lay and intellectual communities read, discussed, wrote about, or wrote according to the schools of thought authorized by the deans. The schools limited, in various ways, the creative strategies and goals of black writers.

The negative light in which I cast deans does not necessarily correspond with the more intentional "censures of realism by vernacular or blues critics of African-American literature," in the words of Kenneth W. Warren. He indicts Henry Louis Gates Jr.'s disparagement of racist social-scientific versions of "black reality." Such "detractors," Warren goes on to say, have demanded genres other than realism for the enactment of "social change" in racial politics.[34] Responding to these detractors, Warren focuses on, and thereby redeems the intellectual value of, realism to decode the racial anxieties of American authors, black and white, in the postbellum nineteenth century. He also examines the ideological role of race in the discursive constitution of aesthetic and political expressions.

Despite their differences, Warren and Gates both recognize the thematic significance of race and realism to African American literary studies. Indeed, this field has always been attuned to the history of readers and writers holding African American literature accountable for addressing social and racial-political conditions. This history presupposes racial realism as a paradigm for studying the pragmatic accountability of African American literature, despite and because of its checkered past.

My theory of African American literary history seeks to avoid the various conceptual pitfalls that imperiled the critical thinking of previous historicist accounts of African American literature. Many of these pitfalls had little to do with developing literary theories or histories that covered a broad swath of texts and drew attention to the role of literary intertextuality in the constitution of "tradition." Rather, the totalizing or generalizing tendencies of this approach tended to lead to redundancy and reductionism. Wahneema Lubiano notes that "critics of Afro-American literature feel the need to speak to each other with the uninformed audience constantly in mind, a dilemma that often results in producing criticism that of necessity reinvents certain wheels of our discourse instead of focusing on the complexities of history and interpretation." One consequence of this anxiety over audience is that "[b]ooks written by Afro-Americanists are frequently structured to engage, explain, account for, redefine, or reconstruct a 'tradition.'"[35] Likewise, Adolph Reed Jr. notes that, since the "disciplinary practice of contemporary literary studies centers on construction and examination of text-based notions of tradition, or canon, it underwrites an approach to intellectual history that [can be] idealist and ahistorical. This approach produces typically 'thin' accounts that emphasize purportedly transhistorical relations of writers and texts," or relations that cut across history.[36]

By contrast, the object of my book is to interrogate the notions of "blackness" and "tradition," not to concretize them as one monolithic, uncontestable piece; to stay historically specific, not to generalize for the sake of theorization. The cultural coherence or cohesiveness that tends to characterize literary tradition—from which a theoretically coherent or cohesive canon of "great" texts can emerge—belies the degree to which its aesthetic-cultural value is constantly under pressure, always being contested both from within and without. The way in which traditions experience ideological struggle and tension, the way they serve as the by-product or producer of debate between and among groups, is itself a controversial story as worthy of being told as the more hagiographic story that traditions exist and warrant celebration.

The number of literary movements (four) and authors (eight) examined at length in this book, however, encourages broad claims about historical trends in the nature and implications of anomalies. Anomalies unsettle conventional notions of a distinct African American literature. The literary characterology of race determines how these texts subvert our expectations for racial realism. Characterology means not simply a study of the properties and narrative implications of literary characters, but also how literary characterization elicits certain responses from readers, although it should not be used to homogenize these responses. Characterology has long ignored the racial subjects permeating and central to an understanding of literary texts and have tended to focus on Anglo-American and Anglo-British literary texts. Characterology, as this book demonstrates, needs more diverse perspectives attentive to race.[37]

This book intersects characterology and the methodology of literary history. Constructions of the "real" vary from era to era, as do those of race. But anomalous texts consistently disrupt the literary taxonomies of racial realism by usually (but not always) casting blacks in minor roles, if they appear at all. At the same time, these texts mark the main characters as racially white, neutral, or ambiguous. In some cases, the texts talk about race in subordinate thematic ways. Schuyler's *Black No More*, for instance, features a protagonist who turns from black to white in racial phenotype. Morrison's "Recitatif" features two main characters, one black and the other white, but the reader is never certain of the racial identity of either one. In both cases blacks play a major role.

Authorial intention, or the reason *why* certain authors characterize race in certain literary ways, cannot be so easily theorized or generalized. Each author and her or his text must be analyzed on a case-by-case basis. I hope in this book to achieve this sort of analytic specificity by providing the extra attention that the truant authors and their anomalous texts so deserve. But to repeat, certain trends are discernible. From the perspective of deans, anomalous texts are outlaws; from the perspective of truants, however, these texts are rebels. Truancy turns out to be a conscious effort on the part of an author to indict the authority of certain figures or the institutions that grant them power. Anomalies refer to the literature written by truant authors to contest the authentic exclusivity of racial realism.

Bear in mind that I do not merely want to redefine the word "anomalous" positively to denote resistant agency, so that the phrase "anomalous African American literature" is no longer pejorative. I anticipate a day when this phrase is no longer self-contradictory or oxymoronic, when it has become simply "African American literature" or "American literature" or "literature." But anomalies can lead to a beneficial readjustment of paradigms. Thomas S. Kuhn theorizes that "awareness of anomaly opens a period in which conceptual categories are adjusted until the initially anomalous has become the anticipated. . . . The more precise and far-reaching that paradigm is, the more sensitive an indicator it provides of anomaly and hence of an occasion for paradigm change."[38] In due time and if taken seriously, anomalies can compel African American literary studies to sharpen its rationale for examining or dismissing certain texts.

Healthy Tension

One should refer to Katya Gibel Azoulay's idea of a "healthy tension" to historicize the debate between deans and truants on the idea of African American literature. There is a healthy tension between literary identities imposed on authors and texts, on the one hand, and discourses capable of counteracting this imposition, on the other. My book is designed to describe the tensions that existed between Howells and Dunbar, Locke and Schuyler, Wright and Yerby, and Baraka and Morrison.

Chapter 1 begins by outlining the post–Civil War historical context of Howells's approach to African American literature. During this period, the racialism of blackface minstrelsy (performed by whites) created a cultural precondition for "minstrel realism," a term I have coined to define a postbellum phenomenon in which audiences regarded the romance and sentimentality of black minstrelsy (performed by blacks) as racially authentic and realistic.[39] An analogous reaction occurred when Howells reviewed Dunbar's second book of poetry, *Majors and Minors* (1896), in *Harper's Weekly* on June 27, 1896. A leader in determining the critical expectations and reading practices of postbellum nineteenth-century America, Howells puts Dunbar on the mainstream American literary map as he lauds the "Humor and Dialect" section of *Majors and Minors*. Howells appreciates the demonstration of minstrel realism in Dunbar's poetic re-creation of black folk language, culture, spirituality, and psychology.

Howells's approval and sponsorship of Dunbar's dialect poetry helped to dictate the terms by which subsequent reviewers and literary critics, in the United States and abroad, defined and interpreted Dunbar's dialect poetry as the authentic product of the "pure African type." The racialism of this critical paradigm merged both biological essentialism and cultural essentialism in classifications, interpretations, and aesthetic judgments of African American literature.

I must pause here to say a brief word about the inclusion of Howells in this book. He shared the critical discourse of blackness ("entirely *black* verse from [Dunbar] would succeed" [Howells's emphasis]) regardless of the fact that he was white. More important than his biological difference, and how this difference translated into a distinctive socioracial experience and literary prerogative, is the discursive and therefore ideological *consistency* of his criticism and commercialization of African American literature with those of critics of later generations and even of different races. Claudia Tate is mostly correct when she states that "it comes as no surprise that canonical authors bear a striking resemblance to those who endorsed (or canonized) them."[40] But Tate's idea, particularly the phrase "striking resemblance," must be clarified to account for Howells. This resemblance is primarily ideological and discursive, not so much racial in the biological sense of the word. For this reason, Howells deserves inclusion in my dean-truant paradigm of African American literary history.

This is not to suggest, however, that because Howells deserves examination for his impact on black authors during the 1890s, so too does, say, Carl Van Vechten, another white male critic, for his patronage of black authors of the Harlem Renaissance. It is not enough merely to influence the careers of black authors. More important are the specific ways in which the literati associated deanship with a particular figure, and how that prestige instituted structures of thought and feeling around the idea of African American literature.

Howells has almost always been regarded as the dean of American letters, a term which encodes the priority of white writers, since it was assigned to him in the late nineteenth century. Yet his influence over American cultural taste extended to, even if it did not entirely dictate the evolution of, African American literary culture. Howells directly affected the careers of Dunbar and Charles W. Chesnutt, even if his power did not sit well with the likes of Victoria Earle Matthews and other ideologues of racial uplift who were skeptical of literary perpetuations of black stereotypes. By contrast, Van Vechten, according to David Levering Lewis, was at best a literary celebrity and enthusiastic patron in New York City, "white America's guide through Harlem, what Osbert Sitwell described as 'the white master of the colored revels.'"[41] Van Vechten encouraged black authors (Rudolph Fisher and Nella Larsen, to name but two), but he never reached Howells's status. Van Vechten *could not*, in fact, given the presence of Alain Locke and other eminent "midwives" during the Harlem Renaissance. In his era, Howells's status was influential enough to dictate a school of racial realism.

Chapter 2 examines why and how Dunbar played truant from the Howellsian school of racial realism and published an anomalous first novel in 1898, *The Uncalled*. Dunbar's truancy makes sense, first, in the context of his subscription to and literary practice of racial-uplift ideology, or the doctrine which argued that the "folk" could be morally, intellectually, and physically (or culturally) elevated to the level of civilization. By subscribing to a "New Negro" version of racial realism, Dunbar critiques the minstrel representations of the folk in the so-called plantation tradition of postbellum Anglo-American literature. The racial-uplift ideology that motivates this critique also underwrites what Victoria Earle Matthews in 1895 called "Race Literature," a genre of African American literature that is anomalous in two senses: the texts critique and resist minstrel realism, but they are "not necessarily race matter," that is, they do not have to express New Negro realism per se.

The taxonomic and thematic paradigm of Race Literature frames my claim that Dunbar's first novel, *The Uncalled*, is anomalous for the way it encodes class and regional markers of realism while submerging the conventional markers of racial realism. This does not mean that racialism is absent from the novel. Indeed, its presence corresponds to Dunbar's novelistic exposure of the thematic limitations of Anglo-American local-color writing, whose trademark idealism tended to elide African American histories of racial oppression and conflict. In the end, the novel anticipates the pointedly anti-Howellsian romantic naturalism of Frank Norris.

Chapter 3 suggests that Locke's status as dean of the Harlem Renaissance empowered him to promote New Negro modernism as a revision of the retrograde versions of racial realism discussed in the previous two chapters. Locke's derivation of this supposedly avant-garde cultural genre replicated Howells's racially essentialist discourses of biology and culture. Locke's own discourse appropriated ethnic pluralism, which imagined the ameliorative potential of American cultural nationalism to foster peaceful contact and relations between U.S. ethnic groups. Nonetheless, he still stratified cultures with "color lines" in order to define, interpret, and assess cultural representations of ethnicity. Accordingly, he identified Henry Ossawa Tanner as the descendant of a cosmopolitan tradition of black painters trained in academic institutions in Europe who consistently avoided or complicated representations of blacks. Tanner's cosmopolitanism and ethnocentric academicism, Locke warned, threatened to lead astray—away from New Negro modernism—the early twentieth-century generation of black painters whom he had sought to affiliate with the Harlem Renaissance. In the end, Locke not only misperceived eclectic black creativity as abominable truancy, he also misunderstood critiques of the racial and cultural normativity of "whiteness" as utter, unreflexive, and uncritical self-submission to Anglo-Saxon racial hegemony.

Chapter 4 shows how Schuyler devised an iconoclastic campaign against the protocols of racial essentialism, ethnic pluralism, and racial realism that underpinned Locke's New Negro modernism. Schuyler's admitted truancy from the Harlem Renaissance included the production of anomalous, if satirical, aesthetic and cultural criticism that sought to expose the fundamental pitfalls of New Negro modernism, namely, the blurring of biology and culture in racialism and the intrinsic chauvinism of the Harlem Renaissance. He promoted cultural monism, which exaggerated the cultural similarities or sameness of blacks and whites at the expense of the historical reality of racist and socioeconomic inequity between the two groups. The result was a philosophical disagreement between his 1926 essay, "The Negro-Art Hokum," and New Negro modernism.

An examination of "The Negro-Art Hokum" guides an interpretation of Schuyler's novel of science fiction, *Black No More*. We learn that the technological "whitening" of blacks so that they could pass as white raises the question of whether racial "passing" involves cultural transformation as much as it exploits biological traits. The way in which passing destabilizes whiteness and marks an anomalous moment within the narrative—a moment when the protagonist exists as neither black nor white yet both—supports the novel's metanarrative suggestion that *Black No More* becomes a black (novel) no more as Schuyler remains racially fixed. The taxonomic line separating African American literature and something else turns out to be a color line fraught with the problems and politics of applying racial essentialism to literary texts.

Chapter 5 tracks the radical permutations of New Negro ideology in the literary and cultural criticism of the dean of the Chicago Renaissance. Through such proletarian, Marxist, Communist, and black nationalist doctrines of leftist radicalism, Richard Wright tried to revise Lockean New Negro modernism in order to build a more class-inflected discourse of racial authenticity. This discourse valued the construction of a pragmatist bridge between the working class and the black intelligentsia. Wright's critical discourse of racial realism, which endorsed a sort of New Negro radicalism, resembled Locke's critical discourse in the late 1930s. At that time, the former dean of the Harlem Renaissance self-effacingly recognized the fatal flaws of the movement's cultural leadership and aesthetic philosophy.

Locke also hailed the promise of the Chicago Renaissance not to repeat these flaws.

The perpetuation or endorsement of Wright's discourse of New Negro radicalism in reviews of his work in the American press ended up limiting the commercial opportunities and creative strategies of black writers. Certain writers broke out of the Wrightean paradigm. They participated in an American cultural nationalism that did not simply celebrate an assimilationist black aspiration toward Americanness. Rather, they called for a literary aesthetics in which universal depictions or avoidances of conventional modes of racial realism supported black claims to national citizenship. Frank Yerby was one of the leaders of this post–World War II movement toward the American cultural nationality and commercial popularity of black-authored literature.

Admittedly, Wright's postwar life and work complicate the dichotomy I seek to establish between deans and truants, racial realism and anomalies. Wright shows that my attempt at a relatively straightforward, comprehensible model of African American literary history may encounter cases of authorial intention and readerly expectation that resist any analytic flattening of his character and career. For example, how do we reconcile Wright's persona in the late 1930s and the 1940s and his persona in the 1950s, when he wrote *Savage Holiday* (1954)? There is a clear change in his literary philosophy. While working on the novel in the early 1950s, Wright delivered lectures on literature, compiled as *White Man, Listen!* (1957). The most relevant essay in the collection is "Literature of the Negro in the United States," in which he describes African American literature according to two philosophical concepts: "entity" and "identity." "Entity" characterizes works that struggle for entrance into a racially transcendent, universal tradition; "identity" pertains to the subjectivity of literature, asserting a worldview colored by a particularly racial-political lens.

Although a simplistic binary in many ways, Wright's philosophical differentiation of anomalous and traditional African American literature along lines of entity and identity, respectively, provides insight into the formal strategies of *Savage Holiday* and the existentialist treatises he was reading while an expatriate in France. The figures of Søren Kierkegaard, Friedrich Nietzsche, and Martin Heidegger (to whom H. L. Mencken's writings had introduced Wright in 1927 and whose work he revisited more intensively in 1940) as well as French existentialists like Albert Camus, Simone de Beauvoir, and Jean-Paul Sartre (whom Wright began to examine in 1947) were instrumental to Wright's vision of *Savage Holiday* as a "universal" story.[42]

At the same time, Wright imported his vision of the novel from the United States. By the time he left the United States permanently in 1947, black writers had already begun to grapple with the prospect of racial integration in the post–World War II era. Wright's reconciliation of these two ideologies, the existentialist and the integrationist, in *Savage Holiday* generates a provocative narrative for scholarly studies of Wright and of black expatriate novelists in general.[43] Wright's legacy teaches us the importance of extensively referring to correspondence, biographical data, cultural history, and literary criticism to account for the ideological and practical contradictions that easily complicate the dean-truant paradigm. Such contradictions also illustrate, as I elaborate in Chapters 5 and 6, that the paradigm breaks down, to a certain degree, between the postwar 1940s and the Black Arts Movement.

Chapter 6 explores the complexity of Frank Yerby. According to Yerby's understudied letters and various literary works from the 1930s to the 1950s, his development of ambivalence toward racial representation in African American literature tempts one to characterize his entire legacy solely in these terms. But the details of his early career urge us to think otherwise. The chapter is broken into four investigative contexts: Yerby's early career as a poet; his shift to short stories in the genre of New Negro radicalism; the failure of his yet-unpublished first novel, *This Is My Own*; and the trend of "costume" novels he wrote early in his career, beginning with his first published novel, *The Foxes of Harrow*. This novel depicts the rugged kind of American individualism that, thematically, runs counter to the tendency of naturalism, one protocol of Wrightean New Negro radicalism, to deny the individual agency within an environment. In order to make this case, the novel revisits and revises the myths about race relations, blacks, and the antebellum South. It refuses to resign the reader to the inevitable southern tragedy of racism, manifested in the national crisis of the Civil War.

Yerby's emphasis on American cultural nationality in *The Foxes of Harrow* connects to the commercial popularity he achieved in the post–World War II era. At this time, demonstrations of national identity or "Americanness" in "universal," "raceless," "white," or multiethnic African American literature were so widespread that they marked the greatest proliferation of such literature at one definable historical moment. Black writers were embracing American cultural nationalism instead of continuing to wrestle with the stressful relationship, if not the contradiction, between this doctrine and racialism.

Yerby's marginality was especially remarkable, if unfortunate. He was the most prolific and commercially successful writer in African American history, yet his thirty novels with nonblack protagonists remain absent from literary anthologies and scholarship. His marginal status, perhaps more than that of any other writer, forces us to confront the principles of African American literary studies since the 1970s. This book is an ideal context in which to introduce or reintroduce Yerby to readers and to address some of the issues of authorship, racial identity, literary aesthetics, and audience that have surrounded his work and African American literature.

In doing so, I raise questions about the long-standing aesthetic devaluation of popular fiction in academic literary studies.[44] This sort of critical elitism has persisted in the field of African American literary studies. "The field of popular fiction is a relatively unexplored terrain in African American as well as American literary history and criticism," according to Susanne B. Dietzel. "In the fields of literary criticism and the teaching of African American literature, for example, scholars and critics alike have restricted their efforts to reviewing, promoting, and canonizing only those texts that fit the prevailing aesthetic and literary standards." As a consequence, a "rigid division" exists between "high and low, or elite and mass culture," and, by extension, between popular fiction and canonical fiction.[45] Dispensing with such critical elitism and addressing both the "literary" and the "popular," which I elaborate at the end of Chapter 6, is prerequisite to asserting the legitimacy of popular fiction (such as Yerby's) as evidence for a scholarly argument on (African American) literature.

I suggest in this book that African American literature's demonstration or disregard of racial realism further influences how and why these "standards" continue to exist. My making this claim does not necessarily mean that I must henceforth declare whether a piece of anomalous literature is bad, mediocre, or great, and thereby determine whether its exclusion from the canon is justified. Proving that Dunbar's first novel is aesthetically superior to his widely cited fourth novel, *The Sport of the Gods* (1902), for example, has little if anything to do with my purpose in this book. More important is the examination of the historical record of readers judging the aesthetic merits of a literary work according to its avoidance or application of racial realism. I explain why the aesthetic judgments of these reader's took certain forms and how discourses of literary criticism reflected and articulated them.

The book closes with a comparative reading of Amiri Baraka's introduction to *Confirmation: An Anthology of AfricanAmerican Women* (1983) and a short story Toni Morrison contributed to the volume, entitled "Recitatif." In light of the fact that men have almost always been anointed deans in African American literary history, I examine the extent to which the historical tension between deans and truants, racial realism and anomalies, dovetails with the historical tension between patriarchs and those who are discontented, such as black women writing against social and cultural expressions of patriarchy, masculinism, and male privilege. "Recitatif" captures this double tension. The story not only unsettles the fixed notions of racial identity in the Black Aesthetic that Baraka incorporated into *Confirmation*, it also depicts strong relationships between women at the expense of conventional heterosocial paradigms in African American literature.

The hermeneutical self-consciousness of "Recitatif," which indeed must be interpreted as a postmodernist trait, coincides with but also pressures the contemporaneous principles of African American literary theory, led, in hindsight, by Henry Louis Gates Jr. and framed by his notion of the "hermeneutical circle" of blackness.[46] Gates argued that critical valuations of African American literature resorted to meditations on black racial or intellectual authenticity. Though brilliant and useful, this formulation of the hermeneutical circle of blackness obscures the concept's original philosophy about how various assumptions can predetermine readings of texts and why understanding parts of texts presupposes understanding their entirety. Morrison's short fiction captures an amazing attempt to critique not only the traditional hermeneutical circle but also the neologistic hermeneutical circle of blackness. In the process, she exposes the racial presumptions and interpretive practices often associated with African American literature and racial identity. "Recitatif" belongs to Morrison's current vision of a world where she can question racially inflected hierarchies of human power, celebrate the inclusivity of Americanism, and yet remain sensitive to the history of race and racism in the United States.

The Gender Politics of Deans and Truants

My examination of "Recitatif" reflects my broader interest in the fact that Baraka and most of the earlier deans of African American literature have something in common: they are men. Indeed, men were almost always anointed the de facto deans of past African American literary movements or renaissances. During the century after slavery ended, patriarchy maintained the supremacy of deans as "father figures," underwriting their acquisition of critical and commercial authority and encoding male or masculine privilege in literary theories and practices of racial realism. Wahneema Lubiano theorizes that "[r]ealism as the bedrock of narrative is inherently problematic. Realism poses a fundamental, long-standing challenge for counter-hegemonic discourses, since realism, as a narrative form, enforces an authoritative perspective." This viewpoint distinguishes between "true" or "false," "concrete" or "abstract" versions of the living world. When held or promoted by a dean, such a perspective can support what Lubiano calls "male cultural and political hegemony." Lubiano uses this phrase to describe the Harlem Renaissance and to situate the writers who have contested it, but it is also applicable to other movements in African American literary history.[47]

During the periods covered in this book, black women writers have produced literature indicting the intrinsic gender assumptions of racial realism and their hegemonic implications. At the turn of the twentieth century, black women novelists employed "domestic allegories"—namely, those of genteel love, courtship, matrimony, and family formation—in order to acquire "authority for the self both in the home and in the world," an authority arising from "woman-centered values, agency" and catering to "distinctly female principles of narrative pleasure."[48] The post-Reconstruction circumstances of black aesthetic and political culture determined the literary production and reception of those novelists. Authors ranging from Frances Ellen Watkins Harper and Pauline E. Hopkins to Amelia E. Johnson, Emma Dunham Kelley-Hawkins, and Katherine D. Tillman crafted empowering iconography and narratives of black women to critique the dominance of masculine ideology. They also exposed the masculinist causes of social and legal inequities and proposed alternative social roles acknowledging the interests and importance of women. Such strategies typified the gender politics of African American literature not only during the post-Reconstruction era but also during the Harlem Renaissance, the Chicago Renaissance, and the Black Arts Movement. The reason for such gender-political motives must point to the roles of deans in creating the critical and commercial conditions that black women writers found burdensome, restrictive, or counterproductive.

Gender politics is crucial to our understanding of the historical dialectic between deans and truants, racial realism and anomalies. As the following chapters will show, Howells's canon of Afro-Western authors praised only men, ignoring (as many other critics have, then and since) the post-Reconstruction "Woman's Era" of African American literature. Locke's canonical genealogy of African American literature anointed mostly men as the ancestors or the "youth" of the Harlem Renaissance. Wright's allegation that Zora Neale Hurston represents black folk in retrograde fashion in *Their Eyes Were Watching God* (1937) borders on antagonistic chauvinism. Finally, any discussion of the Black Arts Movement must account for its encoding of masculinism and patriarchy in its apparently gender-neutral discourse of "the people" or "the race" as well as its studies and anthologies of African American literature.

I must state here that the anomalous texts of Dunbar, Schuyler, and Yerby in some ways perpetuate sexism, or the belief that men are superior to women. Indeed, as much as they are fascinating for their respective critiques of Howells's minstrel realism, Locke's New Negro modernism, and Wright's New Negro radicalism, the anomalous texts mostly adhere to the patriarchal and masculinist conventions of their time. For example, women have little agency in Dunbar's *The Uncalled*, except for the guardian of Fred Brent, Miss Hester Prime, whose tough-love religious approach to parenting comes across as an impediment to Fred's self-individuation. The women of Schuyler's *Black No More*, similarly, possess little agency. In an era of racial homogenization caused by Black No More, Incorporated, they are merely procreative spectacles whose racially "pure" or mixed children incite white male anxieties over female sexuality and miscegenation. Finally, Stephen Fox in Yerby's *The Foxes of Harrow* becomes an American not only by acquiring wealth through the ownership of land and slaves, but also by encouraging a heterosexist culture of patriarchy, adultery, procreation, dynasty, and violent expressions of masculinity. From these works of fiction, we obviously cannot learn how anomalies can contest the literary norms of both racial realism and gender.

A cursory look at other examples of anomalous African American literature, however, reveals the presence of feminist politics. Zora Neale Hurston's *Seraph on the Suwanee* (1948), according to Hazel Carby, "involved a challenge to the literary conventions of the apartheid American society in which Hurston lived—conventions she felt dictated that black writers and artists should be concerned only with representing black subjects." In support of this claim, Hurston wrote a letter discussing her "hopes of breaking that old silly rule about Negroes not writing about white people." At the same time, Hurston's novel "concentrate[s] on complex questions of female sexuality and the sometimes violent conflict between men and women that arises from the existence of incompatible and gender-specific desires."[49]

The issues of sexuality and gender relations appear as well in other anomalous texts published in the century after slavery. They include Frances E. W. Harper's *Sowing and Reaping* (1876–77), Nella Larsen's "The Wrong Man" and "Freedom" (1926), Ann Petry's *Country Place* (1947), and James Baldwin's *Giovanni's Room* (1956). Baldwin's novel represents what Mae G. Henderson calls "racial expatriation." "Baldwin's flight to Paris and his all-white novel," according to Henderson, "must be regarded as attempts to open the space of black literary expression to subjects and experiences not deemed appropriate for black writers in the 1940s and 1950s."

However, the novel asks not only "[w]hat it is to be a (white) American and an expatriate," but also "what it is to be a homosexual and a man."[50]

Respectively, *Seraph on the Suwanee* and *Giovanni's Room* reflect the reactions of Hurston and Baldwin to gender and sexual norms, specifically to the roles of patriarchy and homophobia in the degradation of their identities as a woman and as a gay man. Patriarchy conspired in the enforcement of heterosexual norms such as procreation and family while skewing interpersonal power relations in favor of maleness and fatherhood. For these and other writers, patriarchy and homophobia were linked. At the same time, these writers were aware of—to repeat Hurston's words in a letter—"that old silly rule about Negroes not writing about white people." In this book I not only historicize this "rule," I also remain aware of the political role of gender in why and how people wrote for or against it.

Chapter 1

"Entirely *Black* Verse from Him Would Succeed"

In the early months of 1896, James A. Herne returned to his hotel in Toledo, Ohio, the city where he was directing and performing in his most popular play to date, *Shore Acres*. The hotel clerk informed the preeminent actor and playwright that one Paul Laurence Dunbar had left him a gift. Indeed, after attending and enjoying *Shore Acres*, Dunbar had decided to leave Herne a complimentary copy of his second and latest book, *Majors and Minors* (1896).[1]

Fortunately for the black poet, Herne was well acquainted with the most authoritative literary reviewer, cultural critic, editor, and publisher of the time, the so-called dean of American letters, William Howells. Howells was already a household name for mentoring and helping to publish the works of such well-known writers as George Washington Cable, Henry James, Sarah Orne Jewett, Joel Chandler Harris, and Mark Twain. Readers of *Harper's Weekly*, in particular, had come to know and appreciate Howells's columns, which for a decade had epitomized the magazine's long-standing identification and review of instructive and entertaining literature.

Howells ascended the professional ranks from assistant editor (1866–71) to editor (1871–81) of *Atlantic Monthly* and, subsequently, as a writer of columns entitled "Editor's Study" (1886–92), "Life and Letters" (1895–98), and "Editor's Easy Chair" (1899–1909) for *Harper's*. Further enhanced by his reputation as a gifted and prolific writer of fiction, Howells's name became synonymous with literary realism. According to one contemporary, William Roscoe Thayer, in an essay entitled "The New Story-Tellers and the Doom of Realism" (1895), "perhaps no higher compliment can be paid to Mr. Howells than to state that those who undertake to write about Realism in America will inevitably find themselves dealing with it as though it were his private property, instead of with the doctrines and assertions of a system."[2] When Dunbar dropped off the book at Herne's hotel, any thought that Herne would hand *Majors and Minors* to Howells, who could then review the book for *Harper's Weekly* and thereby launch Dunbar's literary career, was far-fetched, to say the least.

Figure 1. Paul Laurence Dunbar in 1890. (Brown University Library, Providence, R.I.)

Remarkably, these events occurred in this exact way. Herne did not respond to Dunbar while *Shore Acres* was playing in Toledo but he did later, in Detroit, where the play relocated and from which he sent the poet a letter. "While at Toledo a copy of your poems was left at my hotel by a Mr. Childs," Herne wrote; "I tried very hard to find Mr. Childs to learn more of you. Your poems are wonderful. I shall acquaint William Dean Howells and other literary people with them. They are new to me and may be new to them."[3] Herne passed *Majors and Minors* on to Howells, who decided to review the book in the June 27, 1896, issue of *Harper's Weekly*.

Majors and Minors was new to both Herne and Howells not because of its two main genres, British Romantic and American local-color poetry. Herne was well read in American literature, while Howells specialized in both classic and contemporary Western literature. Actually, the frontispiece of *Majors and Minors*, an image of Dunbar at age eighteen, is what made the poems "new" (Fig. 1). Howells found the image so compelling that, for the benefit of his readers, he decided to describe Dunbar's phenotype and physiognomy, those biological traits that affirmed the poet as a "pure African type":

There had come to me from the hand of a friend, very unofficially, a little book of verse, dateless, placeless, without a publisher, which has greatly interested me. Such foundlings of the press always appeal to one by their forlornness; but commonly the appeal is to one's pity only, which is moved all the more if the author of the book has innocently printed his portrait with his verse. In this present case I felt a heightened pathos in the appeal from the fact that the face which confronted me when I opened the volume was the face of a young negro, with the race traits strangely accented: the black skin, the woolly hair, the thick outrolling lips and the mild, soft eyes of the pure African type. One cannot be very sure, ever, about the age of those people, but I should have thought that this poet was about twenty years old; and I suppose a generation ago he would have been worth, apart from his literary gift, twelve or fifteen hundred dollars, under the hammer. My sense of all this was intensified when I came to read the little book, and to recognize its artistic quality; but I hope that the love of dramatic contrasts has not made me overvalue it as a human event, or that I do not think unduly well of it because it is the work of a man whose race has not hitherto made its mark in art.[4]

So captivated was Howells by the image and its racial implications that, reportedly, he wrote a substantial portion of the review—the sections regarding the *idea* of someone like Dunbar—without yet reading all of the poems in the book.[5]

For Howells, the frontispiece verified Dunbar's identity as an African descendant born in the postbellum New World. The image influenced Howells's encounter with *Majors and Minors* in much the same way that a paratext, as I mention in the Introduction, influences a reader's encounter with a text, although Dunbar's book lacks a comprehensive paratextual frame. Aside from the printer's information ("Hadley & Hadley, Toledo, Ohio") and the dedication to Dunbar's mother,[6] *Majors and Minors*, as Howells puts it in the review, was "dateless, placeless, without a publisher." Initially unable to "place" the work, Howells focused on the discernibly African physiognomy and dark phenotype in the frontispiece to place Dunbar and his work.

The frontispiece created certain expectations for Howells about the kind of writing that should exist in *Majors and Minors*. Whenever Dunbar's book defied these expectations, skepticism tempered Howells's enthusiasm. In the review, he suggests that, in order to assure both critical acclaim and commercial success, the poet should dedicate himself to writing verses only in "black" dialect, similar to those filling the second, and shorter, section of *Majors and Minors*. Dunbar is most himself, Howells insists, when he writes in such informal or colloquial English. Accordingly, he maintains that Dunbar should refrain from writing poems in formal, or literary, English, such as those filling the first, and longer, section of the book.

Howells subtly reiterates this assessment one month later in a letter to Ripley Hitchcock, then serving as literary editor and adviser at D. Appleton and Company. Dated July 29, 1896, the letter belongs to a long-running correspondence between Howells and Hitchcock about promising American writers, most notably, Stephen Crane. After informing Hitchcock of his laudatory review of Crane's *Maggie: A Girl of the Streets* (1893) and *The Red Badge of Courage* (1895), in the previous Sunday's *World*, Howells closes the letter with a couple of sentences about Dunbar: "Major Pond is going to platform young Dunbar next winter, and I believe a book of entirely *black* verse from him would succeed. My notice raised such interest."[7]

These words are remarkable for three reasons. First, Howells is referring to Major James A. Pond, a prestigious literary agent who had previously directed the lecture tours of Mark Twain and George Washington Cable, among other popular American writers. Dunbar had secured Major Pond as an agent by the time he decided to travel to England in February 1897 to lecture and recite his poems. Second, the reason that Dunbar interested Major Pond in the first place had much to do with that "notice"—Howells's term for his review of *Majors and Minors* in *Harper's Weekly*. Third, and most important, Howells's assertion that "a book of entirely *black* verse from [Dunbar] would succeed" values the racial authenticity of African American literature, particularly the orthography of dialect that came from the pen of a "pure African type." This appreciation belongs to a larger critical and commercial demand for minstrel realism in postbellum nineteenth-century American culture.

"Minstrel realism" sounds oxymoronic, but it makes sense when placed within the context of how racialism and realism interacted in the nineteenth century. The racialism of blackface minstrelsy, performed usually by white individuals darkened by burnt cork, created a cultural precondition in which audiences regarded black minstrelsy, that is, minstrelsy performed by blacks, as realistic. This reaction resulted from the commercialization of black minstrelsy in American culture as an avant-garde cultural performance of racial authenticity.

An analogous reaction occurred on the publication of *Majors and Minors* in 1896. At this time, racial caricature was central to the so-called plantation tradition of Anglo-American literature and to American literary realism. Howells and other reviewers, editors, and publishers appreciated the section of *Majors and Minors* called "Humor and Dialect" for what happened to be the protocols of minstrel realism: the humor and dialect of black culture. Minstrel realism united racialism and realism in a romantic relationship that flies in the face of the historical conflict between these genres in American culture. While characterizing Anglo-American literary realism as the eschewal of romance and sentiment, Howells, in particular, defined African American literature in these very terms. This apparent inconsistency points to the racialism that helped to perpetuate this definition in the dramatic and literary cultures of minstrelsy.

Thus, I urge another recategorization of American literary realism. Elizabeth Ammons already recommends an "expansion" of this genre to include a variety of realisms, to move beyond the "white, middle-class ideas" of Howells, Henry James, Stephen Crane, and Edith Wharton, among others, and to accommodate the diverse approaches of black, Native American, and Chinese American authors.[8] But Howells's notion of literary realism included Dunbar as well as other "ethnic minority" writers, such as Charles W. Chesnutt and Abraham Cahan. In order to explain, then, Howells's citing of both Crane and Dunbar in the same letter to Hitchcock as the avant-garde of American literary realism, I suggest that, for Howells and his contemporaries, racial or ethnic authenticity determined the aesthetic value of literary realism. The contrasting racial identities of Crane and Dunbar, for example, created different sets of expectations for the kinds of realism that they could and should have produced.

By focusing on the racial politics of such expectations and the concomitant reading practices of postbellum nineteenth-century America, in this chapter I encourage American literary and cultural studies to move beyond the routine indictment of the racial inauthenticity and discrimination of minstrelsy.[9] W. T. Lhamon Jr. notes that such declarations have bogged down this academic field in the past and no longer prove intellectually productive.[10] Accordingly, Howells's critical impressions of Dunbar—impressions molded by the cultural experience of minstrelsy—should not be dismissed merely as racist, although Howells's racist slips do factor into his interpretation of Dunbar's poetry. More important, we must explore Howells's discussions of accurate or truthful representations of black experiences in the context of the minstrel industry. This approach involves determining the ideological roles of minstrelsy and realism within racism and how these roles determine the place of his criticism in the larger discursive and ideological trajectory of African American literary criticism.

Ultimately, the relationship between Howells and Dunbar and the implications for black writers confronting a white-dominated literary marketplace might be an overwhelmingly familiar story. Less intuitive or obvious, however, are the precise ways in which the racialism of Howells and this marketplace arbitrated the realism of certain examples of African American literature.

Minstrel Realism

From the 1820s until the 1930s, American culture was anchored in what George Fredrickson has described as "the romantic racialist view [that] simply endorsed the 'child' stereotype of the most sentimental school of proslavery paternalists and plantation romancers."[11] The cultural consequences of romantic racialism crystallized during Reconstruction. Starting after the Civil War, the daunting federal program tried to transform the antebellum "Old" South from an isolationist Democratic region that endorsed slavery and racial inequality into a "New" South, or a nationalist Republican entity that promoted free labor and racial equality. The racial-political progress afforded by Reconstruction incited antiblack feeling among many white citizens, many of whom developed strategies for undermining the federal program. Such racial and political upheaval influenced the way in which Americans engaged popular culture, especially minstrelsy.

Of course, minstrelsy was not always a site of racial politics, anxiety, and iconography. Before 1842, it was primarily what Dale Cockrell calls the "culture of the ear."[12] An aural, traditionally European concept of minstrelsy prevailed in which whites, not yet in blackface, represented national bards or sang folk tunes in concerts before predominantly white bourgeois audiences. However, Dan Emmet's self-description as "Ethiopian Minstrel" in December 1842—as opposed to Tyrolese or Tyrolean Minstrel, German Minstrel, Alpine Minstrel, Boston Minstrel, or Cambrian Infant Minstrel, names that were already circulating at the time—anticipated the "culture of the eye," or the employment of racial and racist visual tropes for entertainment. "From a marketing perspective," according to Daniel H. Foster, "at this turning point the minstrel show had the advantage of being readable from two contrary perspectives: as descriptive by the middle class and as satire by African Americans and the working class," who became its subject. Minstrels thus "became more and more 'realistic,' that is, they were interpreted as being more representational but also racist."[13]

Early nineteenth-century minstrelsy was not especially racist (though racist examples do exist) but was especially classist in parodying the social, cultural, and ideological differences between the poor and the rich. However, the increasing American social anxieties over racial transgression and conflict in areas as far apart as the southern plantation (e.g., the Nat

Turner–led revolt) and the northern street (fugitive slaves and abolitionism) historically coincided with minstrelsy's reprioritization of class and racial symbolism to maintain the privilege, and to alleviate the anxieties, of the dominant white society.

By the mid-nineteenth century, minstrelsy was drawing on the wealth of racial and racist iconography in American culture. The images included "Old Negro" uncles, mammies, and "chillun'" dressing, talking, behaving, and thinking in inferior ways. Ranging from theatrical to literary exaggerations of "reality," caricatures of this sort oversimplified black perspectives and experiences while lampooning the idea of black assimilability in to American civilization.[14] The many audiences who embraced white minstrel performers in blackface as realistic portrayers of black life sustained this cultural phenomenon.[15]

Things changed when blacks entered the minstrel stage, however. In his monumental 1974 study, *Blacking Up*, Robert C. Toll examines more than any other scholar of minstrelsy, the phenomenon and implications of black minstrel performers in nineteenth-century America.[16] According to Toll, "colored" troupes between 1855 and 1890 developed a couple of self-marketing strategies that cemented the link between black performance and American popular culture. The first strategy included framing their advertisements with extensive quotes or paraphrases from reviews that praised the equal entertainment value of black minstrels and white minstrels in blackface. The second involved asserting, again in their advertisements, the racial realism and authenticity of their shows by selling the idea that black minstrels had lived on the plantation and were incorporating their experiences into their performances.

Such approaches led to remarkable results in the public perception of black minstrel performers. "Endlessly using the terms 'novelty,' 'curiosity,' 'genuine,' and 'bonafide,'" Toll notes, "reviewers grasped for words to express the unique appeal of these 'authentic' ex-slaves." Toll goes on to say that black minstrels often played out the racial stereotypes of blacks that, with the help of blackface minstrelsy, were already entrenched and deemed credible in American culture. Thus, white audiences viewed the black minstrels "as natural, spontaneous people on exhibit rather than as professional entertainers," and "as simply being themselves on stage, without artifice, cultivation, or control." As a result, throughout the nation "many white critics questioned the white minstrels' qualification to perform Negro, especially plantation, material." Spreading in white public circles, this doubt became "one of the major reasons white minstrels sharply decreased the plantation material in their shows and moved toward variety."[17] Black minstrelsy was culturally produced and consumed as a clear, unobstructed window into African American life, primarily because it conformed to preset expectations for minstrel performance.

Thinking about the racial realism of minstrelsy helps us to understand the marriage, at the turn of the twentieth century, of caricature and American literary realism. Writers such as Mark Twain, Edith Wharton, Frank Norris, Charles Chesnutt, Stephen Crane, William Howells, and Paul Laurence Dunbar connected their practices of realism to caricatures of racial or ethnic minorities. And this connection occurred despite the intuition, then and now, suggesting that caricature was incompatible with the ethics, aesthetics, and politics of American realism. According to Henry B. Wonham, realists and caricaturists conspired to demarcate "the outer edges of an inherently privileged bourgeois identity, reserving the ideal of an autonomous, sympathetic, and creative self as the racial prerogative of white middle-class Americans."[18]

In retrospect, the cultural phenomenon of minstrel realism among white middle-class audiences in the mid- to late nineteenth century anticipated the subsequent cultural value of caricature in the project of American realism. More than any other writer during the American realism movement (including Chesnutt, a fellow writer), Dunbar negotiated, exploited, and suffered from the ideological force of minstrelsy. Indeed, American cultural consumers were already attuned to the realist metaphors of racial caricature, but Dunbar's status as the "pure African type" lent his work an aura of racial authenticity unattainable by literary contemporaries identified as nonblack or mixed race.

Furthermore, the improvement in racial realism and authenticity applicable to the transition from blackface minstrelsy to black minstrelsy is analogous, as I will soon show, to the transition from the plantation tradition of Anglo-American literature to marketable African American literary realism. It goes without saying that the plantation tradition was borrowing from the same pool of racial stereotypes that enabled minstrel realism and American literary realism.[19] The phrase "plantation tradition," coined by Francis Pendleton Gaines in *The Southern Plantation* (1925), perhaps the first book-length scholarly treatment of the subject, developed in particular response to the racial politics of Reconstruction. David W. Blight explains:

In an era of tremendous social change and anxiety, a popular literature that embraced the romance of the Lost Cause, the idyll of the Old South's plantation world of orderly and happy race relations, and the mutuality of the "soldiers' faith" flowed from mass-market magazines as well as the nation's most prominent publishing houses. The age of machines, rapid urbanization, and labor unrest produced a huge audience for a literature of escape into a pre–Civil War, exotic South that, all but "lost," was now the object of enormous nostalgia.[20]

The plantation tradition referred mostly to the popular literature produced by white southerners. That literature included the poetry of Thomas Dunn English, the brothers Sidney and Clifford Lanier, and Irwin Russell; the novels of George Tucker, James Ewell Heath, Harriet Beecher Stowe, Francis Hopkinson Smith, and Mark Twain; and the shorter fiction of John Esten Cooke, John Pendleton Kennedy, William Gilmore Simms, and, most notably, Joel Chandler Harris and Thomas Nelson Page, both of whom, incidentally, regarded Irwin Russell as a literary mentor. While the works of these authors were not entirely homogeneous, Blight suggests that their plot constructions, characterizations, settings, symbolism, and themes consistently romanticized the plantation society and culture of the Old South in order to communicate and alleviate national anxieties over sectional reunion.[21]

Toward the end of the 1890s, along with the plantation tradition, Anglo-American literature, such as Thomas Nelson Page's *Red Rock: A Chronicle of Reconstruction* (1898) and Sarah Barnwell Elliott's *An Incident, and Other Happenings* (1899), demonstrated a shift toward the extreme expressions of white supremacist anxiety over brutish and unyielding slaves who rejected the concept of white superiority. Nonetheless, the romantic brand of racial representation peculiar to the plantation tradition remained a viable protocol of marketable African American literary realism. The broad appeal of such stereotypes resulted not simply from racism.

For example, Howells, whom I indict in this chapter for being one of the leading arbiters of minstrel realism, actually criticized the plantation tradition for trying to "tickle our prejudices and lull our judgment, or . . . coddle our sensibilities, or pamper our gross appetites for the marvelous." Arguably, Howells is denouncing the potential culpability of literature in perpetrating racism.[22] More important, however, than whether Howells and his critic contemporaries were racist is the broad ideological tradition of romantic racialism that anointed authenticity, both of authorship and textual representation, as the determinant of African American literary realism.

In this vein, the American literary market of the 1890s—particularly general readers, literary critics, acquisition editors, and publishers—welcomed black writers to the plantation tradition because of the accuracy of their orthographies of dialect. Dialect, the linguistic medium connecting the spiritual interior to the observable exterior, served minstrel and literary claims to realism, although, at best, it approximated and stereotyped the language of ethnic or racial groups.

Using a close reading of the text and context of Howells's "discovery" of Dunbar in *Harper's Weekly*, I will attempt to prove this point. It serves as a case study for how and why the continued appreciation for minstrelsy in American literary criticism unified realism with romantic racialism in characterizations of postbellum African American literature. Contrary to recent scholarly arguments minimizing his complicity, Howells ushered in this aesthetic union for the sake of African American canon formation in the late nineteenth century, although he had rejected this union for Anglo-American literature.

"The Pure African Type"

An extraordinary set of circumstances enabled Howells to influence the direction of African American literature. First of all, the June 27, 1896, issue of *Harper's Weekly* sold out on newsstands everywhere. Numerous readers demanded the magazine's report on the nomination of William McKinley at the Republican National Convention in St. Louis, Missouri. Even Dunbar failed to secure a copy of the "journal of civilization," which also detailed current events and featured editorial columns by prominent U.S. and foreign writers. Second, Howells's reviews wielded enough power to make or break an emerging writer's career. According to Van Wyck Brooks, "Howells was perhaps the only critic in the history of American literature who has been able to create reputations by a single review."[23] The wide circulation of this issue of *Harper's Weekly* empowered Howells to reach readers beyond the regular audience for his column or the magazine in general. More than most, he was effective in swaying readers' expectations and interpretations of Dunbar and *Majors and Minors*.

The special circumstances of *Harper's Weekly* led to the commercialization not only of Howells's hyperbole about the racial authenticity and precedence of *Majors and Minors*, but also of his inaccurate and therefore problematic insinuations about African American literary history. In his declaration that, prior to *Majors and Minors*, Dunbar's "race has not hitherto made its mark in his art," Howells neglects several black writers who were notable in various intellectual circles, both in America and abroad. They included Phillis Wheatley and George Moses Horton at the turn of the nineteenth century; William Wells Brown and Frederick Douglass in the mid-nineteenth century; Albery Allson Whitman, James M. Whitfield, Charles Chesnutt, and Frances Ellen Watkins Harper in the latter part of the century; and international writers of African descent, including early nineteenth-century authors Alexandre Dumas (*père* and *fils*) in France and Aleksander Pushkin in Russia. Wheatley, Horton, Whitman, Whitfield, and Harper, in particular, published substantial amounts of

Figure 2. Charles W. Chesnutt in 1879. (Fisk University John Hope and Aurelia Elizabeth Franklin Library Special Collections, Nashville, Tenn.)

poetry, while Dunbar's black contemporaries, who wrote primarily dialect poetry, included James Edwin Campbell, Daniel Webster Davis, and J. Mord Allen.

Of all these writers, only Douglass, Chesnutt, Dumas, and Pushkin appeared in essays Howells wrote elsewhere. None, as we shall soon see, could match Dunbar's literary potential in Howells's eyes—not even Chesnutt. Though Chesnutt was a writer well respected for publishing, in the *Atlantic Monthly*, several black-dialect short stories (which he later compiled for his first book, *The Conjure Woman* [1899]), he did not appear to Howells as racially authentic as he sounded in these volumes. In a November 10, 1901, letter to Henry Black Fuller, a Chicago novelist, Howells suggests that Chesnutt could pass for white: "You know he is a negro, though you wouldn't know it from seeing him."[24] Thinking similarly, anthologists in the early twentieth century tended to omit Chesnutt from the African American canon, due to his ostensible lack of black authenticity (Fig. 2).[25] Thus, Dunbar's impact on African American canon formation at the turn of the century—a period spanning his rise to prominence in 1896 to the eventual disappearance of his work from national periodicals and from anthologized canons of American literature by World War I—exceeded Chesnutt's. Dunbar's perceived racial "purity" enabled the literary marketplace to authenticate his dialect writing in ways initially inapplicable to the dialect writing of Chesnutt and other black authors of ostensibly mixed racial ancestry.[26]

In Howells's eyes, the sort of interracial complexion that characterized not only Chesnutt, but also Dumas and Pushkin, disqualified them from the tradition of authentic African American literature. In his introduction to Dunbar's third book of poems, *Lyrics of Lowly Life* (1896), an introduction that incorporates but also modifies his review of *Majors and Minors*, Howells argues that, though Dumas and Pushkin antedate Dunbar as renowned writers of African descent, "these were both mulattoes, who might have been supposed to derive their qualities from white blood . . . and who were the creatures of an environment more favorable to their literary development."[27] Dunbar, by contrast, was more authentic:

[T]he father and mother of the first poet of his race in our language were negroes without admixture of white blood. . . .

Paul Dunbar was the only man of pure African blood and of American civilization to feel the negro life aesthetically and express it lyrically. . . .

There is a precious difference of temperament between the races which it would be a great pity ever to lose, and . . . this is best preserved and most charmingly suggested by Mr. Dunbar in those pieces of his where he studies the moods and traits of his race in its own accent of our English.[28]

Howells's investment in the discourse of blood in his introduction to *Lyrics of Lowly Life* followed in the wake of the Supreme Court decision in *Plessy v. Ferguson*, which legalized the biological discourse of interracialism—that is, legally sanctioned ideas about descent from blacks and whites—and supported public notions that one could subject racial identity to biological measurement.[29] This discourse both pervaded the literary criticism and art of black authors and determined the politics of racial representation. By the time Howells was writing his introduction to *Lyrics of Lowly Life*, between September and December 1896, the biological language of *Plessy v. Ferguson* had already been seeping into American popular consciousness for close to half a year.[30] For Howells, one drop of "black blood" did not so much detract from the intellectual potency of "white blood" as it became, in its "unmixed" state, a racial virtue, just as it was in the minstrel industry.

Dunbar's status of "Poet Laureate of the Negro Race," the highest distinction enjoyed by any black author in the late nineteenth century, resulted from Howells's authenticating review. At the same time, Dunbar's *Majors and Minors* utilized the strategy of racial self-authentication behind the authorial frontispieces of, for example, Douglass's three autobiographies, *Narrative of the Life of Frederick Douglass* (1845), *My Bondage and My Freedom* (1855), and *Life and Times of Frederick Douglass* (1881, 1892). Just as Douglass, according to John Stauffer, "relied heavily on portrait photography and the picture-making process in general to create an authentic and intelligent black persona," Dunbar achieved a similar effect and became, in the eyes of contemporary reviewers, an icon of black authenticity.[31] The section entitled "Humor and Dialect" in *Majors and Minors* tantalized Howells and his contemporaries with minstrel realism, the cultural genre best capable of inaugurating a postbellum tradition of authentic African American literature.

The appeal of minstrel realism and the characterization of black minstrel performers in the postbellum nineteenth century help to explain Howells's phenotypical and physiognomic interpretation of Dunbar's frontispiece in *Majors and Minors*. Howells's description belonged to a long-standing Western intellectual discourse that defined racial authenticity as a mythic preservation of African purity across genealogical space and time. This discourse influenced Howells's embrace of *Majors and Minors* as a potential artistic manifestation of black authenticity. The book was an unprecedented "human event" for a race only one generation removed from slavery and striving for cultural acknowledgment in the New World. But "Majors and Minors," the first and largest section of the book, is the moment when Dunbar is, in Howells's words, "least himself" or least the "pure African type." The frontispiece and this section, in short, contradicted one another and complicated Howells's expectations.

Majors and Minors

Ironically, Dunbar is arguably "least himself" for most of *Majors and Minors*. The section entitled "Majors and Minors" comprises approximately seventy prayers, lyrics, odes, ballads, and sonnets, amounting to nearly 75 percent of the book's ninety-five poems. Demonstrating formal, or what Howells calls literary, English, most of the poems in this section employ and sometimes play with the conventional diction, rhyme schemes, and metrical structures of classical Western poetry. Themes of art, love, loss, family, and nature explored in poems such as "Ione," "The Change Has Come," "A Drowsy Day," "The Sparrow," "The Meadow Lark," and "A Creed and Not a Creed" hark back to the work of British Romantic poets like Percy Bysshe Shelley, Lord Byron, John Keats, William Wordsworth, and Samuel Taylor Coleridge.

Several poems, at the same time, counterbalance these universal narratives with specific racial and historical references to events, concepts, and figures. "Frederick Douglass" mourns the passing of Frederick Douglass on February 20, 1895, when the black abolitionist, orator, editor, and writer died of a heart attack just after delivering a fabulous speech at a convention for women's rights. Other poems in the "Majors and Minors" section are likewise racially significant. The speaker of "We Wear the Mask" suggests that the "grins and lies" of blacks—perhaps those in black minstrelsy—disguise collective inner pain and resentment toward their oppressed status. "Ode to Ethiopia" hails Ethiopians as the "Mother Race" from which blacks are descended. "The Colored Soldiers" reimagines the effort of black soldiers in the Civil War. "A Corn Song" envisions field hands returning home at dusk and resting their weary bodies.

The thematic and technical range of "Majors and Minors" reflects the range that one finds in Dunbar's other books of poetry. In most of them he is "least himself," too. His first three books are poems in "literary English" 78 percent of the time. Fifty of the fifty-six poems in his first book, *Oak and Ivy* (1893), are in formal English. Dunbar's third book, *Lyrics of Lowly Life*, a combination of the poems of *Oak and Ivy* and *Majors and Minors*, contains eighty poems in formal English. Poems in formal English likewise fill his later books, *Lyrics of the Hearthside* (1899), *Lyrics of Love and Laughter* (1903), and *Lyrics of Sunshine and Shadow* (1905). Over the course of his professional literary career, Dunbar committed himself more to this kind of poetry than to any other.

The finding that Dunbar tends to be "least himself" in *Majors and Minors* bothered Howells. In his review he transcribes the poem "Conscience and Remorse" prior to expressing his reservations:

"Goodbye," I said to my conscience—
"Goodbye for aye and aye,"
And I put her hands off harshly,
And turned my face away,
And conscience smitten sorely
Returned not from that day.

But a time came when my spirit
Grew weary of its pace;
And I cried: "Come back, my conscience,
I long to see thy face."
But conscience cried: "I cannot,
Remorse sits in my place."[32]

Such pieces, Howells complains, resemble "most of the pieces of the most young poets, cries of passionate aspiration and disappointment, more or less personal or universal, which except for the negro face of the author one could not find specifically notable." Granted, the poem is not Dunbar's best, but it is "notable" not just because of his "negro face" but because it belonged to a postbellum tradition of what Joan Sherman calls "neoclassical" black writers. Indeed, Islay Walden, Henrietta Cordelia Ray, Eloise Thompson, George Marion McClellan, and Timothy Thomas Fortune, among others, produced enough poems to suggest that their literary tradition was not an anomaly but a racial fixture. Their achievement was "specifically notable" not as a sole result of their common racial identity but due to their formal and tropological interest in more traditional British and American Romantic poetry. But, in Howells's eyes, the classical formal structures and "universal" romantic themes associated with white American and British poets read by both Howells and these black writers ran counter to his expectation of and investment in minstrel realism.

Howells often disregarded literary sentiment and romance in the promotion of realism, whose fundamental aspects he defines in *Criticism and Fiction* (1891). More specifically, Howells's endorsement of the "economy" of realism consistently included a critique of the "excess" of romance and sentiment. He degraded sentimentalism by resorting to such feminine stereotypes as "romantic," "melodramatic," "bizarre," and "sensational." "As the spokesman for American realism," Hildegard Hoeller notes in her study of Edith Wharton, "Howells uses the terms *economy* and *excess* to advertise realism's proportionate view of the world to correct the falsifying, excessive vision of the sentimental" that had historically been attributed to the domestic woman reader.[33] However, while characterizing Anglo-American literary realism as the eschewal of romance and sentiment, Howells permitted African American literary realism to embody both of these genres, despite his own gender politics. Thus, even if historical evidence proves that Howells was aware of "neoclassical" African American poetry, it is safe to assume that he would have disliked it, just as he had disliked Dunbar's. Herein lies Howells's racism, by the way: his implicit belief that African American poetry in formal English is inferior to Anglo-American poetry in formal English, simply because of what the author looks like.[34]

What is more, how could such poems as "Conscience and Remorse" come from the pen of a "pure African type"? Of course, the formally written "Frederick Douglass," "We Wear the Mask," "Ode to Ethiopia," "The Colored Soldiers," and "A Corn Song" arguably could have, due to their references to African American history. For Howells, though, even more appropriate and authentic examples of African American poetry are located in "Humor and Dialect," the short second section of *Majors and Minors*, where Dunbar is "most himself." The primary prosodic difference between "Humor and Dialect" and "Majors and Minors" lies not in the degree to which the latter is "literary" and the former is not. "Humor and Dialect" is literary, for it incorporates the same complex metrical structures and rhyme schemes in the formal poems of "Majors and Minors." The difference lies in the racial aesthetics of literary orthography.

"Humor and Dialect" recalls the local-color traditions of American dialect poetry, which includes the works of James Russell Lowell, Ella Wheeler Wilcox, Eugene Field, and James Whitcomb Riley. Dunbar studied the essential phonetic nuances distinguishing the vernacular of blacks and whites, midwesterners and northeasterners, Virginians and Mississippians, even the Irish and the British. In the nineteenth century, literary orthography encapsulated not only racial but also regional and national identity politics, since several kinds of ethnic and regional dialects were being spoken all across the United States.[35] The regional origin and experiences of writers, it was said, predetermined the exactitude, credibility, and aesthetics of their local-color dialect writing.[36] According to this definition, "Humor and Dialect" should have qualified for this genre of American literature.

The historical record shows, however, that local color signified something quite different for ethnic minorities. By the late nineteenth century, vaudeville shows exoticized Jewish, Irish, German, and Ethiopian language and culture. By reiterating the belief that true Americans descended from Anglo-Saxon England, these shows conspired in "othering," or making nonnormative, certain races or ethnic nationalities. The performance of dialect in American popular entertainment facilitated this cultural conspiracy, especially directed toward blacks.[37] Minstrelsy, in particular, associated black dialect with the romanticizing myths of black intellectual inferiority and verbal inarticulateness. At the heart of this connection was the racial essentialism of dialect. Dialect played an irrevocable role in the prevailing cultural myths of black society as a racial group and, subordinately, a regional group of traits and values.

Howells's *Harper's Weekly* review draws on these myths. In it he plays up the racial authenticity of Dunbar's dialect while playing down its local-color possibilities, even though the poet (like Howells) was a native Ohioan and sensitive to regional phonetics. At first, Howells seems to laud both the racial and the regional "ears" of Dunbar: "He [Dunbar] calls his little book *Majors and Minors*; the majors being in our American English, and the Minors being in dialect, the dialect the middle-south negroes and the middle-south whites; for the poet's ear has been quick for the accent of his neighbors as well as for that of his kindred."[38] This praise, however, belies the degree to which Howells is quick to racialize Dunbar's dialect, regard him as more African than American, and dismiss as more anomalous than the norm his formal English poems in the "Majors and Minors" section of the book.

Infatuated with the poetic potential of otherness, Howells creates an analogy between Dunbar and Robert Burns, the late eighteenth-century Scottish poet who once wrote lyrics in Scottish dialect. Like Dunbar, Burns achieved a command of dialect through his childhood engagement with orally transmitted folk songs and folktales. An autodidact, Burns soon mastered the art of versification and trope. His 1787 *Poems, Chiefly in the Scottish Dialect* demonstrates a poetic expertise applauded by Scottish lay folk and intellectual critics alike, elevating Burns to the status of premier Scottish dialect and realist poet of his country in the late eighteenth century. But Howells recommends that one read "Burns when he was most Burns, when he was most Scotch, when he was most peasant." Likewise, one should read Dunbar because he was, in Howells's words, "so far as I know, the first man of his color to study his race objectively, to analyze it to himself, and then to represent it in art as he felt it to be: to represent it humorously, yet tenderly, and above all so faithfully that we know the portrait to be undeniably like." Dunbar was most Dunbar when he was most Negro, Howells would have said. Dunbar resided in the folk, literally living among its members, near enough for intimate reportage. Yet Dunbar also belonged to the folk, was emotionally, psychically, and spiritually attached to them. In the dialect poems of his own "kindred," Howells suggests that Dunbar possessed his greatest racial "authority."

In the review, Howells recognizes and even transcribes many lines or stanzas of four poems that to him best illustrate the romantic and sentimental effects of Dunbar's dialect poetry. Respectively, "The Party" (which Howells mistitles as "The Pahty"), "When de Co'n Pone's Hot," "When Malindy Sings," and "Accountability" focus on a party attended by black folk from local plantations, the blessing of freshly cooked cornbread, one woman's overwhelming vocal talent, and the significance of human individuality and destiny. The laborious transcription of these poems—whose nearly fourteen hundred words constitute about half of the text typed for the review—affirms Howells's remarkable investment in exhibiting as much of Dunbar's poetry as the space of his column, "Life and Letters," allowed. This exhibition is not only literal, in the presentation of the dialect text as block quotations, but also figurative, as it exoticizes the dialect text within Howells's own book review.

Respectively, Howells describes the four poems—"The Pahty," "When de Co'n Pone's Hot," "When Malindy Sings," and "Accountability"—as examples of "primitive human nature," "rich, humorous sense," "fond sympathy," "purely and intensely black . . . feeling," and a "black piece" replete with "fine irony" and "neat satire." (Howells also mentions, but does not transcribe, another poem, "The Deserted Plantation," a postemancipation account of former slave territory.) Howells's descriptions of these representative poems in the "Humor and Dialect" section echo the interpretive language that had surrounded black minstrelsy a couple of decades earlier.

Howells celebrated the romantic excess of racial realism both in his own writings and in his criticism of African American literature. For example, Michele Birnbaum, Jeffory A. Clymer, M. Giulia Fabi, Joseph R. McElrath Jr., Elsa Nettels, Kenneth W. Warren, and Henry B. Wonham have shown that Howells's earlier fiction, namely, the short story "Mrs. Johnson" (1868), and the two novels *A Hazard of New Fortunes* (1890) and *An Imperative Duty* (1893), portray blacks in romantic, sentimental, or other problematic ways. The fiction manifests Howells's vulgar proclivity for minstrel realism and his subtle prejudices (not all pejorative) about racial difference. Moreover, according to Wonham's investigation of the letters between Howells and Twain, as late as 1908, Howells was advising Twain to read for literary inspiration George Ade's *Pink Marsh* (1897), a "novel about a black shoeshine boy in Chicago" who spoke in admirably "rich dialect, a version of the quaint broken English spoken by the 'resplendent darkeys in livery' who populate the dim backgrounds of Howells's own fiction."[39] Finally, in his late critical writings, especially in his criticism of Chesnutt's fiction and Booker T. Washington's autobiographical writing, he romanticizes black psychology and sociology.[40]

Howells's *Harper's Weekly* review of *Majors and Minors* also links to his later commentary on racial purity. In "An Exemplary Citizen," a 1901 review of Booker T. Washington's work, Howells expresses his long-standing conviction that three kinds of black writers exist, according to concentrations of African blood: "Mr. Dunbar is entirely black, and Mr. Chesnutt, to the unskilled eye, is entirely white. Mr. Washington, as Douglass was, is a half-blood. But they are all colored people, and it is only just to credit their mother-race with their uncommon powers and virtues."[41] These men constitute Howells's African American canon. Aside from Dunbar, Chesnutt, Douglass, and Washington, he also discusses Alexandre Dumas (*père* and *fils*) and Aleksander Pushkin. But Dunbar stands above the rest in racial purity. Granted, Howells could be viewed as contradicting those of his era who attributed the "uncommon powers and virtues" of the aforementioned black authors to white blood. Yet the ambiguity of the phrase "uncommon powers and virtues" still leaves open the possibility that he was valuing racial purity in a way consistent with his earlier praise of the racial authenticity of Dunbar's dialect poetry.

In the *Harper's* review, Howells's obsession with this idea of "entirely black verse" causes him to misrepresent certain verses in "Humor and Dialect" as "black." In one of the section's poems, "When Malindy Sings," the only marker of racial realism is the spiritual that Malindy sings, "Swing Low, Sweet Chariot." The song does not guarantee that Malindy, or any of the other figures in the poem, descends from Africans. In fact, along with the poems that Howells calls ostensibly "non-negro dialect pieces"— "Speaking o' Christmas" (which he mistitles as "Speakin' o' Christmas"), "After a Visit," "Lonesome," and "The Spellin' Bee"—several other dialect poems are not "black," though their location in the section "Humor and Dialect" compels lumping them together as such.

Howells's review generated much critical excitement over the implications of *Majors and Minors*. The repercussions were immediate when the readers of *Harper's Weekly* learned that Dunbar represented the "Robert Burns of Negro Poetry" and was a poet who wrote with the authentic voice of his race. In the wake of Howells's review, various lay and intellectual communities read, discussed, or wrote about the review, appreciating Dunbar in a way analogous to the way in which advertisers and audiences appreciated black minstrel performers. Cultural institutions like journals, magazines and newspapers, and marketing apparatuses turned Dunbar into a racial phenomenon.[42]

Between September 1896 and May 1897, reviewers of Dunbar's book echoed the viewpoint that Howells had discovered the most promising poet of his race. One reviewer regarded *Majors and Minors* as a "remarkably hopeful production" and a "triumphant demonstration" of the potential of the black race for verbal rhyme and melody. Another believed that the book "was not great, but it had, in its dialect verse at least, a certain homeliness of sentiment which challenged attention."

Greater proof of Dunbar's phenomenal status appears in reviews of his next book of poems, *Lyrics of Lowly Life.* Printed between January 1897 and April 1898 in major U.S. and British periodicals, the ten reviews praised Dunbar's orthography of dialect as an accurate and authentic re-creation of black vernacular. The critics stated that the dialect poems were "on the whole, excellent"; examples of a Negro being "thoroughly spontaneous and natural"; "pure Negro songs"; "not overloaded . . . with ornaments of culture so heavy and costly that the slender thought can stagger beneath the weight"; and, finally, contributions to his "becom[ing] an interesting phenomen[on]. He is a full blood Negro. These phrases characterizing the dialect poems of *Majors and Minors* echo those phrases previously applied to black minstrel performance, and those phrases central to Howells's review of Dunbar's *Majors and Minors.*"[43]

Howells did for Dunbar what various prefatory or concluding letters, signatures, guarantees, and tales had done for former-slave authors: he authenticated a "newfound black voice."[44] Most authenticators of slave narratives were white, and they commanded this literary industry as amanuenses, editors, or ghostwriters. Just as important as the authenticator's racial identity were the rhetorical strategies they employed to convince a predominantly white readership that former slaves could read as well as write, and even do so at high intellectual levels. Authenticators counteracted public doubts about black authorship, legitimized the slave narrative as well written and historically accurate, and established the aesthetic value of that narrative. Although Howells valued dialect, not just formal English, as the literary vernacular of choice, the slave-narrative paradigm applies to his authentication of Dunbar.

The *Harper's Weekly* review was not attached to *Majors and Minors* in the way that authenticating documents were literally appended to slave narratives. But the article functioned as a symbolic authenticating document whose "attachment" to Dunbar's literary work became literal. Indeed, a few months after the review's publication, Howells revised and reprinted it as the introduction to *Lyrics of Lowly Life*, making the review an authenticating appendage used to market the book far and wide. The review helped to elevate Howells to the commercial influence of Walter Hines Page and Richard Watson Gilder, editors who encouraged black authors to write literature in dialect to get published.[45]

Dunbar's association with the dean of American letters did not end with *Majors and Minors*. He published and circulated his next book, *Lyrics of Lowly Life*, with Howells's introduction, to the delight of readers much greater in number and regional span than those who might have personally come across *Majors and Minors* or even the book review in *Harper's Weekly*. The New York publisher Dodd, Mead, and Company released *Majors and Minors* for the first time in the United States in late 1896, and the Young People's Missionary Movement of the United States and Canada reprinted it that same year. An English edition of *Majors and Minors* appeared a year later under the imprint of London's Chapman and Hall Publishers, and Toronto's G. N. Morang Company reprinted it yet again in 1898. Letters sent from Howells to Dunbar while the poet was lecturing in England (from February to August 1897) encouraged British publishers to consider publishing *Majors and Minors*.

Hardly any of the black writers at the turn of the century were as nationally and internationally commercial as Dunbar, because both the personnel and the geographic reach of their presses were remarkably limited. Black writers such as Anna Julia Cooper, Frances Ellen Watkins Harper, Pauline Hopkins, Amelia Johnson, Emma Dunham Kelley-Hawkins, and Sutton Griggs published, respectively, with Ohio's Aldine Printing House, Philadelphia's Garrigues Brothers, Boston's Colored Co-operative Publishing Company, Philadelphia's American Baptist Publication Society, Providence's Continental Printing Company, and Cincinnati's The Editor Publication Company. None of these presses, though, possessed the national prestige of those publishing Dunbar's books of poetry.

The two black writers who worked with publishing companies equal in prestige to Dunbar's were Charles Chesnutt and Booker T. Washington. Chesnutt released *The Conjure Woman* (1899) and *The Wife of His Youth* (1899) through Boston's Houghton, Mifflin, and Company. Washington revised and reprinted his first autobiography, *The Story of My Life and Work* (1900), which Illinois's J. L. Nichols and Company first released, as *Up from Slavery* (1901) with Doubleday, Page, and Company. But despite Chesnutt's and Washington's emergences in U.S. periodicals and politics, respectively, Dunbar was the first black writer born after slavery to achieve both national and international acclaim and commercial success for his literary work.

The black poet William Stanley Braithwaite, in an October 7, 1899, letter to Howells, captures Dunbar's phenomenal success. Braithwaite introduces himself to Howells as "Your Ob[edient]. Servant" and addresses
him as "Most Reverend Sir": "I am an American Negro in my twentieth
year who has just come to New York with a *MS* with the hope of disposing
of it to a publisher . . . To you as the 'Dean of American Literature' I make
an application for assistance, hoping that you will evince the same interest
in me and my work (if you find it worthy of your consideration) as you revealed in behalf of Paul L. Dunbar."[46] Evidently, Dunbar's "entirely black
verse" had succeeded.

"Irrevocable Harm"

By associating Dunbar with minstrel realism, I depart from twentieth-
century debates over whether he sold out to inherently racist mainstream
literary and publishing tastes. Currently, the most popular scholarly argument on this subject emphasizes Dunbar's disenchantment with Howells
and American literary criticism and shows that the poet was more polemical than his mainstream readers might have realized.

Dunbar held mixed feelings about Howells's review. Sixteen days after it
appeared, he sent Howells a July 13, 1896, letter, stating that he had read
the article and "felt its effect."[47] Less than a year after thanking Howells,
however, on October 22, 1896, Dunbar lamented: "One critic says a thing
and the rest hasten to say the same thing, in many instances using the iden-
tical words. I see now very clearly that Mr. Howells has done me irrevocable harm in the dictum he laid down regarding my dialect verse. I am
afraid that it will even influence English criticism."[48] Dunbar realized that
Howells was no different from most audiences of minstrel shows. The dean
was one of many "intelligent people . . . unable to differentiate dialect as a
philological branch from the burlesque of Negro minstrelsy." Such statements have been well documented and examined.[49]

Scholars have also argued that Dunbar's dialect poems were, all along,
protesting minstrel realism even as they seemed to be perpetuating it.[50]
This is analogous to the argument that black minstrelsy imitated blackface
minstrelsy as a way to seek vengeance against Old Negro stereotypes. The
public interpretations of Dunbar's dialect poetry and black minstrelsy were
also analogous. Audiences tended to miss the protest of black minstrelsy,
just as readers often failed to detect the protest by Dunbar and black authors of dialect literature.[51]

Dunbar's polemical interests are conceivable. Records show that minstrel realism bothered him well before Howells catapulted him into literary

prominence. To his wife of forty-three days, Alice Ruth Moore, Dunbar sent a letter wondering if he and other black writers were obligated to contest the plantation tradition.[62] Little did Dunbar know that one year after writing this letter, the critical and commercial success of *Majors and Minors* would conspire in the standardization of minstrel realism for African American literature. Consequently, Dunbar battled early in his literary career against minstrel realism as well as against readers who pigeonholed his dialect poetry into this cultural genre. Eventually, he used the weapons of racial uplift against romantic racialism, New Negro realism against minstrel realism, and, when these weapons failed, his anomalous first novel.

Chapter 2

"We Must Write Like the White Men"

On February 12, 1899, Paul Laurence Dunbar was reciting poems at New York City's Waldorf-Astoria Hotel in celebration of Hampton Institute, a decade-old black college. His reading attracted the attention of a reporter curious about the poet laureate's opinion of "poetry written by Negroes." The *New York Commercial* (February 14, 1899) printed an excerpt of this interview:

"In the poetry written by Negroes, which is the quality that will most appear, something native and African and in every way different from the verse of the Anglo-Saxons, or something that is not unlike what is written by white people?"

"My dear sir," replied [Dunbar], "the predominating power of the African race is lyric. In that I should expect the writers of my people to excel. But, broadly speaking, their poetry will not be exotic or differ much from that of the whites."

"But surely, the tremendous facts of race and origin——"

"You forget that for two hundred and fifty years the environment of the Negro has been American, in every respect the same as that of all other Americans."

The reporter still objected: "Isn't there a certain tropic warmth, a cast of temperament that belongs of right to the African race, and should not that element make its lyric expression, if it is to be genuine, a thing apart?"

"Ah, what you speak of is going to be a loss. It is inevitable. *We must write like the white men.* I do not mean imitate them; but our life is now the same." Then the speaker added: "I hope you are not one of those who would hold the negro down to a certain kind of poetry—dialect and concerning only scenes on plantations in the south." This appeared to be a sore point, and the questioner at once truthfully denied having any such desire.[1] (Italics mine)

In his statement that blacks "must write like the white men," Dunbar's use of the modal "must" was not a way of insisting what blacks *should* do. Rather, he meant that blacks necessarily wrote like white men, because both wrote from within and in response to a sharable national culture. Dunbar's subordination of racial difference to cultural similarity was therefore at odds with his interlocutor's rather Howellsian racialism. In his writing, Dunbar searched for strategies to counter the influences of minstrel realism and its literary dean over the nature, reception, and direction of African American literature.

Dunbar's main strategy was the racial doctrine of "uplift ideology," or "racial uplift." Asserting that human races could be "elevated" in moral, intellectual, and physical terms, racial uplift enabled African American writers to combat minstrel realism in at least two ways. The first, New Negro realism, provided a literary language for discussing race relations, critiquing minstrel iconography, and portraying blacks as uplifted in culture, morality, intellect, and spirit. The second kind of realism deviated from these previous two mergers of racialism and realism. Accommodated by what Victoria Earle Matthews called "Race Literature," this anomalous realism encoded the markers of class and region while submerging that of race. This special aesthetic applies to Dunbar's first novel, *The Uncalled* (1898).

Dunbar's oeuvre suffers from the scholarly reflex to treat anomalous texts as if they never existed. He is well known for his dialect poetry and novel of racial uplift, *The Sport of the Gods* (1902), but less known for his many poems in formal English and his collections of short stories and novels about the Midwest. Accordingly, *The Uncalled*, set mostly in the province of Dexter, Ohio, has fallen through the cracks of African American literary studies. Scholars who do refer to this novel do so in problematic terms. Peter Revell regards both *The Uncalled* and Dunbar's second novel, *The Love of Landry* (1900), as "'white' novels, in which all the characters are white and virtually no reference is made to the presence of black people in the society [these novels] depict."[2] For Kenny J. Williams, *The Uncalled* is "'race-less' in the sense that Dunbar does not specify what race his characters are; neither does he by speech or other mannerisms identify them more than to make clear that they are all small-town Midwesterners with the speech patterns of that locale."[3] As Williams suggests, Revell is wrong in assuming that the novel's failure to depict "black people" automatically means that it employs "white characters" alone, to the neglect of African American history. On the other hand, Williams's assumption that the novel prioritizes region and class underestimates the importance and complexity of racial identity among "small-town Midwesterners."

The Uncalled is neither white nor simply raceless; its racialism lies in its historical depictions of class hierarchy and regional culture. Specifically, the novel incorporates African American histories of racial unrest and inequity to expose the thematic limitations of local color, then regarded as a more idealistic version of literary realism. Implicitly, it deviates from traditional Anglo-American literature, which tends to overlook the racial politics of local color while stereotyping nonindustrialized rural spaces as good and urban spaces as evil.

Dunbar's novel also complicates the kind of literary realism Howells associated with Anglo-American literature. It does so by addressing such ideas as spirituality, heritage, destiny, and the environment in ways that contradict Howells's protocols for literary verisimilitude, namely, simplicity, naturalness, and honesty. In several ways, the novel anticipates the so-called romantic naturalism of Frank Norris, a white writer who called for profound literary forays into the minds and hearts of the lower class.

Unlike Norris's version of literary naturalism, however, *The Uncalled* contradicts the conventional masculinist "plot of decline." Jennifer L. Fleissner describes this plot as the "fatalistic" depiction of "modern individuals [as] bereft of agency or vitality, dwarfed by a cityscape of soulless mechanical dynamos," and thus as ultimately tragic. By contrast, Dunbar's novel illustrates the importance of individual will to overcoming environmental forces, even within the city. It shows how Fred Brent can ultimately embrace modern civilization not despite but because of a respect for—or an anticipation of interaction with—women in his life. Women, Fleissner shows, had come to mark the strained relationship between men and modernity.[4] Dunbar alleviates this tension through discourses on human interiority. Thus, while worthy of the term "second-generation realist," then assigned only to white writers such as Norris and Stephen Crane, Dunbar demonstrates in this novel that he was more talented and philosophical as a novelist than writers and critics in his era gave him credit for, and more so than present-day scholars have realized.

Racial Uplift and African American Literary Character

In nineteenth-century America, racial uplift focused on the civilization of the folk. Antithetical to the prevailing "romantic racialism," discussed in Chapter 1, racial uplift asserted that blacks could be "elevated," "uplifted," "developed," or "improved" toward "respectability," a term then associated with the white upper classes. Moral uplift signified growth in ethical sophistication as well as spiritual or religious consciousness. Intellectual uplift involved formal and informal education and the development of cultural literacy. Physical uplift improved dress, hygiene, and social conduct, exterior qualities that supposedly stabilized the interior psyche, emotions, and spirit. Nineteenth-century black assemblies and conventions articulated these three dimensions of racial uplift in their struggle against racism, in demonstration of black pride, and in aspiration toward national acceptance. Consisting of various northern communities, religious groups, and literary organizations, these conferences usually featured elite race representatives who subordinated both the regional sectionalism and the patronizing classism fracturing the race from within.[5]

Dunbar viewed the world through racial-uplift ideology. As early as 1890, at the age of eighteen and as the only black student at Dayton's Central High School, he published an editorial in the *Dayton Tattler* pleading with local black readers to subscribe to the newspaper (December 13, 1890). The paper was designed to keep readers abreast of the progress of black communities in Dayton, in Ohio, and in other regions of the United States. Essays Dunbar wrote later in life followed in this same vein. In "Of Negro Journals" (1894), he claims that mid-nineteenth-century black journals such as *Freedom's Journal* and *North Star* were the first signs of black intellectual progress. In another essay, "England as Seen by a Black Man" (1897), he states that his trip to England and his experiences with British citizens prompted the development of "some ideas to inform and elevate Negro family life."[6] To drive home the importance of racial uplift, Dunbar wrote "Recession Never," an essay so scathing to the white majority that *McClure's* magazine, which originally commissioned it, refused to publish the piece. The essay contends that the 1898 riots in Wilmington, North Carolina, would encourage black "growth, the inevitable" result of "going forward."[7] In another essay, "The Negroes of the Tenderloin: Paul Laurence Dunbar Sees Peril for His Race in Life in the City" (1898), Dunbar's imagined district of black "denizens" between Twentieth and Fifty-third streets in midtown Manhattan is the object of racial-uplift analysis: "[I]f the better-class Negro would come to his own he must lift not only himself, but the lower men, whose blood brother he is. . . . [T]he fate of the blacks there, degraded, ignorant, vicious as they may be, is his fate."[8] Dunbar's critique of the disastrous impact of northeastern urbanity on human character is a major component of his racial-uplift argument.

Dunbar's poetry and fiction also take up the subject of racial uplift. Aside from the poems in *Majors and Minors* mentioned in Chapter 1— "Frederick Douglass," "We Wear the Mask," "Ode to Ethiopia," and "The Colored Soldiers"—Dunbar wrote "The Ordeal at Mt. Hope." A short story included in his collection *Folks from Dixie* (1898), "The Ordeal at Mt. Hope" critiques Booker T. Washington's prioritization of industrial over intellectual labor in his conception of uplift. Furthermore, Dunbar's fourth novel, *The Sport of the Gods*, focuses on the role of migration from the South to the North, the country to the city, in the black search for social and economic opportunities. While indicting white southern patriarchy, this novel criticizes the black intelligentsia for hanging out with gamblers and night owls in the clubs of New York City. The club in the novel contributes to the moral decline of Joe Hamilton, the protagonist, while the "gamblers [continue] to sermonize in their unlikely role as purveyors of the moral discourse of Darwinian determinism and social control, cynically abdicating responsibility for their exploitation of Joe."[9] *The Sport of the Gods* thus operates both within and against the theme of racial uplift. It addresses the importance of racial uplift as much as it portrays the black intelligentsia as hypocrites of racial progress.

Although he belonged to the racial-uplift category of black authors, Dunbar also countered minstrel realism through the presentation of "literary character." "Literary character," Elizabeth McHenry elaborates, "offered black Americans a way to refute widespread claims of their miserable, degraded position; examples of it, made visible at meetings of African American literary societies or through the pages of a black newspaper, would counter assumptions of African inferiority with displays of black genius."[10] Literary character, in other words, was a trope of the New Negro and a means of reconstructing and thereby uplifting the image of blacks. "New Negroes rewrite the iconography of the black body itself to effect the bodily intrusion they see as the sole means to personal and collective uplift," notes Marlon Ross. "The energetic force of the black body is indicated in its very composition and stance—the serious countenance of the face, the concentrated intentness of the eyes, the upward bearing of the head, the alert posture of the limbs."[11] Discourses of the New Negro emerged principally to contest the caricatures of the Old Negro, discussed in Chapter 1. Literature, photographs, illustrations, drama, theatre, and speeches were some of the contexts in which blacks declared that the race could be elevated.

Black authors infused New Negro ideology into literary character. They eyed the development of a special kind of racial realism—a New Negro realism—that formalized the language, dignified the appearance, and refined the culture of blacks. New Negro realism sought to prove by stylistic and tropological means that blacks could assimilate into American society.[12] Yet in the court of public opinion, New Negro realism was losing, to minstrel realism, the battle over racial representation. White critics called the bourgeois and articulate (New) Negro literary protagonists "amorphous," "artificial," and "bitter." By contrast, the protagonists of minstrel realism were ostensibly more graspable and servile, and hence realistic.[13] The heightened language of New Negro realism, which included recitations of Western canonical literature, failed to capture what most readers claimed should have been the authentic cadences of black voices. The consistent dismissals of New Negro realism, it turns out, veiled a deeper anxiety over the threat of racial uplift to white supremacy.[14]

Ultimately, black intellectuals hoped that Dunbar's poetry would help to advance the race. One article in *Woman's Era* hails Howells's review of *Majors and Minors* as an important step for African America: "Paul Laurence Dunbar is recognized as a true poet by the first critics of America and his little volume, 'Majors and Minors,' will be welcomed as a contribution to real literature. There is hardly a recent circumstance that means more to the race than this. As Mr. Howells says it is probably through the arts that nations are to be brought together and hostilities and prejudices to disappear."[15]

But this opinion was in the minority. For many black intellectuals, the polemical underside of African American literature written in dialect likely could not emerge visibly enough to deal with the stigma of minstrelsy. An article in *A.M.E. Church Review* (October 1896) worries that, in the wake of Howells's review of *Majors and Minors*, "titillated" editors "with the commercial side well developed will besiege [Dunbar] for a copy in a 'minor' view."[16] White readers had similarly mistaken the polemics of black dialect literature for the racism of minstrel realism. For this reason, the black press—*Colored American Magazine, Voice of the Negro, Horizon,* and *Woman's Era*—mostly regarded the racial uplift in dialect literature as ineffective.

By contrast, other black periodicals claimed that African American literature should combat minstrel realism by avoiding racial realism altogether. In the January 7, 1848, issue of *North Star*, Frederick Douglass tries to rally black readers around two causes: "we must do just what white men do"; and "we must take our stand side by side with our white fellow countrymen, in all the trades, arts, profession[s] and callings of the day."[17] An article published in *Woman's Era*, "Negro Folk-Lore" (September 1894), reiterates this point. Quoting George Washington Cable, the article proposes that "the colored people [should] make all haste to drop those marks distinctly Negroid, to strive to write like a white man, dress like a white man, and talk like one, and so hasten on the day when they will be distinguished only as 'Americans.'"[18]

Although almost half a century apart, these articles express a goal shared by countless other writers of racial uplift in the postbellum nineteenth century: for black writers to prove their literary dexterity and their creative and intellectual comparability with white writers. It was no longer good enough simply to write slave narratives. Douglass once accused this genre of being "a form of verbal bondage" that shackled African American literature to a particular kind of aesthetics and limited its readership, criticism, and commercial appeal.[19] Mindful of these limitations, intellectuals in the black press embraced the literary art of such writers as Henry Wadsworth Longfellow, James Fenimore Cooper, Henry

Beecher Ward, Lydia Maria Child, and Ralph Waldo Emerson. Certainly as a direct result of their racial identities and positions in American society, these white authors were free to explore the possibilities of individualism and democracy without the obligation to address the problems of slavery, racism, and institutionalized racial oppression. Some black authors wanted to write literature with this sense of freedom and with universal themes in mind.[20]

These authors discovered that they could not escape the racial meaning of their writing. It was in "The Value of Race Literature," a lecture delivered by black writer and feminist Victoria Earle Matthews at the First Conference of Colored Women of the United States, in Boston, Massachusetts, on July 30, 1895, that the term "Race Literature" was coined to refer to what we now call African American literature.[21] Race Literature, however, includes not only those works that flaunt racial realism—or "race matter," in Matthews's words—but also those that do not. When "developed," according to Matthews, this tradition not only would "compare favorably with many, but [would] stand out pre-eminent, not only in the limited history of colored people, but in the broader field of universal literature." Race Literature also pitted itself against minstrel caricatures of blacks who were "the wrongly interpreted and [whose frailties were] too often grossly exaggerated." Matthews hoped that Race Literature would "enlarge our scope, make us better known wherever real lasting culture exists, [would] undermine and *utterly drive out the traditional Negro in dialect,*—the subordinate, the servant as the type representing a race whose numbers are now far into the millions."[22]

Less than one year after Howells's review of *Majors and Minors*, Dunbar began writing a novel without "race matter," so to speak, at a time when race especially mattered for African American literature. While lecturing and reciting poetry across England between February 6 and August 7, 1897, as "Poet Laureate of the Negro Race," he began to wonder what would happen if he wrote a novel that avoided all the conventional types of race matter—not only minstrel realism but New Negro realism as well. During early to mid-March 1897, in "the heart of a typical English home among the hills of Somerset," he began to write that novel. Soon he became so invested in the project that, over the course of a "few" evenings, he wrote "sixteen thousand words in prose."[23] He entitled the novel *The Uncalled* and published it first in *Lippincott's Monthly Magazine: A Popular Journal of General Literature, Science, and Politics* (May 1898). Several months later, Dodd, Mead, and Company, a major New York–based publishing house, released the novel in book form. *The Uncalled* was the first novel by an

African American writer to be nationally marketed, sold, and reviewed in the wake of Howells's praise of *Majors and Minors*.

The Uncalled

Book reviewers in American and British periodicals expressed disappointment that Dunbar had written about Dexter, Ohio, without invoking the conventions of minstrel realism. As one *Bookman* reviewer put it, in "*The Uncalled* [Dunbar] is an outsider . . . Mr. Dunbar should write about Negroes."[24] Indeed, for the most part, *The Uncalled* avoids the racially explicit dialect that had made Dunbar the preeminent black poet.[25] The best example lies in an early section of the novel. Six elderly women—Mrs. Mandy Warren, Miss Melissy Davis, Miss Austin, Miss Hester Prime, and two other women whom Dunbar leaves unnamed—gather at a local house after having departed the funeral of Margaret Brent, the deceased mother of the novel's protagonist, Fred Brent. Together, the women ponder the fate of Margaret's only son, Fred:

"It's a pity we don't know some good family that 'ain't got no children that 'ud take him an' bring him up as their own son," said a little woman who took *The Hearth-side*.

"Sich people ain't growin' on trees no place about Dexter," Mrs. Warren sniffed.

"Well, I'm sure I've read of sich things. Ef the child was in a book it 'ud happen to him, but he ain't. He's a flesh and blood youngster an' a-livin' in Dexter."

"You couldn't give us no idee what to do, could you, Mis' Austin?"

"Lord love you, Mis' Davis, I've jest been a-settin' here purty nigh a-thinkin' my head off, but I ain't seen a gleam of light yit. You know how I feel an' just how glad I'd be to do something, but then my man growls about the three we've got."

That's jest the way with my man," said the little woman who took her ideas of life from the literature in *The Hearthside*. "He allus says that pore folks oughtn't to have so many childern."

"Well, it's a blessin' that Margar't didn't have no more, fur goodness knows it's hard enough disposin' o' this one." (24–25)

Dunbar's reputation for black dialect poetry, in *Majors and Minors*, invites a racial interpretation of this conversation. The identities of the speakers and their speech, however, are not delineated with sufficient clarity to do so. While *The Hearthside* reference confirms the literacy of the unnamed "little woman," her affinity for learning clashes with her dialect, which consistently subordinates her and the other characters to the more educated ones who speak in formal English.

Regional culture, it turns out, marks this literary rendering of dialect. Over the course of his career, Dunbar consistently conceived of dialect in this way, writing in New Orleans Creole (or French English), German American, Irish American, and midwestern (Kentucky, Ohio, Indiana) dialects. *The Uncalled* shares the same tendency to experiment with regional dialects that transgress racial and ethnic boundaries.[26]

Race figures implicitly in the resistance of *The Uncalled* to conveying the democratic idealism of conventional local-color writing. In Dunbar's era, local-color writing celebrated regional speech, etiquette, habits, vistas, and atmosphere at a time when the nation was reeling from the Civil War's disruption of national stability and community. While such authors as Thomas Sergeant Perry, George Pellew, Hamlin Garland, and William Dean Howells regarded local color as a more democratic and idealistic version of literary realism, *The Uncalled* illustrates a bleaker side of local color and, by extension, literary realism.[27] The novel focuses on how industrialism produces not only moral conflict between and within provinces but also cultural differences between small-town and urban values. It complicates the polarity of good versus evil, which American literature often invested in provinces as opposed to cities.

Dexter is not the idyllic rural town it appears to be, as one learns from the description of a "mean" section where Mrs. Brent, Fred's mother, once lived. "Mean" connotes the personal characteristics of spite, unkindness, or aggression; it also symbolizes the social conditions of shabbiness and impoverishment. Within this sort of abode once lived Margaret Brent, the exact cause of whose "affliction" and death remains vague (5). For all the reader knows, Margaret was a "pore creature" simply because she suffered from personal misfortune and a lack of money (4). Consequently, the Dexter community stigmatizes her son, Fred, for having immoral parents (the father was a deadbeat) who once lived in the "mean" section of town. An unmarried churchgoing woman, Hester Prime, later volunteers not only to rear Fred but also to cleanse his soul and steer him toward the ministry. As such, Miss Prime is the moral antithesis of Fred's mother. In her words, "Margar't Brent was n't my kind durin' life, an' that I make no bones o' sayin' here an' now" (5).

The aesthetic differences between the homes of Margaret Brent and Miss Prime translate into the moral differences between the two women:

At the top of the mean street on which Margaret's house was situated, and looking down upon its meaner neighbours in much the same way that its mistress looked upon the denizens of the street, stood Miss Prime's cottage. It was not on the mean street,—it would have disdained to be,—but sat exactly facing it in prim watchfulness over the unsavoury thoroughfare which ran at right angles. The cottage was one and a half stories in height, and the upper half-story had two windows in front that looked out like a pair of accusing eyes. (32)

The novel's comparison of Mrs. Brent's and Miss Prime's residences connects morality to culture and class to region. Dexter's modernization strengthens these connections. As the streets of Dexter become paved, Margaret's "mean" street is "built up" to look "respectable." The town generates suburban outgrowths. Electric cars begin to roar. Amusement parks sprout across the province. A smoky sewing-machine factory, full of bustling workers, juts atop a central hill. Dexter becomes "the hurrying town" (105–7). By putting cities at the center of local-color writing, *The Uncalled* compromises the genre's tendency to depict provinces as resistant to urbanization and industrialism.[28]

This story about the mean streets leaves open the possibility of a racial reading of *The Uncalled* against the backdrop of American history. Elizabeth Ammons and Valerie Rohy stress that turn-of-the-twentieth-century American literature could not ignore the mass abandonment of rural farms for urban life. Nor could it ignore the influx of millions of immigrants into the United States and the failure of radical Reconstruction. Migration led to rural depopulation and urban population, which created friction between ethnic groups.[29] Such local and national histories of racial unrest and inequity resulting from American modernity should frame our reading of how *The Uncalled* exposes local-color writing's false hope of democracy.

The racial politics of Ohio demographics in the 1890s resonates in the characterization of Dexter's mean streets, where the "denizens of the poorer quarter" live (34). David A. Gerber has shown that black neighborhoods in Ohio cities were often decayed and teeming with inhabitants. Indeed, the tenement housing of Central Avenue and East Thirty-fourth Street in the Twelfth Ward of Cleveland, which, in 1913, the chief of Cleveland's Bureau of Sanitation called the worst housing residence in the United States, resembles Margaret's house, down to the detail of the ramshackle roof. The tenements "were overcrowded and often characterized by dilapidated exteriors, leaking roofs, defective and insufficient plumbing, poor lighting and ventilation, and wooden frames which easily caught fire and wooden backstairs which occasionally collapsed."[30] Of course, the "shiftlessness," "untidiness," and "immorality" of the mean street "denizens" could merely be referring to the moral cancer of a "poorer quarter" that Miss Prime seeks to cure in Fred. But the association between these economic conditions and urban African America is clearly there as well.[31] Class was indeed but one of several cultural contexts in which racism prevented blacks and whites from achieving equal footing in American society and culture. American literature, Dunbar suggests, must address such cultural contexts before it can transition from local-color writing to more historically contingent versions of literary realism.

Moreover, local color and literary realism—as Howells defined them—cannot account entirely for the moral and thematic complexity of *The Uncalled*. The novel traces Fred's development from the mean streets of Dexter to his experimentation with Methodism, then to his secular enlightenment in Cincinnati. In these cultural geographies appear the relationship between human development and the environment at a deep spiritual level often left unexplored by either local color or realism, both of which interpreted the environment through a focal human consciousness. In a letter from London to his fiancée, Alice Ruth Moore, Dunbar discusses his first novel in these terms: "My novel grows apace, though I can hardly call that a novel which is merely the putting together of a half dozen distinct characters and letting them work out their destiny along the commonplace lines suggested by their values and environment."[32] While echoing Howells's realistic discourse of the commonplace, Dunbar advanced beyond this paradigm by participating in a generational shift that resisted this discourse.

In an interview with Howells in 1894, Stephen Crane recognized such "a change in the literary pulse of the country within the last four months . . . a counter wave, a flood of the other—a reaction, in fact. Trivial, temporary, perhaps, but a reaction, certainly." Howells agreed: "What you say is true. I have seen it coming . . . I suppose we shall have to wait."[33] Here, the "other" signifies Frank Norris, considered the forefather of American literary naturalism and, above even Crane and Hamlin Garland, one of the premier rebutters of Howellsian realism and its "high" aesthetic decorum.

In his essay entitled "Zola as a Romantic Writer" (1896), Norris rightly identifies Howells as the institutionalized leader of the realist tradition. He also indicts the genteel ideology informing the latter's novels: "We ourselves are Mr. Howells's characters, so long as we are well behaved and ordinary and bourgeois, so long as we are not adventurous or not rich or not unconventional." Howellsian realism "is the real Realism." In another essay, "A Plea for Romantic Fiction" (1901), Norris further argues that realism is superficial. "For [realism,] Beauty is not even skin-deep, but only a geometrical place, without dimensions of depth, a mere outside. Realism is very excellent so far as it goes" in dramatically detailing the minute, the mundane, the everyday, "but it goes no farther than the Realist himself can actually see, or actually hear."[34] Norris exposes the falsity of Howells's Keatsean claim that "Beauty is Truth, Truth Beauty," an analogy defining realism in pictorial, photographic terms.[35] Truthful portrayals, Norris argues, concern "the unplumbed depths of the human heart, and the mystery of sex, and the problems of life, and the black, unsearched penetralia of the soul of man."[36]

By proposing a "romantic" literary paradigm that could achieve human profundity, Norris was indicting the limitations of Howellsian realism and redeeming a genre that the "genteel" literati would have characterized as "uncivilized," lowbrow. At the same time, Norris was setting the stage for what Jennifer L. Fleissner calls the "remasculinization" of literary realism. In the sense of being both accurate and exceptional, such "true" realism privileged men and their political interests as the bastions of American naturalism. Norris's version necessarily characterized women, whether as authors in a genre or as subjects in fiction, as impeding male progress toward modernity.[37]

Of course, several other versions of this kind of realism existed at the turn of the twentieth century. But no author aside from Norris had fashioned a version so decidedly anti-Howellsian.[38] Norris celebrated Emile Zola's romanticism, despite Howells's influential revision of this outmoded genre in *Criticism and Fiction*, in order to refute Howells. Norris wrote that "[a]ccuracy is realism and Truth romanticism," but this categorization, he believed, was not precise enough. The literary aspiration toward conveying "Truth" should "lie in the middle," striving for both accuracy and truth. For Norris, this intermediate space belonged to naturalism.[39]

Proponents of naturalism tried to expose the bourgeois hypocrisy of Howellsian realism. The genre captured the drama of life "among the lower—almost the lowest—classes; those who have been thrust or wrenched from the ranks, who are falling by the roadway."[40] In Norris's era, the main characters of naturalistic stories tended to belong to the lower class, the undereducated, or the oppressed. Norris's own novels—*McTeague* (1899), *The Octopus* (1901), and *The Pit* (1903)—exemplify this aspect. Theodore Dreiser, through such novels as *Sister Carrie* (1900) and *Jennie Gerhardt* (1911), extended Norris's naturalistic aesthetic into the modern era of the U.S. urban landscape. Naturalistic stories did not discriminate among cultural-geographic settings. At the turn of the twentieth century, however, amid the circumstances of modernization, urban settings did pervade naturalist stories.

Within these stories, literary characters confront the demise of individualism in the face of hereditary and environmental determinism. The preponderance of literary characters serving as human subjects explains the titles of naturalist stories, which often highlight simply the name, traits, or trials of the protagonist. Naturalist protagonists rarely control internal or external forces, just as they rarely narrate the nature and implications of these forces in the first person. More often, third-person omniscient narration, often verging on blatant didacticism, as opposed to the putatively more "detached," "objective," or reportorial kind of realism, guides the reader through these stories.

The formal properties of *The Uncalled* suggest that, before Norris and Dreiser, Dunbar was already experimenting with literary ways of stretching realism in naturalist directions. Howells would have disapproved of this attempt. In a *New York Times* interview with Crane three years after the release of *Criticism and Fiction*, Howells admonishes that a novel "should never preach and berate and storm." "Ineffably tiresome," this kind of novel neglects the more important "business to picture the daily life in the most exact terms possible, with an absolute and clear sense of proportion."[41]

Book reviewers likewise criticized *The Uncalled* for displaying unrealistic incidents and for its intrusively didactic narration, some of the hallmark problems critics recognized then and still recognize in American naturalist fiction. These contemporary critics tended to reiterate Howells's guidelines for realist writing: drama, economic characterization, sparing prose, and streamlined exposition.[42] They also questioned the overly "philosophical" nature of the novel's portrayal of spirituality, heritage, destiny, and the environment.[43]

But these are the very parameters Dunbar needed to tell the story of Fred Brent. In a letter to Alice Ruth Moore, he reveals that he was not opposed to literary philosophizing: "I . . . believe that a story is a story and try to make my characters 'real live people.' But I believe that characters in fiction should be what men and women are in real life,—the embodiment of a principle or idea."[44] By balancing local color, literary realism, and naturalism, *The Uncalled* examines Fred's rise from the mean streets.

Fred's individualistic grappling with determinism constitutes the kind of naturalist story that Howells attributed to Stephen Crane and Frank Norris at their deaths in 1900 and 1902, respectively. Speaking of Crane's *Maggie: A Girl of the Streets* and Norris's *McTeague*, Howells once praised the two men in much the same way that a sympathetic snob would, for becoming "second-generation realists" who explored the "tragically squalid" and the "grotesquely shabby" streets of the modern city and the "half-savage" life existing there.[45] Dunbar had been there, done that, and thus deserved praise, too.

Indeed, Dunbar's novel describes in vivid detail Fred's ascent from Dexter's mean streets and tracks the young man's encounter with desolation in Cincinnati on fleeing his hometown. While searching for a boardinghouse in the city, Fred observes drunken adults and impoverished children lining the streets. Such images horrify Fred, whose family history, in the eyes of Dexter residents, predestines him for this unfortunate way of life. Fred's mother, Margaret, was a housewife stigmatized for living in the dilapidated, lower-class section of Dexter and for marrying an abusive and often inebriated husband, Tom Brent. As an adolescent, Fred suffered through the divorce of his parents, the death of his mother, and the flight of his father. In Cincinnati, he thus seems on the verge of becoming like his unenviable father.

Once at his boardinghouse in the city, Fred meets a young clerk, Mr. Perkins, who invites him to a nightclub of shame and sin, Meyer's Beer-Garden and Variety Hall. At the door of the club, Fred encounters an old man who tries to dissuade him and others from entering. The old man encourages them to attend a meeting later that night about the need for public temperance. Fred agrees to attend the temperance meeting. There, the old man recounts his life for the attendees. Fred infers that the old man is Tom Brent, his father, who plans to return to Dexter to make amends with his wife (who he does not yet know has died) and his son. This epiphany marks a major moment in *The Uncalled* that distinguishes the novel from those of Dunbar's naturalist contemporaries: moral self-reform and spiritual regeneration.

Earlier moments in the novel foreshadow this possibility. The best example occurs in the middle of the novel, when Fred enters the theological seminary and befriends a colleague named Taylor. A literary writer-cum-seminarian, Taylor is the only person to whom Fred confides his reservations about entering the ministry. In a painful monologue, Taylor recounts why he abandoned his long-held desire to be a writer. Since childhood, he had enjoyed writing for his own amusement. "Fools" later pushed him to pursue the craft, even though his verse was "more or less deformed" (138). He circulated his work among periodicals. Some pieces suffered rejection, others were accepted and published. Intermittent success encouraged him to stick with writing. Four years passed before he realized his mediocrity and that "it would have been better just to go on and do the conventional thing" (139). The seminary enabled him to cope with his previous missteps.

Toward the end of the monologue, Taylor waxes philosophic:

If you are a brave man, you say boldly to yourself, "I will eke out an existence in some humble way," and you go away to a life of longing and regret. If you are a coward, you either leap over the parapets of life to hell, or go creeping back and fall at the feet of the thing that has damned you, willing to be third-rate, anything; for you are stung with the poison that never leaves your blood. So it has been with me: even when I found that I must choose a calling, I chose the one that gave me most time to nurse the serpent that had stung me. (140)

Taylor tries to ingrain in Fred the idea that only by subscribing to social conventions—or simply by listening to others—can individualistic pursuits become possible. Ignore spiritual compulsions, Taylor advises Fred, and stay on the academic straight and narrow path toward success.

Taylor's case for subordinating personal will to public conformity did not and still does not work for Fred. Fred's spiritual resistance to conformity strained his interaction with Dexter's citizens and ended up alienating him from them and forcing him to flee to Cincinnati to restart his life. While in the city, through which Mr. Perkins guides him, Fred assumes Taylor's initial professional identity—as a writer—in order to mask his current spiritual turmoil, caused, in part, by his memory of Dexter's provincialism:

"You can talk all about your Chicago," Perkins was rattling on, "but you can bet your life Cincinnati's the greatest town in the West. Chicago's nothing but a big overgrown country town. Everything looks new and flimsy there to a fellow, but here you get something that's solid. Chicago's pretty swift, too, but there ain't no flies on us, either, when it comes to the go."

Brent thought with dismay how much his companion knew, and felt a passing bitterness that he, though older, had seen none of these things.

"Ever been in Chicago?" asked Perkins; "but of course you haven't." This was uttered in such a tone of conviction that the minister thought his greenness must be very apparent.

"I've never been around much of anywhere," he said. "I've been hard at work all my life."

"Eh, that so? You don't look like you'd done much hard work. What do you do?"

"I—I—ah—write," was the confused answer.

Perkins, fortunately, did not notice the confusion. "Oh, ho!" he said: "do you go in for newspaper work?"

"No, not for newspapers."

"Oh, you're an author, a regular out-and-outer. Well, don't you know, I thought you were somehow different from most fellows I've met. I never could see how you authors could stay away in small towns, where you hardly ever see anyone, and write about people as you do; but I suppose you get your people entirely from books."

"No, not entirely," replied Brent, letting the mistake go. "There are plenty of interesting characters in a small town. Its life is just what the life of a larger city is, only the scale is smaller."

"Well, if you're on a search for characters, you'll see some to-night that'll be worth putting in your note-book. We'll stop here first [at Meyer's Beer-Garden and Variety Hall]." (213–14)

Taylor has abandoned writerhood and entered the seminary; in a role reversal, Fred has abandoned the seminary and feigned writerly expertise. Previously confident in his endeavor, Taylor pursued a writing career despite warnings of his literary mediocrity. His failures provided him enough experience to philosophize about his fall from literary grace. By contrast, in Dexter, Fred excelled in the church to the town's delight, but he remained skeptical of his journey. His memory of his previous moral disposition and professional accomplishments only exacerbates his private doubts about his religious calling and later prolongs his meditation in Cincinnati. The story of Fred's defiance of Dexter's norms and its imagining of his calling (hence the title of the novel) functions in terms of Dunbar's own generic experimentation with the norms of literary naturalism.

Later in the novel, while reflecting on his encounter with his father at the temperance meeting, Fred takes "up a little book which many times that morning he had been attempting to read," *The Strayed Reveller, and Other Poems* (1849), by Victorian poet Matthew Arnold. The stanza in the poem "Mycerinus" "seemed to fit his case," elucidating his fateful misery.[46] The recurring metaliterary tropes in *The Uncalled* mark of Fred's maturation. The trope of literature, as suggested in the conversation between Mr. Perkins and Fred, has implications for the thematic intentions of *The Uncalled*. Fred's lying to Mr. Perkins about being a writer and his concomitant striving for a literary understanding of his predicament indicate the particularly reflexive stage of the novel, when the story begins to talk about itself.

Fred and fellow Dexter citizens have deliberated extensively over whether or not his father's intemperance, his mother's social marginality, and his birthplace predestined him for moral impropriety and professional failure. Meditating on his encounter with his father and his previous life in Dexter, Fred puts this idea in succinct naturalist terms while, possibly autobiographically, capturing the intense theological conflict in Dunbar's own ruminations over a possible career in the church: "Is it Fate, God, or the devil that pursues me so?" (222). Dexter has equated Fred's inheritance of familial blood with the inheritance of shameful parental morals and values. In determining Fred's fate by interpreting his blood, however, Dexter has also created a self-fulfilling prophecy: the town always has the potential of willing this prophecy into reality by spreading rumors that the Brents lowered the town's ethical standards.

Ultimately, Fred demonstrates the will to overcome his fate, despite the curse of his family. Tom Brent, on returning to Dexter to make amends with his son and wife, becomes sick. Mr. Hodges learns of Mr. Brent's predicament and takes the ill man into his home; he then writes a letter to Fred urging his return to Dexter. On his deathbed in the home of Mrs. Prime and Mr. Hodges, indeed, in the very room where Fred once slept under their guardianship, Mr. Brent repents before his son. At this final moment, after Fred accuses Mr. Brent of "ruining" his life by leaving him "a heritage of shame and evil," the son forgives the father. Fred then returns to Cincinnati, where he tries to clarify his relationship with God by attending a Congregational church and working in the name of "poor humanity" (239). He commits himself to moral autodidacticism, but it is a self-regeneration not entirely in biblical terms, as Mrs. Hester Prime would have liked: "I've been to a better school than the Bible Seminary. I haven't got many religious rules and formulas, but I'm trying to live straight and do what is right" (254).

The sign of Fred's liberation from tradition, religion, and history and his settlement in civilization (the city of Cincinnati) is his newfound joy in having a girlfriend, Alice, who fills his life with happiness and emotional security. She enables Fred to consummate his detachment from Dexter, for which his forgiveness of his dying father served as the penultimate step. The novel's ending defies the conventional closure of the naturalist novel, which has the protagonist decline and degenerate into a tragic figure.[47] Fred's appreciation of Alice turns *The Uncalled* from a novel of tragedy into one of triumph while reminding us that time will tell whether his triumph will remain as Fred continues to navigate his way mentally through memories of loss and pain and, physically, through the unpredictable terrain of modern life.

"We Must Write Like the White Men"

The reviews of *The Uncalled* were not entirely favorable. Dunbar's omission of black dialect and other markers of minstrel realism undermined the contemporary belief that he should dedicate himself to authentic portrayals of his race. One critic expresses disappointment that Dunbar had decided to "forsake his own people." Another laments that the "narrow creed and restricted life of a body of 'church members' in the typical American provincial town is a theme that previous writers have worn threadbare" in local color. The reviewer expresses some "regret that [Dunbar] has abandoned ground on which he possesses unique advantages for one open to all newcomers. It was scarcely worth while to throw over the picturesque, exotic personality of the Negro for such comparatively commonplace people." In other words, Dunbar should have stuck to being a minstrel realist instead of trying to be a literary realist who explored "the habits and feelings of an alien race," namely, whites.

Other reviews of the novel's literary merits were similarly mixed. One critic sighs that *The Uncalled* "does not give promise of a great future" in prose fiction. Another reviewer admits that "*The Uncalled* is not a great novel, but it is a good one." Another reader believes that the "book is evi-

dently a first effort of varying merit." Another says the prose has "force
and vigor" but possesses "little flexibility or imaginative epithet." And yet
another says flatly that the novel is not as appealing as Dunbar's third book
of poetry, *Lyrics of Lowly Life*.[48]

Interestingly, aside from a perceptive review from the *New York Times* regarding the naturalism of *The Uncalled*, "a long way in advance of the Russian school [led by Leo Tolstoy] and of much of the work of the modern
English and American schools," most of the praise for Dunbar's novel
came from the British press.[49] If *The Uncalled* signified more of what was
to come from Dunbar the novelist (it did), then most reviewers feared that
his literary career would not turn out to be as promising as expected when
Howells lauded his poetry in *Harper's* in 1896. If Dunbar returned to his
old form, the novel could be considered just an anomaly.

Amid these reviews of *The Uncalled*, Dunbar's assertion in the interview
mentioned at the chapter's outset that black writers "must write like the
white men" suggests why he had to write his first novel in such an anomalous way. This statement does not echo Douglass's mantra, "[W]e must do
just what white men do," or Cable's advice to blacks to "strive to write like
a white man," mentioned earlier. Douglass and Cable were perpetuating
what Winston Napier calls the "cultural monism" of racial-uplift ideology,
an idea I elaborate in Chapter 4.[50] Proponents of cultural monism believe
that whites represent "America" in the most general sense, when, in fact,
according to Dunbar, they represent only one ethnic group of American
people. In the nineteenth century, proponents of racial uplift elevated this
group to the top rung of the ladder of civilization as the standard by which
all ethnic participants in the United States judged themselves and others.
Similarly, Douglass and Cable equated the literary absence of New Negro
realism with the presence of whiteness, whiteness with universalism, universal texts with American literature, and the production of American literature with the black demonstration of national assimilability.

By contrast, Dunbar was annoyed at how the reporter of the *New York
Commercial*, like Howells, could essentialize "the poetry of the Negro" as
being different from "the verse of Anglo-Saxons" while associating white
"blood" with intelligence. Dunbar countered these racialist and implicitly
racist ideas with the contention that the New World diaspora of "the
African race" would write poetry that would "not be exotic or differ much
from that of Whites." For Dunbar, the decisive factor was that the races
shared a national culture.

Accordingly, *The Uncalled* argues that the races can advance a common
national literature through the use of realism. However, the novel also acknowledges that the cultural differences separating blacks from whites can

result from certain kinds of racism that preclude this advancement. One kind, which Howells and many American writers of his day could not overcome, is the fallacy that whiteness is raceless and universal while only blackness is racial and peculiar. Anomalous African American literature—as exemplified by Dunbar's first novel—refutes this belief. Both whiteness and blackness, it turns out, are visible, dialectically engaged with one another, and historically contingent constructions of racial, cultural, and national identity. Dunbar, in particular, tried to disrupt the stereotypical thesis and antithesis, namely, that white privilege and black underprivilege necessarily implied, in terms of his own profession, white intellectual achievement and black intellectual underachievement. For Dunbar, blacks and whites had more in common than met the eye, than what the cultural media portrayed, and than what most of America wanted to believe.

Chapter 3

"The Conventional Blindness of the Caucasian Eye"

On March 21, 1924, at a dinner held for luminaries at Harlem's Civic Club, Alain Locke expressed his belief that the newer generation of black writers possessed "enough talent now to begin to have a movement—and express a school of thought."[1] Appointed as master of ceremonies by Charles S. Johnson, his friend and the organizer of the dinner, Locke presided over the event in the early stages of his career as an aesthetic and cultural critic—as a young man whose reputation rested on having been the first black Rhodes scholar, in 1907; a PhD from Harvard a decade later; and a contributor of editorial advice and intelligent essays to the journal Johnson founded in 1923, *Opportunity*. Locke did not belong to the older generation of black intellectuals, a generation he identified with W. E. B. Du Bois during the dinner. Nor did he, at thirty-eight years of age, belong to the far younger generation of black writers bursting onto the Harlem scene. Betwixt and between these two groups, Locke began to envision himself as an esteemed interlocutor within the black race and as ambassador of the race to America.

The dinner represented Johnson's vision of an influential role for Locke, because the stakes for the younger generation were so high. Two weeks before the dinner, Johnson asked Locke "to present this newer school of writers. There seems to be insistence on getting you to assume the leading role for the movement. I regard you as a sort of 'Dean' of this younger group."[2] Locke also served as a "midwife" and "father" of the movement.[3] He was, simultaneously, the intellectual president of a cultural institution, a nurturer of black artistic "youth," and a demanding figure who tended to historicize African American literature in patrilineal terms.[4]

The dinner underscored Locke's newfound status. If, before the dinner, he was merely writing about Negro art and culture, afterward, his abundant corpus of aesthetic and cultural criticism resonated with the symbolic authority he earned from the 1924 event. One year later, Locke's leadership received another boost. He edited and published two widely circulated and critically respected volumes, "Harlem: Mecca of the New Negro," in the March 1 issue of *The Survey Graphic* and an expanded version released later that year in book form as *The New Negro*. Examining and exhibiting the efflorescent black artwork of the 1920s, these 1925 collections served—and still serve—as the most critically acclaimed, commercially successful, and canonized texts of black culture during the movement they embody, the so-called Harlem Renaissance. Of all the essays Locke published over his career, the ones he included in these volumes were his most influential, and therefore his most important.

Two essays in *The New Negro*—"Negro Youth Speaks" and "The Legacy of the Ancestral Arts"—are especially meaningful. At a climactic moment in the first essay, a comprehensive introduction to the literary component of the Harlem Renaissance, Locke declares that "realism in 'crossing the Potomac' had also to cross the color line" in order to consummate the literary movement.[5] At a crucial section of the second essay, Locke accuses the dean of American painters, black artist Henry Ossawa Tanner, of perpetuating "the conventional blindness of the Caucasian eye with respect to the racial material at their [painters'] immediate disposal."[6] These two incidental statements link discursively and conceptually. The first encapsulates Locke's appreciation of avant-garde and multiethnic conventions of racial realism; the second segues into his criticism of cosmopolitan and academically trained black painters who tended to avoid or complicate such conventions. These two statements are keys to reinterpreting the historical assumptions, the principles of canonical selection, and the stakes in Locke's ambassadorial vision of the Harlem Renaissance and its predominant school or genre of racial realism, New Negro modernism.

The lore cycle of racial realism determined New Negro modernism. Modernism does not necessarily correspond with the "high" American modernism often attributed to avant-garde writers like Ezra Pound, T. S. Eliot, and Gertrude Stein, although scholars have shown that these and other white writers influenced black literary theories and practices of racial realism during the Harlem Renaissance.[7] Nor does it necessarily mean the "Afro-modernism" of a poet like Sterling Brown, known for experimenting with the blues and folklore in ways that writers of the Harlem Renaissance could not yet handle.[8] Nor, finally, does it pertain to the kind of (neo)modernism attributable to the 1930s and the 1940s, in the works of Richard Wright and Ralph Ellison, among others, or to the 1950s, in the African American literature of the period.[9] Rather, New Negro modernism pertains to young black writers, ranging from Jean Toomer and Langston Hughes to Zora Neale Hurston and Eric Walrond, whom Locke labeled in 1928 as *both* "modernists" and "race-realists."[10] For Locke, modernism was a special generic-cum-cultural development of racial realism in the post–World War I era.

Locke's notion of modernism was highly problematic within the paradigm of racial realism. His appreciative association of a "lusty vigorous realism" with New Negro culture was consistent with a more general "cultural logic" of modernism that, according to Elisa F. Glick, envisioned "black identity as a supposed counterforce to the rationality and sterility of capitalist modernity."[11] Subjecting both modernism and modernity to the same level of critical analysis does not ignore the theoretical differences between what was mainly, on the one hand, an aesthetic and cultural ideology that had burgeoned between the two World Wars, and, on the other hand, a historical demarcation of the rise and transformations of capitalism, technology, and industry over the past two centuries in the United States and the rest of the world.[12] New Negro modernity, as Marlon Ross puts it, represented a moment when the black "race [was] seen in the spotlight of modernity, the arena in which the future of civilization [was] fought-over, negotiated, claimed, and reclaimed." It was a moment when "the New Negro [gained] control of the circulation of his [or her] own image in the urban media (publishing houses, magazines, newspapers, advertising concerns, and sociological studies)."[13] If New Negro modernity refers to the cultural materiality and marketability of New Negro ideology, then New Negro modernism pertains to the cultural aesthetics and discourses through which New Negro ideology articulates and contests strategies of racial representation in the era of modernity.

By merging intraracial and interracial critical approaches to the Harlem Renaissance, in this chapter I analyze Locke's New Negro brand of modernism.[14] New Negro modernism tried to "control" racial images by overcoming cultural stereotypes of the folk, as well as by confronting the vogue of primitivism that came to delimit the nature, audience, and commerce of "Negro art" during the Harlem Renaissance. The racialism intrinsic to Locke's modernism resisted the historical perception of the folk as inherently inferior to those of white ancestry. Nonetheless, his racialism accepted and perpetuated nearly Howellsian ideas of folk authenticity that blurred the biological and cultural essentialism of Negro art and artistry.

Locke's racialism also drew color lines between cultures and thereby accepted the premise of ethnic pluralism. Proponents of this doctrine believed that the sense of American cultural nationalism was attainable through the equal valuation, cooperation, and diversity of racial groups. At the same time, New Negro modernism attempted to advance beyond the retrograde models of racial realism. In being both ethnically pluralist and progressively racially realist, Locke's cultural genre for the Harlem Renaissance captured the idea of racial realism "crossing" the Potomac from south to north and the color line from black to white.[15] Sounding much like the racial-uplift ideologue he criticized, Locke envisioned the moral uplift of Anglo-American writers, and, analogously, Anglo-European painters, with the help of New Negro modernism and the interracial cooperation it encouraged. Equally important, Locke placed the burden of racial responsibility on *all* artists of the African diaspora, in the United States and abroad, to "speak as Negroes" or construct the folk in ways progressive, pragmatic, and authentic.

Locke realized that, of all the ways that culture could represent the race, perhaps the most "arresting display," to borrow Marlon Ross's phrase, appeared in photographs and illustrations. Their more "eidetic" qualities tended to achieve greater "visual impact" on readers than did written narratives.[16] Visual images could immediately display the composure, elegance, formality, meditation, and determination of which the race was capable. Anne Elizabeth Carroll and Martha Jane Nadell elaborate this point in their studies of the relationship between written words and visual images in the long New Negro era between the Civil War and World War II. Both scholars show that black artists exploited the immediacy of visual images to achieve political effects that they believed were impossible, stifled, or suboptimal if restricted solely to the realm of the written word. According to Carroll, Locke, in particular, designed the *Survey Graphic*'s New Negro issue in the visual footsteps of the magazine's special issue on Mexico a year earlier and commissioned the same artist and theme (Winold Reiss and the exotic ethnic minority). When Locke considered additional works by Aaron Douglas and Miguel Covarrubias for *The New Negro*, he remained in an experimental struggle for the appropriate visual aesthetic to complement the poetry, fiction, and nonfiction heralding the Harlem Renaissance while refraining from stereotyping.[17]

Accordingly, Locke bastardized Negro visual art and artists who failed to support the cultural politics of New Negro modernism. For example, he condemned Henry Ossawa Tanner for encouraging the early twentieth-century generation of black painters to avoid or complicate New Negro modernism. Locke regarded Tanner's cosmopolitanism—the imagination of oneself settled in the world, away from one's native home—as coincident with an ethnocentric academicism that favored whiteness over blackness. Cosmopolitanism contradicted the racial-nationalist protocol—as slight as it may have been—in New Negro modernism. To repeat Locke, cosmopolitanism caused "the conventional blindness of the Caucasian eye with respect to . . . racial material." Scholarly portrayals of Locke as an advocate or representative of cosmopolitanism are thus inaccurate or incomplete. They fail to acknowledge that he was quite critical of the ethnocentric valuation of whiteness in cosmopolitan claims to universalism.[18] By analyzing Tanner's personal and professional commitment to black communities, however, one can detect the flaws in Locke's critique of cosmopolitanism despite his correct assessment of Tanner's anxiety over racial identity and the responsibility of black artists to their race.

New Negro Modernism

During and even after the Harlem Renaissance, Locke freely regarded modernism as an avant-garde movement of racial realism. In "The Beauty Instead of Ashes" (1928), he states that the "younger Negro artists as modernists have the same slant and interest, as is unmistakably shown by Jean Toomer's 'Cane,' Eric Walrond's 'Tropic Death,' Rudolph Fisher's and Claude McKay's pungent stories of Harlem, and the group trend of *Fire*, a quarterly recently brought out to be 'devoted to younger Negro artists.'"[19] And these are the same writers, along with Zora Neale Hurston, Willis Richardson, and Langston Hughes, whom Locke praised three years earlier in *The New Negro* for "declar[ing] for a lusty vigorous realism, the same that is molding contemporary American letters, but their achievement of it, as it has been doubly difficult, is doubly significant."[20] Locke also applied the term "modernist" to black painters for their excellence in racial realism. In "The American Negro as Artist" (1931), Locke states that it "is this saccharine, romantic quality [of the previous generation of black art] that has given the younger modernists their foil; they aim at hard realism and verge at times on the grotesque and the satirical."[21]

Locke's modernism always encouraged favorable cultural representations of the race. The ideologies intrinsic to his endorsement of more respectable racial representations, however, did not entirely refute the prevailing notion that blacks were essentially different from their white counterparts. In discussions of Negro art and culture, Locke consistently employed an essentialist postbellum discourse of folk authenticity—or the putatively genuine, trustworthy, and almost mythic quality of lower-class black experiences—as the foundation of his cultural thought.

Ironically, while contrasting Dunbar and Brown in his review-essay "Sterling Brown: The New Negro Folk-Poet" (1934), Locke appreciates the folk authenticity of Brown's first book, *Southern Road* (1932), in almost the same way that William Howells appreciated the folk authenticity of Dunbar's second book, *Majors and Minors* (1896). Locke claims that *Southern Road* never resorts to the "jingling and juggling of broken English" attributable to Dunbar's dialect poetry. Brown "has listened long and carefully to the folk in their intimate hours, when they were talking to themselves, not, so to speak, as in Dunbar, but actually as they do when the masks of protective mimicry fall." Brown is "more reflective, a closer student of the folk-life, and above all a bolder and more detached observer."[22]

Nearly four decades earlier, Howells had boasted that Dunbar was "the first man of his color to study his race objectively, to analyze it to himself, and then to represent it in art as he felt it to be: to represent it humorously, yet tenderly, and above all so faithfully that we know the portrait to be undeniably like." At the same time, *Majors and Minors* includes lyrical "expressions of a race life from within the race" that are "indefinitely more valuable and significant."[23] Locke and Howells, though separated by nearly half a century, both defined racial realism in terms of the black author's social, emotional, psychological, metaphysical, and cultural proximity to the folk.

Generally, Locke tried to detach such privileging of black cultural insight from the essentialist ascription of differences in human phenotype and physiognomy—or skin color and facial features—to inherent biological and intellectual traits differentiating human beings. In short, he was aware of the thin line between cultural racialism and biological racialism. But Locke slipped in and out of defining racial communities based on biological connections while clinging to race as a cultural category. "The Legacy of the Ancestral Arts," Locke's essay in *The New Negro* most concerned with the idea of an African diaspora, describes blacks as "blood descendants, bound to [Africa] by a sense of direct cultural kinship," and as cultural relatives, consenting to embrace one another as New Negroes and New World Negroes.[24] Locke's utterance of both "blood" and "cultural kinship" in the same sentence straddled the fine line between biological and cultural constructions of race. Sometimes he planted his philosophical feet on both sides simultaneously.

When he was discussing the African diaspora in the U.S. context, Locke's cultural valuation of race translated into ethnic pluralism. Ethnic pluralism asserted the equal importance of black and white culture to the cohesion and progress of the nation. While flawed for drawing strict racial boundaries around cultures, this concept proved useful to Locke, at least rhetorically. It enabled him to explain that different races or ethnicities produced and consumed culture in different ways and held unique senses of ethics and aesthetics, self-pride and self-respect. Thus Locke could say that the lives of blacks in Harlem, the "race capital," were fundamentally distinct from the lives of whites living there and elsewhere.[25] Locke's discourse of racial collectivity and nationalism was not as extreme as Marcus Garvey's in the 1920s or the Black Arts Movement's in the 1960s and the

1970s. The theoretical connections Locke saw uniting blacks, however, served his imagining of a cooperative climate in which ethnic individuality could cause interethnic or interracial peace.

Locke's essay entitled "Enter the New Negro" asserts the point that cultural and racial diversity facilitates national unity. In it he states that, while the "multitude [of blacks] perhaps feels as yet only a strange relief and a new vague urge. . . . the thinking few know that in the reaction the vital inner grip of prejudice has been broken."[26] In the revised version of the essay, "The New Negro," Locke adds another section in which he subordinates the post-Reconstruction historical reality of Ku Klux Klan terrorism, the mass lynchings that reached their height in the early 1890s, and the horrors of Jim Crow segregation laws while favoring socioeconomic approaches to the Negro in American democracy and industrialism.[27] Optimism often framed his vision of an interracial America and a New Negro modernism whose pragmatism hinged on interracial alliances.

New Negro modernism also attended to the cultural history of racial realism. To begin with, Locke, in both "Harlem: Mecca of the New Negro" and The New Negro, assaults the Old Negro of minstrel realism. The romantic and sentimental protocols of minstrel realism certainly bothered him, but the more current and equally racist portraiture of Negroes in early twentieth-century Anglo-American literature also irked him. The black characters found in the novels of Thomas Dixon elicited anxiety from white readers over the perceived insolence of postbellum blacks toward white superiority. Eldred Kurtz (E. K.) Means's short stories also sought to amuse readers within the grotesque and comic traditions of blackface minstrelsy. Commercial fascination with this sort of caricature persisted during the 1920s, with an abundance of folktale anthologies and the more popular and sensational "Negrophobic" stories of Dixon, Octavus Roy Cohen, and Hugh Wiley.

By reiterating notions of the general inferiority and servility of blacks to modern white society, the novels of Cohen and Wiley thrived in the wake of Madison Grant's notorious The Passing of the Great Race (1916). Their novels exploited and contributed to Grant's Nordic supremacist, eugenic, and anti-immigration philosophies as well as his racist mythologies about darker-skinned native people and foreign nationals. Between Grant's pivotal study and the publication of "Harlem: Mecca of the New Negro," filmmaker D. W. Griffith modeled his film The Birth of a Nation (1915) after Thomas Dixon's sympathetic treatment of the Ku Klux Klan in The Clansman (1905). White and foreign-born essayists ranging from Charles W. Gould and Lothrop Stoddard to Houston Stewart Chamberlain and Count Arthur de Gobineau supported this intellectual tradition of white supremacy. Unsurprisingly, Locke was eager to leave such literature behind.[28]

Locke also believed in scrapping black literature written in dialect, regardless of its polemical potential and the popularity it created for black writers, because of its close connection to minstrel realism. Certain black writers in the early 1920s were already dismissing Paul Laurence Dunbar for this reason. James Weldon Johnson notes, in his preface to the first edition of *The Book of American Negro Poetry* (1922), that the "qualities that gave [black dialect poetry] vogue—tenderness, sentimentality, homely humor, genial optimism—are the very qualities that now bring disparagement upon it."[29]

Four years later, Locke echoed this point. In "The Negro Poets of the United States" (1926), he admits that he admires Dunbar's achievement of critical and commercial success and his establishment of a vernacular "folk-expression." But the minstrel realism that readers celebrated in Dunbar's poetry caused black contemporaries to be "held back somewhat by the dilemma of dialect,—wishing not to desert the race spiritually but at the same time not to be hampered by the Dunbar tradition, which was gradually deteriorating from minstrelsy, to buffoonery."[30]

Two years later, Locke was still putting Dunbar's "popular school of Negro dialect poetry" in context. Dunbar stood "for the race at a certain stage of its history and a certain class at that stage," Locke stressed, but "Dunbar himself rebelled against this overemphasis upon his dialect poetry, and thought more both of his legitimate English lyrics and his fiction, in both of which fields he is not a negligible figure."[31] Alas, Locke could have added, as I imply in Chapter 1, that Dunbar's writing of poetry in formal English and his anomalous fiction could not entirely overcome the reputation that dictated his life and career.

The overt racial uplift of New Negro realism in the postbellum nineteenth century, finally, tended to be so "stiltedly self-conscious" and "racially rhetorical" that for Locke it hampered the development of "fine" and "true" black culture. From such examples of New Negro realism, Locke explains, "we have lately had an art that was stiltedly self-conscious, and racially rhetorical rather than racially expressive. Our poets have now stopped speaking for the Negro—they speak as Negroes."[32]

Of course, Locke's critique rings with hypocrisy. The equality of all blacks, he believed, might be more improbable than "putting the premium upon the capable few, and thus of accelerating the 'levelling up' processes in American society." As far back as 1918 Locke supported the notion that "successful peoples are rated, and rate themselves, in terms of their best."[33] For New Negro modernism, however, Locke tried to understate his elitism.

His own stature notwithstanding, he tried to repudiate expressions of "conscious motive" in Negro art that were more performative than natural, more fantastic than realistic, more imposing than suggestive, more highbrow than folkloric.

Although a strategic rejection of previous cultural genres of racial realism, Locke's modernism did accept the pragmatism of racial realism, in much the same way that the racial-uplift ideology underwriting New Negro realism suggested that art could impact life. New Negro literature since the nineteenth century had tried to convey the properly eloquent personality for black intellectual debate on race relations, for refuting minstrel stereotypes, and for conveying uplifted black morality, intellect, and spirit. Pragmatism similarly contended that ethics, aesthetics, and knowledge could engage the historical and material experiences of cultural consumers. By these means, culture could help to improve interracial understanding, deepen societal respect for the diversity of American subcultures and ethnicities, and strengthen American democracy and the sense of national unity. New Negro modernism could function to access, articulate, and ameliorate the lived experience of New World Negroes and even Negroes abroad.

How did New Negro modernism, then, capture Locke's succinct phrase "realism in 'crossing the Potomac' had also to cross the color line"? New Negro modernism was prospering with the help not only of authors born, bred, or writing in the North (who had therefore crossed the Potomac), but also of those who happened to be white (who had crossed the color line). Most crucial to Locke, in this context, was the abolition of racial stereotypes, not necessarily an author's racial identity. Unsurprisingly, between 1929 and 1953, in the magazines *Opportunity*, *The Crisis*, and *Phylon*, Locke published annual reviews that concentrated on "the literature of the Negro." This phrase mainly signified for Locke literature *about* the Negro, which either blacks or whites could have written. His cultural pragmatism remained focused on the larger picture of the gradual movement of American literature away from minstrel realism.

The younger, post–World War I white writers in the era of the Harlem Renaissance were indeed revising this genre. Ridgeley Torrence and Eugene O'Neill in drama, as well as T. S. Stribling, H. A. Shands, and Clement Wood in fiction, had all, in Locke's words, "helped in the bringing of the materials of Negro life out of the shambles of conventional polemics, cheap romance and journalism into the domain of pure and unbiassed [*sic*] art."[34] When Locke wrote these words in 1925, he considered New York City, as many others did, to be the most modern metropolis in the most powerful nation of the world. Just as the "opposition of northern and southern, rural and urban, [was] nothing new in terms of the cultural representations of blackness," according to Elisa F. Glick, and dated back to antebellum minstrelsy and continued into the Renaissance, this opposition determined the ideological categories to which the authors of these representations belonged. The prevailing depiction of New York City as a "World City" in the post–World War I era referred to its evident urbanity, cultural capitalism, and symbolic modernity.[35]

Locke's cultural polarization of white writers of the North and the South, mythically separated by the Potomac River, perpetuated the idea that the North was progressive and the South was not. This ideological circumstance lent credence to Locke's graphing of racial realism along historical and geocultural axes of progression. He portrayed the modernist and sophisticated emergence of white writers of racial realism as a movement born or bred in the North. Ridgeley Torrence, Clement Wood, and Waldo Frank accordingly revised the racial realism of Harriet Beecher Stowe, Joel Chandler Harris, Thomas Nelson Page, George Washington Cable, and Thomas Dixon.

In making this claim in 1925, Locke was welcoming white writers of racial realism more readily than were several of his black contemporaries, including Benjamin Brawley, Jessie Fauset, William Stanley Braithwaite, Nella Larsen, Walter White, and some of the participants in *The Crisis* symposium in 1926 entitled "The Negro in Art: How Shall He Be Portrayed?" In an article he later wrote for *The Nation*, "The Beauty Instead of Ashes" (1928), Locke rebukes critics of white artists for "mistak[ing] for color prejudice the contemporary love for strong local color, and for condescension the current interest in folk life."[36] More generally, Locke refused to obsess over the minor infelicities of racial representations in Anglo-American literature. Rather, he concentrated on the more important historical progress and ethical implications of this literature by the 1920s.

Traces of this logic exist in Locke's studies of African art. "The Legacy of the Ancestral Arts" is an essay he derived from his previously published essays on art, including "A Note on African Art" (*Opportunity* [1924]) and "The Art of the Ancestors," which *The Survey Graphic* released only months prior to "Harlem: Mecca of the New Negro." "The Legacy of the Ancestral Arts" praises Anglo-European painters like Belgium-born Auguste Mambour and Bavaria-born Winold Reiss for their sensitivity to African aesthetics. Reiss, in particular, provided sketches for "Harlem: Mecca of the New Negro" and *The New Negro*. His style reportedly inspired Aaron Douglas, a young black painter, to contribute several illustrations reflective of a "truly" Negro perspective. Reiss symbolized for Locke the possibility that European artists could teach the black avant-garde how to achieve that "characteristic idiom" called New (World) Negro art. The legacy of the "ancestral arts" thus operated through an essentialist articulation of the artists and cultural geographies of Europe, Africa, and African America.

However, Locke placed the greatest racial responsibility on artists of African descent to produce revisionist racial realism. When you compare Glasgow with Page, or Frank with Cable, Locke claimed, "you will get the true clue of this [analogous] contrast between the younger and elder generations of Negro literature," between black practitioners of New Negro realism and those of New Negro modernism.[37] Racial accountability, which had everything to do with black writers of racial realism, turns out to have had little to do with white writers of it. Not only was New Negro modernism an aesthetic and ethical means toward interracial cooperation, it could also unify blacks in the United States and around the world.

For this reason, Locke lauds *Batouala* (1921) in "Negro Youth Speaks." *Batouala* made its author, Martinique-born René Maran, the first writer of African descent to win the Prix Goncourt, France's renowned literary prize. For Locke, the novel bridged local and global contexts of the African diaspora through New Negro modernism. Although "*Batouala* is not of the American Negro either in substance or authorship, the influence of its daring realism and Latin frankness was educative and emancipating" for the American Negro. "And so not merely for modernity of style, but for vital originality of substance, the young Negro writers dig deep into the racy peasant undersoil of the race life."[38] The "black internationalism" and pragmatism of *Batouala* were qualities constitutive of New Negro modernism.[39]

The geocultural scope of New Negro modernism ranged far and wide; the renaissance as Locke conceived it was never restricted solely to Harlem. Neither in his edited collections of 1925 nor in his contemporary essays does the term "Harlem Renaissance" appear. A misleading conflation more often attributable to subsequent scholarship on the era, the Harlem Renaissance was at the time consistently called the "New Negro movement" or the "Negro Renaissance." This terminological distinction is significant from a conceptual standpoint: Locke did not necessarily limit the New Negro movement geographically, socially, and culturally, although he did conceive of Harlem as a crucial geocultural node. Instead, he recognized the movement's national (in Washington, D.C.) and even global proportions. Racial realism, one could say, crossed not only the Potomac and the color line, but the Atlantic as well, everywhere and anywhere inhabited or traversed by the African diaspora.

New Negro modernism was poised to organize black societies and cultures and imbue them with racial-political significance. Seven years after saying that "successful peoples are rated, and rate themselves, in terms of their best," Locke declared in 1925 that the younger generation of black artists had "now stopped speaking *for* the Negro," as racial-uplift ideologues had previously done, but "speak *as* Negroes," applying racial consciousness to aesthetic expression. On occasion, Locke self-consciously tried to downplay his own cultural ambassadorship. When he introduced the writings of the younger generation in "Harlem: Mecca of the New Negro" and *The New Negro*, he noted that "it is a presumption to speak for those who have spoken and can speak so adequately for themselves."[40] Locke's edited volumes were positioning this younger generation to lead the cementing of national unity in spite and because of interpersonal and ethnic differences.

New Negro modernism, so defined, discounted one kind of "literature of the Negro," namely, literature written *by* a Negro but not *about* the Negro. This taxonomic exclusion resulted from a large cultural ideology, applicable to Locke and other critical authorities like James Weldon Johnson and Ernest Boyd, that dismissed "nonracial" Negro art as lacking aesthetic power and political relevance. Locke indicted cosmopolitanism as responsible for this kind of art and as antithetical to New Negro modernism.

An early stage in Locke's intellectual career foreshadowed otherwise. In a paper delivered in June 1908 to the Cosmopolitan Club at Oxford University, an organization of international students, according to Paul Allan Anderson, "seemed brought together as much by their marginality at Oxford as by their devotion to the ideal of cosmopolitanism." There, Locke "anticipated the corrective possibilities of a newer cosmopolitanism" that would embrace cultural pluralism within and across nations. Over two and a half decades later, Anderson continues, Locke would style himself a "cultural cosmopolitan, but perforce an advocate of cultural racialism as a defensive counter-move for the American Negro, and accordingly more of a philosophical mid-wife to a generation of younger Negro poets, writers, artists than a professional philosopher."[41]

The seeming equation of cultural pluralism with cosmopolitanism gives the impression that this doctrine of "self in the world" captures the link between the local and the global afforded by New Negro modernism. But there was more than one kind of cosmopolitanism. The kind that Locke associated with harmonious cultural pluralism within and across human societies differed remarkably from the more ominous kind he associated with the ethnocentrism of the Anglo-European academies, even those academies that reared generation upon generation of blacks, including himself and famed black artists. Such academies tended to value not blacks but whites.

The ethnocentrism of the latter type of cosmopolitanism undermined the pluralistic vision of New Negro modernism. It also contradicted the extra racial responsibility Locke assigned to artists of the African diaspora to revise older versions of racial realism. For mainly this reason, Locke accused Henry Ossawa Tanner, the most famous black painter at the turn of the twentieth century, of being the leading culprit in perpetuating "the conventional blindness of the Caucasian eye with respect to the racial material at [his] immediate disposal."

Tanner's Blindness

For much of his career, Henry Ossawa Tanner intrigued audiences in the United States and around the world. Numerous educators, practitioners, critics, patrons, and casual enthusiasts of visual art admired his paintings of animals, seascapes, landscapes, human types, and memorable scenes from the Holy Bible. Critical and commercial success made Tanner the first twentieth-century black painter to earn international acclaim and to bear the name "Dean of American Painters."[42] But Locke never bought into Tanner's fame, accolades, and artistic humanism. The dean of the Harlem Renaissance could not ignore the versions and avoidances of racial realism that catapulted this dean of American painters to stardom.

In "The Legacy of the Ancestral Arts," Locke contends that Tanner created nothing "above the level of the *genre* study" or nothing "more penetrating than a Nordicized transcription" of humanity. Similarly, the work of painters W. E. Scott and Laura Wheeler Waring and of sculptors Meta Warrick Fuller and May Howard Jackson, "competent as it has been, has wavered between abstract expression which was imitative and not highly original, and racial expression which was only experimental." Only Archibald Motley and Aaron Douglas had attained that "new style, a distinctive fresh technique, and some sort of characteristic idiom."[43] In the case of Tanner, Locke is alluding to the painter's attraction to American "genre" realism in the early to mid-1890s. Tanner's genre paintings include *The Bagpipe Lesson* (1892–93), *The Banjo Lesson* (1893), and *The Thankful Poor* (1894) (Figs. 3–5).

Locke's dismissal of these paintings as shallow, if not also stereotypical, neglected their significant racial-political context and themes. Indeed, Tanner produced these paintings when he was visiting Philadelphia and involved with black interest groups in the mid-1890s. After a brief bout with typhoid fever while studying in Paris, he returned to Philadelphia and ac-

Figure 3 (*top*). Henry Ossawa Tanner, *The Bagpipe Lesson* (1892–93). Oil on canvas, 49" x 35½". (Collection of Hampton University Museum, Hampton, Va.)

Figure 4 (*bottom*). Henry Ossawa Tanner, *The Banjo Lesson* (1893). Oil on canvas, 49" x 35½". (Collection of Hampton University Museum, Hampton, Va.)

Figure 5. Henry Ossawa Tanner, *The Thankful Poor* (1894). Oil on canvas. (Private collection. Photograph Art Resource, N.Y.)

cepted an invitation to speak at the Congress on Africa at the World's Columbian Exposition, held in Chicago on August 14–21, 1893. His lecture, "The Negro in American Art," affirmed the competitiveness of blacks with whites in the visual and fine arts.[44]

Lasting until October 1894, Tanner's sojourn in the United States marked his increased participation in and fondness for black communities. In 1894 he attended an African Methodist Episcopal conference in Tallahassee, Florida, as well as a commencement ceremony at Hampton Institute in Virginia. The black press and even black leaders revered him. Booker T. Washington lauded the painter in his autobiography, *Up from Slavery* (1901), and W. E. B. Du Bois, two decades later, heaped comparable praise onto him in *The Gifts of Black Folk* (1924). Coincidentally, the mid-1890s marked Tanner's momentary yet explicit artistic interest in the genre of racial realism.[45]

Tanner's genre paintings were more progressive than Locke realized. Genre was a realist style at the turn of the twentieth century, found in

French painting but even more commonly in American painting, postcards, and cartoons. Produced during the "coon era,"[46] when illustrations of ethnic or racial caricature filled American books and periodicals, genre paintings became the visual transcription of "artists' personal observations of their mundane domestic, workplace, and leisure surroundings." Consequently, the goal of such transcriptions—to "please prospective patrons"—exposed "the dominant values and prejudices, painted by the members of the community who shared them." The goal also implied a promotion of "a socially conscious point of view, purporting to be a straightforward response to everyday realities and yet preserving through sentimental, patronizing, and nostalgic scenes the image of a traditional lifestyle resistant to change and of potentially unruly groups still subject to hierarchical control."[47]

Tanner once stated that he tried to counter the tradition of genre painting by avoiding its derogatory protocols—its "comic" and "ludicrous" minstrel side, in the case of the African American genre. He did this to convey the "sympathy with and appreciation for the warm big heart that dwells within such a rough exterior."[48] *The Banjo Lesson* and *The Thankful Poor*, for example, seem to employ stereotypical tropes, the banjo in *The Banjo Lesson*, religiosity in *The Thankful Poor*, the signs of socioeconomic poverty in both paintings. However, they still show the transmission of knowledge from an older to a younger generation as a form of emotional and intellectual uplift. This theme of uplift also informs his other genre painting of the period, *The Bagpipe Lesson*. Locke's remark that Tanner's genre paintings, by implication, were not "more penetrating than a Nordicized transcription"—in the sense that these works perpetuated white racial prejudices of black subjects and hence failed to meet his criteria for New Negro modernism—thus missed the polemics as much as had the reviews of other critics who had encountered these paintings.[49]

Aside from Tanner's genre works, Locke also had in mind his biblical paintings. Biblical themes characterize the majority of Tanner's oeuvre since his permanent expatriation to Paris in the mid-1890s. These paintings ostensibly avoid explicit representations of blacks in order to tell more universal stories of humanity. In "The Legacy of the Ancestral Arts," Locke suggests that the widespread appreciation for this universalist kind of art threatens to undermine New Negro modernism with an ethnocentric cosmopolitanism, fostered in academic settings traditionally Western and white. The black visual artists working between 1895 and 1915, in his words, were "products of the best American academies," but their "talents" were "forced into the channels of academic cosmopolitanism." This generation comprised "victims of the academy tradition."[50] Tanner's academic training, expatriation to Europe, and biblical approach to painting, according to Locke's reasoning, were influential factors in the direction of black visual art. Locke concludes, cynically, that "race" connotes a "ghetto of isolation and neglect from which Tanner must escape to gain artistic freedom and recognition. And so, except for occasional sentimental gestures of loyalty," as exemplified by the genre paintings, Tanner avoids race "as a motive or theme in [his] art," as demonstrated by the biblical paintings.[51]

After 1925, Locke's criticism of Tanner remained scathing. In "The American Negro as Artist" (1931), Locke historicizes in greater detail the tradition of black visual and fine arts. The early art of this tradition (1860–1890) "was of a purely imitative type, but not without technical merit . . . [T]he Negro artists were isolated and exceptional individuals, imitations though, judged by contemporary American standards, not mediocre and almost entirely lacking in race consciousness. They were artists primarily and incidentally Negroes."[52] Locke traced such hierarchic identity politics to illustrator and sculptor Edmonia Lewis and painters Robert S. Duncanson and Edward M. Bannister. He derided their academic education for its emphasis on (white) formal mentorship (of blacks) rather than on the kind of natural (black) talent born from racial experience. In this sense, Tanner's biblical paintings contradicted the intended pragmatism of New Negro modernism.

Certainly, Locke's criticism of Tanner is both dismissible and understandable. In light of his life and work, first of all, Locke's words once again ring with hypocrisy. As mentioned before, his own academic pedigree included undergraduate and graduate degrees from Harvard and Oxford, respectively. Evidently, in neither institution did Locke resist the academic influences of white teachers. Similarly, the artistic and intellectual gifts of most of the younger generation he anointed as leaders of the Harlem Renaissance—Langston Hughes, Countée Cullen, and Zora Neale Hurston, to name but a few—came just as much from academic cultivation in predominantly white settings as from lived experiences in black communities. Although he did not wholeheartedly support the implications of these relations, namely, that whites almost always enlightened and mentored blacks, Locke and his anointed younger generation benefited greatly from interracial academic relations.[53]

Yet Locke's criticism of Tanner is also understandable. He was not entirely off base about Tanner's racial anxiety. The painter always grappled with his racial identity, even though, according to his son, Jesse Tanner, "My father was . . . a fourth-generation American of Negro extraction. But he always felt himself to be an American first and a Negro second."[54] Other evidence proves that on his expatriation to France in 1895, at the moment when he was ascending to the status of preeminent black genre painter, Tanner rejected America because of its consistently prejudicial, if not hostile, treatment of black citizens. Tanner's creative gravitation toward or away from black genre, scholars have recently agreed, corresponded with his negotiations with his own racial identity.

The culmination of Tanner's frustration spilled over in his often-cited 1914 letter to white poet, novelist, and journalist Eunice Tietjens. In the letter, Tanner assails an article she sent him in which she stereotypes works painted by whites as "clean" and "objective" and works painted by blacks as "mystical" and "subjective"—qualities, she thought, he would appreciate in association with his work. But, according to the painter, these characterizations were nothing less than reductive, misguided, and prejudiced.[55]

Locke's criticism of Tanner's racial irresponsibility was not uncommon in the early twentieth century. The historical tendency of writers in the U.S. media—namely, those in *Harper's Weekly, Ladies Home Journal, Cosmopolitan*, the *Philadelphia Inquirer*, the *Atlanta Constitution*, the *Chicago Daily Tribune*, the *Detroit Free Press*, the *New York Times*, and the *Boston Evening Transcript*—to address Tanner's African ancestry incensed the painter. By contrast, the Parisian media—including *Revue de l'Art, Gazette des Beaux-Arts, International Studio, Fine Arts Journal*, and *Brush and Pencil*—less frequently discussed his racial identity and, at least in Tanner's mind, concentrated more appropriately on the aesthetic qualities of his paintings.[56] Thus, while Locke and his anointed younger generation arguably colluded in the black appropriation and dissemination of certain academic values, at the time such views were within reason.

That said, Locke's belief that Tanner's biblical illustrations were shallow "Nordicized transcription" reduces their aesthetic and generic complexities. True, his biblical paintings tended to dignify what ostensibly seemed to be representations of whites. But there was more to his paintings than that. Traditional critics of visual art, for example, elevated the genre of biblical characters and subjects above secular realism, which was quite popular at the turn of the twentieth century. When Tanner settled in Paris and enrolled in the Académie Julian, he began studying under French masters Jean-Joseph Benjamin-Constant and Jean-Paul Laurens while experimenting with this popular mode of painting. Soon he discovered the Salon de la Société des Artistes Français and submitted his artwork to the salon's annual spring exhibition of the best and brightest painters of Europe and the United States. Unfortunately, the salon rejected his work on the basis of its nonnormative style.[57]

Not until *Daniel in the Lions' Den* (released first in 1895, then in 1907–18) did Tanner settle into a new thematic approach to painting that garnered almost absolute acclaim (Fig. 6). While not his first painting of a religious

Figure 6. Henry Ossawa Tanner, *Daniel in the Lions' Den* (1907–18). Oil on paper mounted on canvas. (Los Angeles County Museum of Art, 22.6.3, Mr. and Mrs. William Preston Harrison Collection. Photograph ©2005 Museum Associates/Los Angeles County Museum of Art)

subject—for that we must consider *Waiting for the Lord* (1882)—*Daniel in the Lions' Den* represents Tanner's decisive turn toward the Holy Bible, especially the New Testament, for stories of humanity.

By the early twentieth century, Tanner's biblical paintings had garnered many awards for their aesthetic merit and thematic nobility. He had earned the right to hold solo exhibitions, and he had achieved several professional milestones, among them, *The Annunciation*, which he completed and the Pennsylvania Museum and School of Art purchased in 1899; *Nicodemus Visiting Jesus*, created the following year and awarded the American Lippincott Prize; *Daniel in the Lions' Den*, which in May 1901 won a silver medal at the Pan-American Exposition in Buffalo, New York, and three years later another silver medal at the Purchase Exposition in St. Louis, Missouri; and *Two Disciples at the Tomb* (1906), which won the Chicago Art

Institute's Harris Prize in summer 1906. Furthermore, his solo exhibitions took place at prestigious galleries mostly in the United States: New York's American Art Galleries in 1908; Chicago's Thurber Art Galleries in 1911 and 1913; New York's Knoedler's Gallery in 1913; Boston's Vose Galleries in 1921; Des Moines's Association of Fine Arts in 1922; and New York's Grand Central Art Galleries in 1924.

Tanner also achieved professional milestones. In 1905, the Pennsylvania Academy selected him to judge its annual exhibitions. Three years later, the National Academy of Design elected him an associate member. In 1914, he became a member of the American Negro Academy in Washington, D.C. During World War I, he worked for France's American Red Cross. Toward the end of his life (1927), the National Academy of Design finally elected him full academician, and the European chapter of the American Artists Professional League inducted him as a member in 1930.

Locke resented the awards and the acclaim for Tanner. He believed it came mostly from white critics who were negatively influencing visual art across the world and within the black artistic community.[58] But according to one acquaintance, Tanner was aware, perhaps more than Locke was, of the importance of religious symbolism to the black community. His father, formerly a prominent bishop of the AME Church, instilled that idea through various sermons and essays about theology, divinity, and religious practice. In order to accommodate the racially specific symbolism of religion without restricting his artwork to it, Tanner resorted to certain humanistic philosophies and personal experiences with religion.

Daniel in the Lions' Den and *The Resurrection of Lazarus* (1896; Fig. 7), for example, could refer to uplifting biblical stories applicable to black experience and possibly of great thematic import to black audiences. Human representation in *Daniel in the Lions' Den*, however, could also be viewed as lacking racial specificity. The physiognomic and phenotypical traits of racial identity in the painting are ambiguous, at best. *The Resurrection of Lazarus* more clearly contrasts the skin tones of Jesus Christ's onlookers, but here, too, Tanner is emphasizing multiracial heterogeneity, not racial homogeneity. His subsequent biblical paintings similarly refrain from restricting humanity to one racial type. Instead, in them he tried to convey a universalism that accommodates the histories and interests of all types of people. He maintained this theme after 1908, when he began to incorporate into his biblical work "Oriental" themes inspired by his visits to Albania, Turkey, Algeria, and the Holy Land of Palestine.

New Negro modernism blinded Locke not only to the extent of Tanner's frustration with racism, but also to the promise of racial liberation that Tanner saw in cosmopolitanism. Tanner was an expatriate for most of his life, be-

Figure 7. Henry Ossawa Tanner, *The Resurrection of Lazarus* (1896). Oil on canvas. (Musée d'Orsay, Paris. Photograph Réunion des Musées Nationaux/Art Resource, N.Y.)

cause, according to his son, Jesse, "he felt the white people in America were not ready to face acceptance of the colored races, especially the Negro race. He believed this acceptance would eventually be worked out through education and equal opportunity, though it might take many years."[59]

Cosmopolitanism, the ideology of feeling at home in the world, allowed the painter to conceive of an international home outside of a country he so desperately wanted to call his national home. After marrying Jessie Macauley Olssen in 1899 and having Jesse four years later, Tanner constantly traveled through the Eastern and Western hemispheres looking for a home, even as he kept a permanent residence in France until his death. Biblical art projected Tanner's vision of what "nation" in the United States would not always allow for blacks.

While Tanner's cosmopolitanism freed him from racism in the United States, Locke disregarded it because it failed to assume the racial responsibility on which he founded New Negro modernism. Tanner's depiction of biblical universalism and humanism captured his optimism about peace. For Locke, by contrast, this optimism posited whiteness as the standard for humanity. It undercut the kind of link between the local and the global demonstrated by Maran's *Batouala*, whose cosmopolitanism is neither European nor academic but African diasporic and pragmatic. Unlike Maran, cosmopolitan truants such as Tanner were bastardized in Locke's canonical version of the Harlem Renaissance.

New Negro Culture: A Sensation

The commercial sensation of "Harlem: Mecca of the New Negro" and its representative claim to New Negro culture assured the influence of Locke's critical views. *The Survey Graphic Number* sold approximately thirty thousand copies of the special edition on March 1, 1925, and nineteen days later sold another twelve thousand copies, more than twice the regular circulation of any one issue of the magazine. Philanthropists such as Albert C. Barnes, George Foster Peabody, and the Spingarns purchased three thousand copies for distribution to black students and organizations.[60]

The critical acclaim justified the commercial success. The May 1925 issue of *The Survey Graphic Number* printed a section entitled "What they say of the Harlem Number," which includes twenty blurbs from white writers about race relations; from public, judicial, religious, political, and philanthropic officers; as well as from the essayists and editors of recognized American periodicals. Effusive was the praise of the high literary and editorial quality and current relevance of Locke's edition. According to the blurbs, the Harlem issue of *The Survey* was "one of the few fine things of the year," "an excellent piece of work," "one of the most important things in many years in American periodical literature," a "superb" "picture of the almost unparalleled achievement of a race," "a human document of great value," a "most fertile, meaty, fascinating magazine," "[a]dmirably done and consistently well written from end to end," "interesting reading matter," "one of the most fascinating achievements in real editing," "far and away the best number," "one of the most important and interesting achievements in contemporary journalism," "an amazing performance," "an extraordinary range," "a splendid thing," and "a notable contribution." The canonical potential of Locke's edition, and of its subsequently expanded version as *The New Negro*, was unquestionable.[61]

Such extraordinary critical and commercial success determined the historical predominance of Locke's vision in the Harlem Renaissance. Some were aware, though, that his vision could eclipse other noteworthy visions of the movement. Marcus Garvey stressed that Locke's idea of the Harlem

Renaissance was "commendable" but still only "partial." In his blurb, also printed in the Harlem issue, the founder and leader of the Universal Negro Improvement Association states that "the effort you [Locke] have made to present partially the life of the race as it strikes you in Harlem is commendable. Your motive is of the nature that will bring about the better understanding that the world needs."[62]

Garvey's reservations anticipate, to an extent, Barbara Foley's recent revelation that the political conservatism of Locke's views obscured the kind of radicalism that he and others, whom Locke called "liberals," represented.[63] Foley has shown rather convincingly that Locke's 1925 editions about the New Negro effectively shifted black intellectual discourse from political radicalism to romantic culturalism, despite his claims that he was distancing himself from the romantic imagery of the folk. Indeed, the cultural ideology of the New Negro movement pivoted, in 1925, on Locke's hegemonic tropes of the folk vis-à-vis his proclamation that black culture was undergoing a rebirth of extraordinary proportions.

Though the detachment of the New Negro from radicalism was only a glimmer in some of his earlier, pre-Renaissance writings and lectures, Locke completed his separation in *The New Negro*. In the collection, Locke buries—by revising certain essays and omitting others that conjure up radical sentiment—the idea that the New Negro is radical both in tone and in purpose.[64] His "turn from class consciousness to class collaborationism" coordinated with the larger black intellectual turn, during the 1920s, from racial antagonism to racial amelioration. Hence Locke's version of the New Negro coincided, unsurprisingly, with the fact that "the production of literature inflected with revolutionary politics had slowed to a near-trickle by the last half of the decade."[65]

One black author whose leftist writings never slowed was George S. Schuyler, who rejected much of what Locke stood for. In the wake of Locke's 1925 publications, Schuyler devised an anomalous canon of lamp-blacked Anglo-Saxons that recovered not only Henry Ossawa Tanner, but also other black artists who showed the impress of nationality rather than race. Schuyler also wrote himself into this canon by producing a novel of science fiction that critiqued the arbitrariness of racial distinctions. Indeed, he enjoyed playing truant in Locke's school.

Chapter 4

"The Impress of Nationality Rather than Race"

In 1922, almost every Sunday, George S. Schuyler attended a forum sponsored by the Friends of Negro Freedom. Held in Harlem, the forum enabled the black journalist, novelist, and critic to associate with other prominent black thinkers, including Asa Philip Randolph and his friend Chandler Owen, coeditors of the leading black socialist magazine, *The Messenger*. Cramped together in *The Messenger* headquarters, two small rooms located on the third floor of a renovated brownstone at 2305 Seventh Avenue, Schuyler and Randolph became "very chummy." In 1923, Owen left the magazine, and Schuyler assumed some of *The Messenger*'s editorial and administrative responsibilities.

On most Saturday afternoons at the brownstone, with other local intellectuals and artists, they discussed anything and everything and, "of course, solved the problems of the world." Spilling over into Sunday morning breakfast at Randolph's home, these spirited talks "acquainted [Schuyler] with most of the people who had any intellectual pretensions, the eggheads of Harlem."[1] Aside from Randolph and Owen, the clique included James W. Ivy, editor of *The Crisis* after the tenure of W. E. B. Du Bois; William Pickens and William Bagnall, field secretaries of the National Association for the Advancement of Colored People; W. A. Domingo, journalist, essayist, editor, and cofounder of the modern Jamaican independence movement; and Theophilus Lewis, regular drama critic for *The Messenger*. The editorials Schuyler wrote for local newspapers derived from his conversations with these figures on weekends.

From the weekly debates Schuyler crafted "The Negro-Art Hokum" and sometime between late June and November 1925 submitted it to Freda Kirchwey, the managing editor at *The Nation*. Stunned by its satire, Kirchwey refrained from printing "The Negro-Art Hokum" without a rebuttal. She sent Schuyler's essay to Charles S. Johnson and James Weldon Johnson, who both stood atop her list of luminaries capable of commenting on it or recommending those who could. After submitting the article, Schuyler began an eight-month tour of the United States for a journalistic series slated for *The Pittsburgh Courier*.[2]

The cautionary review of the essay in typescript continued through March 1926. In this month, Schuyler was sitting at a train junction in Tyler, Texas, when he read a letter from Kirchwey, forwarded from his office at *The Pittsburgh Courier*. *The Nation*, the letter told him, had accepted the article for publication. Usually, *The Nation* took only ten days to determine whether to print an unsolicited article. Since Schuyler was never in the Northeast for more than two days at a time during his travels across the country, he had never had the opportunity to learn through the grapevine that his essay was being passed around and beyond Harlem. For yet another two months after penning the acceptance letter to Schuyler, Kirchwey continued to circulate "The Negro-Art Hokum." Finally, only two weeks before the publication of Schuyler's essay on June 16, 1926, Kirchwey secured a rebuttal from Langston Hughes entitled "The Negro Artist and the Racial Mountain."[3]

The debate was set. In brief, "The Negro-Art Hokum" claims that, since Negroes are not peculiarly racial, they do not produce peculiarly racial art. "Negro art," or what Schuyler called art whose creators were identified as "Negro," bears the cultural imprint of the nation, a pattern discernible in art created by whites, generally called "American art." The idea of considering Negro art "true," or an authentic, singular tradition, is a sham, a "hokum." This argument, Schuyler admitted later, in his autobiography, was "treason at a time when there was so much talk about African heritage."[4]

The "story" behind the genesis of "The Negro-Art Hokum" provides insight into Schuyler's iconoclasm. He purposely assumed any number of ideological guises when the occasion permitted in order to defy easy categorization. His self-conscious desire to play truant translated into the kind of rhetorical satire that encased serious criticism. As much as he insisted in an interview that "[o]f course, I didn't write ["The Negro-Art Hokum"] as a debate, but I mean, *The Nation* made it a debate" between him and Hughes, Schuyler welcomed the potential intellectual discussion the disagreement would stimulate.[5]

Amid the public debates about Alain Locke, his ambassadorial status, and his edited collections published in 1925, "Harlem: Mecca of the New Negro" and *The New Negro*, Schuyler began an iconoclastic campaign. More than with any other contemporary, Schuyler sought to undermine the protocols of racialism, cultural pluralism, and racial realism that Locke promoted in New Negro modernism and during the Harlem Renaissance.

The years 1925 and 1926 mark Schuyler's most explicit rejection of the ethnic and racial particularities implicit in cultural pluralism (that blacks and whites have distinct yet cohabitant cultures in the United States). He favored, instead, a cultural monism (that blacks and whites have the same or a similar kind of culture) dissolving these particularities. Appearing in northeastern mainstream and leftist magazines, Schuyler's satirical essays sought to expose the fundamental problems in the racialism and corollary cultural pluralism of Harlem's status as the epicenter of the New Negro.

In his blunter essays, Schuyler does acknowledge the impact of racism on black culture, politics, and socioeconomic status. He also demonstrates awareness of the black inferiority complexes and identity politics that sociologists recognized at the time. It is important to remember that he is more satirical than sincere, more iconoclastic than honest, in downplaying the historical reality of racism in his most controversial essay, then and now, "The Negro-Art Hokum." More generally, while describing racial differences as incidental in American culture, Schuyler noticed ideological differences in white cultural representations of blacks, differences attributable to race. Schuyler was skeptical of the role of Anglo-American literature in the modernization of racial realism, an idea Locke promoted in New Negro modernism.

Interrogating racialism for the sake of intellectual argument required that Schuyler use satire and cynicism to hide his acceptance of current and historical realities of race. He prioritized region over race in the construction of cultural identity, despite his flawed substitution of one essentialism for another. In his clever statement that "the Aframerican is merely a lampblacked Anglo-Saxon," he racializes Americanism as peculiarly white, just as Locke racialized the New Negro as peculiarly black.[6] And he complicates the authenticity of racial realism by comparing and contrasting its cultural examples with those belonging to artists ostensibly white but supposedly containing one drop of Negro blood.

Schuyler was notorious for poking fun at New Negro modernism and the Harlem Renaissance, but his satire and cynicism should not distract us from the important body of work he wrote in which he was *not* being, prima facie, satirical and cynical. In several of these instances, he acknowledges scientific facts about the socioeconomic plight of the black lower class, a plight that romanticizing images of racial authenticity in American culture tended to obscure. An examination of his letters, interviews, autobiography, and other writings explains the cynicism, satire, and "conservative" racial politics by which his oeuvre has often been characterized.

Such writings frame my close reading of his novel *Black No More: Being an Account of the Strange and Wonderful Workings of Science in the Land of the Free*, A.D.

1933–1940 (1931). A latter-day satire of the tropes of racial passing that began in mid-nineteenth-century African American literature, *Black No More* tells the story of how the sanitariums of Black No More, Inc., "whiten" black skin with great commercial success. In 1931, reviewers of *Black No More*—a list that includes such notables as W. E. B. Du Bois, Alain Locke, Arthur P. Davis, and Rudolph Fisher—applauded Schuyler's use of satire for racial commentary. More recent readings have examined Schuyler's innovative black science, or speculative, fiction, his satirical portraits of the New Negro intelligentsia, and his analysis of passing as a cultural rather than a racial phenomenon facilitated by skin color.[7]

Black No More is a remarkable example of how an anomalous text can be interpreted as a truant for taxonomic passing from African American literature to something else. The fact that one of the novel's main characters, Dr. Junius Crookman, the founder and entrepreneur of Black No More, Inc., does *not* undergo phenotypical treatment supports the allegory of how literature can become "black no more." *Black No More* crosses the literary color line, I want to suggest, even as its author remains "racially" fixed. The novel illustrates the complexity of African American literature's "passing" from one tradition to another.

Schuyler revisits the ideas behind Paul Laurence Dunbar's statement that blacks inevitably must "write like the white men," discussed in Chapter 2. Like Dunbar, Schuyler subordinates the incidence of racial differences, the premise of racialism, to cultural similarities in the comparison of blacks and whites. However, especially since the Black Arts Movement, which celebrated Hughes's "The Negro Artist and the Racial Mountain," Schuyler has usually stood as the antithesis of the Harlem Renaissance. "The Negro-Art Hokum" went against the themes of racial collectivity, beauty, and pride, themes that Hughes's essay supposedly embody and that informed the critical discourses of the movement and subsequent generations of literary and cultural scholars. Schuyler's essay, it has been said, is symptomatic of his "rac(e)ing to the right." That portrayal, however, perpetuates the idea that he was an assimilationist, a believer that the African diaspora had to integrate into and adopt the values of American society at the expense of black heritage, a Negro with an "urge to whiteness."[8] The consequences of such reductive logic have been significant: "The Negro-Art Hokum" has received only minor acknowledgment or utter neglect in African American anthologies; "The Negro Artist and the Racial Mountain," by contrast, has remained a canonical staple.[9]

I do not intend to overstate Schuyler's outsider status or his lack of recognition in African American literary studies. His fiction and nonfiction have generally remained in print since the 1970s. Rather, this point addresses the extent to which literary historians have misrepresented Schuyler's insight into race, culture, nation, and diaspora. Contrary to popular opinion, Schuyler's truancy was born out of a political stance that, in some ways, was not as conservative as Locke's in the mid-1920s. His attack of the racial, cultural, and aesthetic assumptions of Locke's New Negro modernism suggests that he was a more provocative persona than most scholars of the Harlem Renaissance have given him credit for.

Cultural Monism

In the wake of Locke's influential work about the cultural renaissance of the New Negro, debates abounded in New York's newspapers and magazines. Famous artists and intellectuals communicated with each other in periodicals and staked out various positions on race, culture, and nation. Two separate and ideologically opposed debates appeared in *The Crisis* and *The Messenger*.

In February 1926, *The Crisis* began printing public reactions to a questionnaire about the racism of white writers, including Haldane MacFall, Thomas Dixon, Clement Wood, T. S. Stribling, and Octavus Roy Cohen. Entitled "The Negro in Art: How Shall He Be Portrayed?" the seven-month "symposium" of nearly twenty opinions covered "what has long been controversy within and without the Negro race as to just how the Negro should be treated in art—how he should be pictured by writers and portrayed by artists."[10] *The Crisis* symposium mostly attributed ideological differences in racial realism to racial differences between white and black authors.

Perhaps in response to *The Crisis* symposium, *The Messenger* posed its own questionnaire, "Group Tactics and Ideals," and printed public responses in late 1926 and 1927. This symposium scrutinized "the development of Negro social consciousness (a definite group psychology stressing and laudation of things Negro) compatible with the ideal of Americanism (Nationalism)." *The Messenger*'s endorsement of American cultural nationalism contrasted with the racialism of *The Crisis*.[11] *The Messenger*'s symposium resisted the romantic rhetoric of "group psychology," used by Alain Locke, and its assumption that blacks were more racially unique than culturally distinct from their white counterparts.[12] In short, both symposia differed on whether racial difference or cultural similarity best characterized the Negro.

Schuyler embraced the latter portrayal, for ideological and personal reasons. Since joining *The Messenger* staff in 1922, he had written satirical essays endorsing the magazine's political positions. But even in other magazines, including *The Nation, The Pittsburgh Courier, American Mercury*, and

The New Masses, his 1925 and 1926 essays corresponded with the critique of racialism in *The Messenger*'s questionnaire. He specifically examined racialist or color-line demarcations of culture, in which different races possess different cultures. This idea, the basis of Locke's cultural pluralism, lay at the heart of New Negro modernism and thus became the object of Schuyler's attacks.

One American culture permeated the nation. Schuyler supported this claim with hypotheses of cultural monism—an extreme form of American cultural nationalism—that understated skin color and valued whiteness as the cultural norm. The resistance of cultural monism to the protocols of ethnic self-pride and solidarity in cultural pluralism went against what Locke deeply believed in. "Given his arrangement of the critical conceptualistic foundations for a new Afrocentric aesthetic order," according to Winston Napier, "Locke . . . call[ed] for a critique of the cultural monism which inhibits America's democratic ideals, and it is in this mode that he would assert the need for black intellects whose moral responsibility it is to criticize cultural hegemony and consequently contribute to correcting social injustice."[13] Schuyler's cultural monism undoubtedly contradicted Locke's cultural pluralism.

In one essay, "The Negro and Nordic Civilization" (1925), Schuyler refutes the cultural pluralism implicit in calling Harlem a city peculiar to the New Negro. "Aside from varying differences in pigmentation," according to Schuyler, "there is no difference . . . between" blacks and whites. The sameness of the two groups is an interior one: "[T]hey think and feel about the same." He goes on to say that in Africa there is "no eager scrambling out of bed at six o'clock in the morning, six days a week, to the melodious strains of the alarm clock; no bolting of the coffee and rolls in happy anticipation of the pleasant day's work ahead." Nor are there sophisticated transportation, labor, or environmental structures to accommodate society.[14]

Schuyler reiterates these ideas in one of his *Pittsburgh Courier* columns, published in August 1925, "Thrusts and Lunges." He states that "the environment of the Negro in this land of liberty is the same as that of the Nordic. Both live in an environment of hustle and bustle, extreme standardization and militarization of education, work and pleasure; both worship the same and in the same way; both have the same moral and ethical concepts and what is more important, they make their living in about the same way."[15] If taken at face value, Schuyler's 1925 and 1926 essays suggest that he regarded skin color as incidental in interracial contact and in the formation of American culture. A closer inspection of other essays he wrote at the time, however, proves that he believed the role of skin color in racialism and racism was insurmountable.

In the pages of *The Messenger* and *The Pittsburgh Courier*, Schuyler published essays that acknowledge the implications of racism. Some essays examine the capitalist corruption and economic underdevelopment afflicting Harlem's black communities. They expose what Locke's "Harlem: Mecca of the New Negro" and *The New Negro* mostly hid from public view. Schuyler decried the utopian idea of Harlem being a "mecca of the New Negro." In the August 1925 "Shafts and Darts," a monthly "page of calumny and satire" written for *The Messenger*, Schuyler quips that the "literary renaissance" has ignored the city's entrenched capitalist problems: "The Aframerican, we have been informed by gushing white friends and their sable satellites, are [*sic*] entering upon a literary renaissance. Harlem, we learn, is the Mecca of the New Negro. It is also, we might add, the mecca of swindlers, sharks, spiritualists, suckers and strivers."[16]

Schuyler's more comprehensive complaint appears in "New York: Utopia Deferred" (1925). With twenty-two subtitles, the article rivals even the thoroughgoing first section of "Harlem: Mecca of the New Negro," which includes essays by Locke, James Weldon Johnson, Charles S. Johnson, Rudolph Fisher, and W. A. Domingo. Schuyler's rejection of Harlem's utopianism pivots on the idea that, "despite the pious lallygagging of sleek and well-paid professional uplifters, the future will, like the writer's complexion, be very dark."[17]

Schuyler's statements have at least two implications. First, they racialize labor politics by addressing the black proletariat and explaining antiblack oppression in terms of class and capitalism. Schuyler's socialist essays generally commented on race at a time when the more popular magazines devoted to the interests of the working people (*The Masses*, *The New Masses*, and *The Liberator*) did not. (It could be said, however, that the *Liberator* became interested in racial issues once Claude McKay became coeditor in 1921.) Second, Schuyler's statements look at the socioeconomic problems of black societies that Locke subsumed within his romantic construction of "the folk." (Later Locke admitted that the stock market crash of 1929 crippled the folk during the decline of the Harlem Renaissance.)

By 1925 and 1926, Schuyler had embarked on what would become a perennial scrutiny of the black inferiority complexes financing the businesses of skin-lightening creams. As we shall soon see, his 1931 novel, *Black No More*, expounds on this phenomenon, which for him exposed a problematic, if cosmetic, way for blacks to identify with white society.[18] Certain serious essays conflict with his other, more satirical, essays of the era, including those quoted above and in "The Negro-Art Hokum." These underplay the damage caused by racism—or the idea that all things white are superior to all things black—to black psychology and cultural pride.

Schuyler knew full well that the darker-skinned members of American society had lived under circumstances of oppression, poverty, and injustice. And he knew full well that light skin color had historically facilitated the assimilation of certain groups, namely, the Jews and the Irish, into American society by gradually freeing them from the racist mythologies assigned to darker skin color. New (World) Negroes, for the most part, suffered from the social disadvantages historically tied to darker hues.[19]

Schuyler's thematic connection of black inferiority complexes, light skin color, and upward mobility placed him among contemporaneous sociologists interested in making such connections. In 1918, Edward Byron Reuter's influential *The Mulatto in the United States, Including a Study of the Role of the Mixed-blood Race throughout the World* presented so-called empirical evidence that racial skin color lightened in proportion to ascension in class status. Two decades later, E. Franklin Frazier elaborated on this evidence in *The Negro Family in the United States* (1939). Frazier argues that, since the "brown middle-class" had achieved collective self-consciousness only as recently as 1900, this group could not solidify its own cultural traditions. As a result, this group had matured primarily through the cultural mimicry of the dominant white order.[20] Schuyler did not exactly subscribe to Reuter's and Frazier's sociological images of black society. Yet he still probed the ideological rationale, cultural significance, and racist implications behind the desire of certain blacks to lighten their skin color.

Schuyler downplayed the prevalence of racism so that his critique of racialism could work. If he acknowledged the existence of racism, he would also have to acknowledge the existence and necessity of racialism in the identification of the perpetrators and victims of this racism and as an explanation of why and how this circumstance had become a reality. Satire and iconoclasm permitted his disingenuous subordination of racism while providing rhetorical maneuverability for his critique of racialism. This critique, which focused on skin color, refuted the constant racialization of human physiognomy (facial features) and phenotype (skin color) during his era, when, in fact, these morphological traits failed as accurate cultural and ideological indicators. And since such racialization factored so much into Locke's chauvinistic conception of New Negro modernism and the Harlem Renaissance, Schuyler felt that his iconoclasm was justified.

"The Aframerican Is Merely a Lampblacked Anglo-Saxon"

Of all the magazines in which Schuyler could have chosen to publish perhaps his most controversial essay in the mid-1920s, "The Negro-Art Hokum," *The Nation* was the ideal place. Along with *The New Republic, The*

Nation was then one of the few long-standing national magazines to print regular editorials, reports, and book reviews related to the Harlem Renaissance. Thematically, the periodical shifted after World War I from being a voice of white cultural conservatism to accommodating progressive voices aware of the nation's problematic racial politics. In 1925, *The Nation* published a front-page editorial about the renaissance of art, culture, and social activity occurring in Harlem. For years afterward, it printed the work of renowned black artists and intellectuals. By the time *The Nation* printed Schuyler's article, it had already become an invaluable site for critical discussions about Negro art.[21] "The Negro-Art Hokum" would not disappoint.

"The Negro-Art Hokum" resumes the critique of racialism vis-à-vis cultural pluralism that Schuyler had begun in earlier essays. In it he ridicules "the current gabble about a distinctive Negro art and literature," particularly the gabble about New Negro modernism and the Harlem Renaissance.[22] What makes "The Negro-Art Hokum" so controversial, and anomalous, is its climactic statement: "[T]he Aframerican is merely a lampblacked Anglo-Saxon." Some scholars since the mid-twentieth century have called the statement and the essay examples of Schuyler's assimilationism. Others have recommended that we ignore the statement entirely as a poor choice of words.[23] I argue, by contrast, that the outrageous statement subtly captures Schuyler's complex critique of not only cultural pluralism but, indirectly, also the modernist styles of racial realism that characterize New Negro aesthetics and culture. The trope of the lampblacked Anglo-Saxon initiates Schuyler's remarkable intervention into the principles of African American canon formation.

Returning to the theme of cultural monism in Schuyler's 1925 and 1926 essays, "The Negro-Art Hokum" invokes region, not race, as the primary indicator of cultural identity. Rejecting the racial particularity of Locke's insistence on the "group psychology" of Harlem's (New) Negroes, Schuyler counters that, if this group lived in the same locality as whites, it would "think, talk, and act about the same."[24] Spirituals, the blues, jazz, and the Charleston, Schuyler underscores, are not quintessential artworks of black folklore; rather, they are regionally coincidental. Even if one were to grant blacks the authority to proclaim the racial representativeness of these artworks, such de facto ownership would not necessarily render these artworks unique. Other groups, if in that same position, would have been similarly productive. Thus, one motive in "The Negro-Art Hokum" is to dislodge folklore from cultural racialism and instead anchor it in cultural regionalism.

The ideas in this article, it turns out, Schuyler transcribed from another he had published a year earlier in *The Pittsburgh Courier*. In the earlier article, he identifies the blues and spirituals as not simply Negro but as "Southern NEGRO—the expression of the WORKING CLASS."[25] Of course, Schuyler is merely replacing one kind of cultural essentialism (region) for another (race). He assumes that a "true" southern folk culture exists from which evolved spirituals, the blues, jazz, and the Charleston. He also assumes that essential cultural distinctions exist between "Northern, West Indian, and African Negroes," but that, together, they share a body of cultural knowledge that cannot interpret other southern groups. The point of such blatant rhetorical duplicity, however, is to undermine the cultural synecdoche of race, whereby the (cultural) part represents the (racial) whole, and vice versa.[26]

In "The Negro-Art Hokum," cultural regionalism enables Schuyler to counter "the common notion that the black American is so 'different' from his white neighbor," which notion had "gained wide currency" by 1925. A hypothetical world in which blacks and whites, as neighbors, own the same home environments and personal practices emphasizes his point:

> Again, the Aframerican is subject to the *same* economic and social forces that mold the actions and thoughts of the white Americans. He is not living in a different world as some white and a few Negroes would have us believe. When the jangling of his Connecticut alarm clock gets him out of his Grand Rapids bed to a breakfast *similar* to that eaten by his white brother *across the street*; when he toils at the *same* or *similar* work in mills, mines, factories, and commerce *alongside* the descendants of Spartacus, Robin Hood, and Eric the Red; when he wears *similar* clothing and speaks the *same* language with the *same* degree of perfection; when he reads the *same* Bible and belongs to the Baptist, Methodist, Episcopal, or Catholic church; when his fraternal affiliations *also* include the Elks, Masons, and Knights of Pythias; when he gets the *same* or *similar* schooling, lives in the *same* kind of houses, owns the *same* makes of cars (or rides in them), and nightly sees the *same* Hollywood version of life on the screen; when he smokes the *same* brands of tobacco, and avidly peruses the *same* puerile periodicals; in short, when he responds to the *same* political, social, moral, and economic stimuli in precisely the *same* manner as his white neighbor, it is sheer nonsense to talk about "racial differences" as between the American black man and the American white man. . . . In the homes of the black and white Americans of the *same* cultural and economic level one finds similar furniture, literature, and conversation. How, then, can the black American be expected to produce art and literature dissimilar to that of the white American?[27] (emphasis added)

This world is utopian for the black (male) who is from the Northeast, racially integrated into industry and across neighborhoods, economically uniform (middle to upper class), permeated by a common cultural style and language, governed by interracial religious worship, and thriving as a result of mass educational and residential equity. Racism does not exist, not because, as Locke once put it, "the vital inner grip of prejudice has been broken," but, rather, because *there are no races to begin with.*[28] No fundamental differences exist between people except for incidental skin color.

Again, Schuyler's cultural monism, embedded in the idea that black and white environments are the "same" or "similar," distorts historical reality. The slippage in his argument lies in positing this privileged and comfortable black person as representative of *all* blacks. His frequent and strategic use of "when" restricts blacks to an imaginary social, cultural, and economic egalitarianism for the sake of debunking racialism with regionalism. In truth, certain articles he wrote at the time threw into stark relief the two faces of Schuyler: the iconoclast, and the historical realist. In *The Messenger*, he published "These 'Colored' United States" (October–November 1925); "Politics and the Negro" (April 1923); and "Hobohemia" (June 1923) and "The Folks Farthest Down" (August 1923), the last two a two-part series entitled "Lights and Shadows of the Underworld: Studying the Social Outcasts." In contrast to the hypothetical world of "The Negro-Art Hokum," the worlds painted in these serious articles document the lack of opportunities for blacks, including those residing in New York City. These articles expose the politics of racism in the formation of cultural regions, while "The Negro-Art Hokum" downplays these politics in order to critique racialism. (Langston Hughes's rejoinder, "The Negro Artist and the Racial Mountain," indicts Schuyler's satirical conduct in "The Negro-Art Hokum" without mentioning him by name.)

While trying to undermine arguments for racial singularity, Schuyler's paradigm of black and white cultural "similarity" or "sameness" denies that cultural realism can reflect racial singularity. Black culture shows "the impress of nationality rather than race." It is no longer illustrative of "the Negro soul" in even the most racist of Anglo-American literature:

The dean of the Aframerican literati is W. E. B. Du Bois, a product of Harvard and German universities; the foremost Aframerican sculptor is Meta Warwick [*sic*] Fuller, a graduate of leading American art schools and former student of Rodin; while the most noted Aframerican painter, Henry Ossawa Tanner, is dean of American painters in Paris and has been decorated by the French Government. Now the work of these artists is no more "expressive of the Negro soul"—as the gushers put it—than are the scribblings of Octavus Cohen or Hugh Wiley. . . . Coleridge-Taylor, Edward Wilmot Blyden, and Claude McKay, the Englishmen; Pushkin, the Russian; Bridgewater, the Pole; Antar, the Arabian; Latino, the Spaniard; Dumas, *père* and *fils*, the Frenchmen; and Paul Laurence Dunbar, Charles W. Chestnutt [*sic*], and James Weldon Johnson, the Americans. All Negroes; yet their work shows the impress of nationality rather than race. They all reveal the psychology and culture of their environment—their color is incidental.

Why should Negro artists of America vary from the national artistic norm when Negro artists in other countries have not done so?[29]

Calling W. E. B. Du Bois "the dean of the Aframerican literati" was surely a swipe at Alain Locke, because Locke was by most accounts considered the black cultural leader of the day. More important, however, Schuyler's insinuation that these black figures are "lampblacked Anglo-Saxons" points to only one side of the racial double consciousness Du Bois describes in *The Souls of Black Folk* (1903): the idea that "America has too much to teach the world and Africa," to the extent that he would "bleach [the] Negro soul in a flood of white Americanism."[30] (Note that Locke expresses the other side of racial double consciousness in his Africanization of America: "Negro blood has a message for the world.") But by making whiteness the core of black identity and by turning black flesh into the black(faced) flesh of a minstrel performer, Schuyler's figure of the lampblacked Anglo-Saxon reiterates the incidence of ostensible physical traits in the human absorption of culture while cleverly conjuring up memories of the minstrel culture that Locke's version of the New Negro was trying to overcome.

Schuyler's collection of lampblacked Anglo-Saxons attacked the prevailing African American canon formation. He complicated the racial authenticity of cultural works by Harlem Renaissance pioneers (Du Bois, Dunbar, Chesnutt, Johnson, Fuller [later in life]) and the younger generation (McKay) by highlighting their Americanism. Just as radically, Schuyler classified as Negroes those artists previously deemed Anglo-Saxon descendants. To do so, he relied, ironically, on the essentialist one-drop rule—one drop of black blood makes one racially black—in order to distinguish the artists whose likeness, art, and notoriety resisted easy association with those of the African diaspora.

The irony pardons the bioracial implications of Schuyler's distinctions between the ostensibly white artists. If the one-drop rule could racially demarcate the African diaspora, it was highly likely that everyone, whites included, was African in lineage. Schuyler's suggestion in "The Negro-Art Hokum" predates by a decade Rudolph Rocker's anarchist *Nationalism and Culture* (1936). That book produces a Western canon even more controversial in its racial implications:

If it is indisputable that men like Socrates, Horace, Michelangelo, Dante, Luther, Galileo, Rembrandt, Goya, Rousseau, Pestalozzi, Herder, Goethe, Beethoven, Byron, Pushkin, Dostoievsky, Tolstoi, Balzac, Dumas, Poe, Strindberg, Ibsen, Zola, and hundreds of others were mixed race, this is surely a proof that external race-marks have nothing to do with the intellectual and moral qualities of man. It is

really amusing to observe with what excuses our modern race fetishists try to overcome these difficulties.[31]

If the entire Western canon comprises artists whose blood contains one
drop of blackness, Schuyler would ask, what does it mean to have an
African American canon? And who, really, is in a position to determine
someone's race, anyway?

Raised by "The Negro-Art Hokum," such questions unsettle the notion
of racial authenticity so central to the prevailing ideas of Negro art. This
notion, while anchored in cultural racialism, gravitates dangerously close
to the kind of biological racialism that Locke's racist contemporaries were
using to rationalize black inferiority, indeed, the very contemporaries
whom Locke and others were trying to refute. "On this baseless premise,
so flattering to the white mob, that the blackamoor is inferior and fundamentally different," Schuyler warns, "is erected the postulate that he must
needs be peculiar; and when he attempts to portray life through the
medium of art, it must necessarily be peculiar art." Schuyler was fighting
two kinds of "peculiarities," because the public could too easily blur them:
first, the kind of racism that segregated Negro art as peculiar; and, second,
the New Negro kind of racialism that embraced Negro art as peculiar.[32]

The response to Schuyler's "The Negro-Art Hokum" and Hughes's
"The Negro Artist and the Racial Mountain" reverberated for days, weeks,
and even years after the two articles appeared in *The Nation*. Schuyler, of
course, threw fuel onto the fire by writing a letter to *The Nation* pointing out
the weaknesses in Hughes's essay. Penned while he was on journalistic as-
signment in Atlanta for *The Pittsburgh Courier*, Schuyler's "Negroes and
Artists" (published July 14, 1926) opens with the familiar claim that blacks
and whites are culturally similar. This time, however, he criticizes Hughes's
glorification of black-folk life for obscuring its resemblance to the lives of
others who do not belong to this society. White folks, too, "watch the lazy
world go round" and "have their nip of gin on Saturday nights." He counters Hughes's black stereotypes with his own white stereotypes: the "love of
strong liquors is supposed to be a Nordic characteristic."[33]

While "The Negro-Art Hokum" and "Negroes and Artists" reiterate
that art should be defined not by race but by region and nationality, the latter indicts the shaky and hypocritical self-pride of black folk. The Negro is
known for using hair straighteners and skin whiteners "per annum in an effort to reach the American standard in pigmentation and hair texture."
This inferiority complex undermines the development of a racial tradition
of Negro art: "Negro propaganda-art, even when glorifying the 'primitive-
ness' of the American Negro masses, is hardly more than a protest against

a feeling of inferiority, and such a psychology seldom produces art."[34] This criticism belongs to Schuyler's long-standing mission, mentioned earlier, to end the black consumption of self-whitening commercial products.

The local media buzzed about the debate between Schuyler and Hughes. On June 23, 1926, the same day that *The Nation* printed "The Negro Artist and the Racial Mountain," the *New York Amsterdam News* reprinted Schuyler's and Hughes's articles side by side on the "editorial and feature" page, under the title, "Two 'New Negroes' Discuss Negro Art in the 'Nation.'" (Hearing Schuyler called "New Negro" sounds curious, given his reservations about the idea.) On week later, the periodical released "J. A. Rogers Discusses the Schuyler and Hughes Articles," by the heralded Jamaica-born journalist and historian of Africa and U.S. racial politics. Between 1926 and 1928, letters to the editor also began to flood into newspapers such as *The Nation*, *The Amsterdam News*, *The Negro World*, *Social Forces*, and *The Pittsburgh Courier* in response to the debate.

Some respondents agreed with Hughes. "I Am a Negro—and Beautiful" (1926), a column by the wife of Marcus Garvey, Amy Jacques, praises Hughes's "splendid article" for condemning "want-to-be-white" Negroes everywhere. Aside from Hughes's own letter to the editor, "American Art or Negro Art?" (1926), however, many responses published in *The Nation* appreciated Schuyler's prioritization of nation over race as a cultural determinant of Negro art.[35]

Respondents in other periodicals agreed with Schuyler, furthermore.[36] Hughes, they said, did not contest the premise of Schuyler's argument, namely, that the racial politics of authentic Negro art failed to account for the omnipresent cultural influence of Americanism. Contrary to what the present-day canonization of the Harlem Renaissance suggests, a substantial portion of editorial respondents portrayed Schuyler's "The Negro-Art Hokum" as a manifesto at least as representative of black and white intellectual opinion as was Hughes's "The Negro Artist and the Racial Mountain," if not more so.

Black (Literature) No More

The public discourse on the Schuyler-Hughes debate and on the possibility of a racial basis for Negro art continued into 1931, the year Schuyler published his first satirical novel, *Black No More*. Shortly after the novel's release, *The Nation*—unsurprisingly, in light of its previous associations with Schuyler—printed Dorothy Van Doren's review, "Black, Alas, No More!" Van Doren bemoans Schuyler's novelistic demonstration of the very truancy he trumpets in "The Negro-Art Hokum." She claims that Schuyler desires to become that very lampblacked Anglo-Saxon who "engaged whole-heartedly in an attempt to be as much like the white man as possible. He will be whiter than white; he will, without a thought for the virtues of his own kind, embrace the white man's virtues, although they are foreign to his nature and beyond his comprehension. . . . This, of course, is one way of saying that the Negro will never write great literature while he tries to write white literature. . . . Mr. Schuyler has written white satire."[37]

Van Doren's allegations compelled Josephine Schuyler, three months later, to defend her husband, who was then traveling throughout Liberia and could not reply with his usual immediacy. In *The Nation*, she repeated almost verbatim what Schuyler had stressed in 1926: "It is rather surprising that well-read people still assume there is such a thing as a distinct Negro literature. . . . There is not, and never has been, such a thing as 'racial' literature; there is only national or sectional literature."[38] Certainly, either Schuyler would have been proud of his wife for asserting a position he evidently held, or she was a critic in her own right, having helped him formulate his intellectual opinions and taken advantage of this opportunity to emerge from behind the scenes as a voice to be reckoned with.

Black No More elicited Van Doren's criticism because the novel tries to debunk the values that she and other traditionalists of Negro art held so dear. Schuyler's novel about the "Black No More" machine, which permits the main characters to cross the color line and change in racial phenotype from black to white, was, in Josephine Schuyler's words, an allegory of how the African American novel could cross the taxonomic color line from "racial literature" to "national or sectional literature." *Black No More* becomes black (literature) no more not because it simply becomes "white literature" or "white satire." Rather, the novel "passes" in the most complex and broadest senses of the word. "In creating a novel in which almost all the black characters are actually 'white' and all the white characters 'black,'" according to J. Martin Favor, "Schuyler is able to examine the question of 'birthright' . . . by modifying the theme of passing in such a way as to render it an issue of culture rather than color." But this modification to "denaturalize race," Favor goes on to say, to make race "a highly unstable category" through the invocation of class, gender, and geography, also has profound implications for *Black No More* as a self-reflexive literary agent of passing.[39] Just as passers complicate their racial-historical backgrounds, *Black No More* complicates its own birthright, its own taxonomic relationship to an African American literary tradition then appreciated and commercially successful for its brand of racial realism. A latter-day companion piece for "The Negro-Art Hokum," *Black No More* forces readers to realize their interpretive discomfort when racialism is unsettled by cultural monism; realism, by science fiction; and racial realism, by literary-taxonomic passing.

The protagonist of passing in the novel is Max Disher, a man of "negroid features" who initially loves "high yallah women" (3).[40] At the outset of the novel, he is hanging out with his good friend Bunny Brown in Harlem's Honky Tonk Club. There, Max spots a "shimmering strawberry blonde" woman with "cool green eyes" who sounds like a "cracker" from Atlanta, his hometown (6). He cannot deny his attraction to her. After the woman rejects his flirtatious entreaty to dance ("I never dance with niggers!" [8]), Bunny tells Max about a press release about one Dr. Junius Crookman opening up a sanitarium in Harlem that, Max learns later, will whiten blacks in three days.

The experiment, Dr. Crookman admits at a press briefing Max attends, exacerbates vitiligo, a disease that destroys melanocytes, the skin cells responsible for producing the melanin for pigmentation. As a result, skin color lightens or becomes almost completely white. While the phenotypical disease is actually not known to affect physiognomic features, bone structures, and hair, Dr. Crookman claims that the hair (somehow) happens to change, too, consummating the scientific whitening of the black race into the white race. As long as there are no Negroes to speak of, there can be no "Negro Problem," Dr. Crookman rationalizes (11). Max agrees to participate in the experiment, with an eye toward tracking down that belle he first drooled over in the Honky Tonk Club.

The novel, in the person of Dr. Crookman in particular, encapsulates several views that gave Schuyler an iconoclastic reputation during the Harlem Renaissance. When questioned about the fact that the Black No More treatment fails to affect "darky dialect," Dr. Crookman argues that "[t]here is no such thing as Negro dialect, except in literature and drama. It is a well-known fact among informed persons that a Negro from a given section speaks the same dialect as his white neighbors. In the South you can't tell over the telephone whether you are talking to a white man or a Negro. The same is true in New York when a Northern Negro speaks into the receiver. . . . There are no racial or color dialects; only sectional dialects" (14). This claim echoes the rumor circulated during the Gilded Age that the speech of southerners and Negroes was indiscernible to a third party listening at nighttime and unaware of the speakers' identities.[41]

In "The Negro-Art Hokum," Schuyler's critique of the racial chauvinism of (New) Negro art also hinges on the notion that blacks and whites are the same because they share a national environment and vary only by degrees of region and class. This claim echoes throughout the articles that form the basis of "The Negro-Art Hokum." Reiterating the opinions expressed in this essay, Crookman asserts that, even if the Black No More treatment cannot change physiognomy, this inability is unproblematic: "[A]s a matter of fact there has been considerable exaggeration about the contrast between Caucasian and Negro features" (15).

In the novel, Disher has premonitions about the change, but in the end he enjoys the results, although on occasion he suffers from bouts of boredom with his new white life and nostalgia for the black life he left behind. Now an "ex-Negro," Max Disher changes his name to Matthew (Matt) Fisher in order to complete his change in identity and, indirectly, to try to render his past life untraceable. He then tries to profit from his newfound whiteness.

In search of that woman from the club, he travels to Atlanta. While there, he joins the Knights of Nordica, a white-supremacist organization, in order to make quick money. He awes the organization with orations that, ironically, appeal to the hearts and minds of white supremacists by criticizing Black No More, Inc., for permitting blacks to pass into and pollute the blood of white society (23). To his luck, Max/Matt also finds the woman he has long sought: Helen, the daughter of the Rev. Henry Givens, the Imperial Grand Wizard of the Knights of Nordica.[42] Not only does Max/Matt marry Helen, but his power also grows in the face of the success of Dr. Crookman and his venture.

By the mid-1930s, Black No More, Inc., has opened at least fifty sanitariums, earned close to twenty million dollars, gained legislative support, and whitened almost every black person in the United States. The growing white-supremacist and southern resentment toward this scientific enterprise determines the nation's sectionalism along regional and racial-political lines. Fisher profits from this sentiment, acquiring yet more power and money. He facilitates the unification of the Knights of Nordica and the Anglo-Saxon Association of America to produce Democratic presidential candidates advocating white supremacy.

A statistical analysis of the racial ancestry of American citizens conducted by the purist Anglo-Saxon Association of America, however, questions this association's claim that it can trace its members' white blood back two hundred years. Though intended to strike enough fear in whites to compel them to vote for the Democratic Party candidates, the statistical research instead portends the undermining of white-supremacist claims to racial purity. Predictably, the Democratic presidential candidate suffers a political debacle when the report is published anonymously after it is stolen from the vault of the association's headquarters.

Fisher, at the same time, is enduring travails of his own. Helen's pregnancies—the first child is miscarried, the second is born—stir up

Max/Matt's anxieties over the possible genetic exposure of his African ancestry in the child. Before the publication of the report, the birth of an ebony child would have aroused suspicion that he was one of those whitened Negroes. The recently publicized statistics about the undeniably multiracial nature of American citizens, however, exonerate him, since his white-supremacist family and peers cannot purport racial purity, either.

At the end of the novel, he and his family move to Mexico City. By this time, the public is noting that the recently whitened blacks are paler than their white counterparts, who do their best to tan their skins to imply racial purity. Thus, Max/Matt and his family try to appear "quite as dusky as little Matthew Crookman Fisher," their son, who was born "very, very dark" (150, 180).

Black No More touches on a host of issues about the importance of human difference and identity politics to America. It addresses colorism, or the discrimination-cum-superiority complex perpetrated by individuals within races—as opposed to across races, which is racism—on the mythic basis of phenotype. It interrogates the hegemony of various forms of whiteness in American conceptions of aesthetics and power. It revisits the idea that the black consumption of skin-whitening creams and hair-straightening treatments only reaffirms the aesthetic valuation and racial aspiration toward whiteness, at the heart of which is an inferiority complex.

Backtracking from his earlier suggestion, in "The Negro-Art Hokum," that blacks possess no unique culture, Schuyler explores, in the transition of the protagonist from Max to Matt, the degree to which racial transformations actually involve social, cultural, and mental transformations, marked by changes in behavior, values, and attitudes. He foregrounds such issues as ancestry and genetics in the formation of racial identity. He underscores the predication of American local and national politics on individual and sectional anxieties about racial difference, intermixture, and threats to white supremacy and genetic purity, all of which have worked to disempower blacks. Yet he also suggests the possible hypocrisy of black organizations that exaggerate stories of and capitalize on racism for personal gain instead of offering achievable solutions. Ironically, these black organizations, whose leaders (W. E. B. Du Bois and Marcus Garvey, among others) Schuyler caricatures, might have much in common with the white-supremacist groups also in the "business" of racism.[43]

The particular concentration of *Black No More* on the nature of white-supremacist groups playfully incorporates many of the racist and racialist tropes of Thomas Dixon, Octavus Roy Cohen, Hugh Wiley, and other "Negrophobic" white writers of the time. Mindful of the obstacle of these writers to black attempts at the time to revise stereotypical racial iconography, Schuyler, iconoclast and satirist that he was, could not help but write a novel with two main goals in mind: first, to expose and poke fun at the assumptions about African America that were central to Negrophobic Anglo-American literature; and, second, to tease the similarly intense anxieties of black intellectuals as expressed in their theories and praxes of racial uplift.

When Max/Matt speaks before the Knights of Nordica for the first time, he raises the controversial issues that affiliates of the New Negro Renaissance (including Schuyler) have condemned time and again. Ironically, Max/Matt seems to support these issues as much as the racist audience does: "For an hour Matthew told them at the top of his voice what they believed: i.e., that a white skin was a sure indication of the possession of superior intellectual and moral qualities; that all Negroes were inferior to them; that God had intended for the United States to be a white man's country and that with His help they could keep it so; that their sons and brothers might inadvertently marry Negresses or, worse, their sisters and daughters might marry Negroes, if Black No More, Incorporated, was permitted to continue its dangerous activities" of whitening blacks (54–55).

Schuyler shows, however, that the articulation of these issues derives not from Max/Matt's profound and historically racist commitment to them. Rather, it comes from his deliberate performance, aimed at feeding his greed for professional self-empowerment, money, and a "titian blonde" (55). Later in *Black No More*, Schuyler implies that material and selfish prizes underwrite the collaboration of black political groups and white-supremacist groups in the destruction of Black No More, Inc. Albeit for different and not entirely accurate reasons, the simultaneous investment of white-supremacist and black political groups in the "Negro Problem"—or, more generally, in maintaining racial difference—shows, in Schuyler's view, that the capitalistic attraction of these two clubs to one another has always threatened to overrule the kinds of racialism and racism that have historically kept them apart.

Schuyler's satire about the similarities and differences between whites and blacks depends mostly on ostensible racial characterology. Special descriptive portraiture enables *Black No More* to tell a story about the implications of a sanitarium that has the scientific ability to alter black phenotype. Schuyler goes to great lengths to draw the reader's attention to skin color prior to satirizing the person, the groups, and the social and cultural contexts often associated with its mythic quality.

At the outset of the novel, we learn that Max Disher is a man with "negroid features [that] had a slightly satanic cast" (3). As Max and his friend Bunny Brown, "a short black fellow," eyed the "motley" of "blacks, browns, yellows, and whites . . . rubbing shoulders in the democracy of nightlife," they "swore that there were three things essential to the happiness of a colored gentleman: yellow money, yellow women and yellow taxis" (4, 5). Toward the end of the novel, according to a monograph by Dr. Crookman "on the differences in skin pigmentation of the real whites and those he had made white," we learn that "to the consternation of many Americans, . . . in practically every instance the new Caucasians were from two to three shades lighter than the old Caucasians, and that approximately one-sixth of the population were in the first group. The old Caucasians had never been really white but rather a pale pink shading down to a sand color and a red. Even when an old Caucasian contracted vitiligo . . . the skin became much lighter" (176–77). All this is to say that blacks became whiter in skin color than white people who, ironically, tried to darken their skins to prove that they were the whitest, or the purest in terms of Anglo-Saxon blood. Thus, the scientifically whitened blacks tried to follow suit and continued to hide their racial background.

Interestingly, Dr. Junius Crookman, the author of this monograph and founder of Black No More, Inc., does not participate in this racial contest. We, as readers, do not know whether Dr. Crookman, first described as a "colored fellow" and a "tall, wiry, ebony black, with a studious and polished manner," ever allows his sanitarium to whiten his body (9, 10). We only know that he supervises its experiments. Presumably, he is one of a select group of blacks who have *decided* to remain black. This circumstance contrasts that of those denied the opportunity to whiten their bodies, including people in "prisons, orphan asylums, insane asylums, homes for the aged, houses of correction and similar institutions," and those "mulatto" babies "charming" for their "beautiful color" (58, 60, 101).

His simultaneous detachment from and exasperation with the values of a country dealing with the phenomenon of whitened blacks come across at the end of *Black No More*. Here, Dr. Crookman reads a newspaper reporting the anxiety caused by his monograph on white phenotype:

One Sunday morning Surgeon-General Crookman, in looking over the rotogravure section of his favorite newspaper, saw a photograph of a happy crowd of Americans arrayed in the latest abbreviated bathing suits on the sands at Cannes. In the group he recognized Hank Johnson, Chuck Foster, Bunny Brown and his real Negro wife, former Imperial Grand Wizard and Mrs. Givens and Matthew and Helen Fisher. All of them, he noticed, were quite as dusky as little Matthew Crookman Fisher who played in a sandpile at their feet. (179–80)

The last line of *Black No More* reads: "Dr. Crookman smiled wearily and passed the section to his wife" (180).

Dr. Crookman's position as both author and reader of the circumstances reported by the newspaper, circumstances involving the very characters of *Black No More*, prompts us to view Schuyler's novel from a special interpretive angle, one that does not seduce us into believing that only the whitened and racially passing blacks experience identity in motion. Dr. Crookman's identity is just as dynamic as these characters'. Despite remaining constant in ostensible physical traits, he "passes" into white society.

More precisely, Dr. Crookman profits from the cultural, class, and political benefits of this society. His situation demands a more complex, performative notion of passing that subordinates its historical meaning of racial assimilation to its politics of cultural assimilation. The millions of blacks who line up at the Black No More, Inc., sanitariums look forward to saying what Max/Matt would come to say a few days after his transformation: "Yes, indeed there were advantages to being white" (27). Yet Schuyler targets both blackness and whiteness, the supposed extremes of racial difference, in order to achieve a more culturally sophisticated notion of "the color line."

Black Harlemites whiten themselves to obtain privilege, but Dr. Crookman does not have to whiten himself to gain the privileges of whites: "Dr. Crookman prided himself above all on being a great lover of his race. . . . He was so interested in the continued progress of the American Negroes that he wanted to remove all obstacles in their path by depriving them of their racial characteristics." But he has no need to deprive himself of his own "racial characteristics" (35). A more profitable "crook" than those who sell hair-straightening and skin-whitening creams to blacks, Dr. Crookman reaches the height of privilege by exploiting the black inferiority complex that rationalizes self-deracination as the ironic means toward racial uplift.

Thanks to this complex, Dr. Crookman becomes a millionaire and the owner of a monoplane, limousines, and sanitariums around the country. Just as important, his entourage (of probably whitened blacks) represents his privileged status, as one observer notes: "'Sfunny . . . how he don't have nuthin' but white folks around him. He must not like nigger help" (58). He does not pass into white society through the manipulation of his own phenotype. Instead, he does so through the acquisition of the social, cultural, and economic capital historically denied blacks. But despite his acquisition of capital, he is still prey to racism, which operates on all class levels, including his own.[44] He might have been passing alongside his patients while remaining ostensibly fixed in phenotype, yet racism still limits his privileges and those of his patients, who anxiously work to keep their racial history secret.

The implications of Dr. Crookman's station as a black person—in spite and because of the power of Black No More, Inc., to whiten black people—could frame our examination of Schuyler's station as a black author and of how *Black No More* whitens black characters and becomes, as Dorothy Van Doren worried in 1931, "white literature." The supposed color passing of blacks as whites signals the taxonomic passing of *Black No More* from African American literature into something else.

The last sentence of chapter 1, "It was either the beginning or the end," marks this generic traversing. It identifies a crucial, liminal moment in the transformation of Max Disher into Matt Fisher, a moment concluding with Disher's nostalgic reflections about experiencing life as a black man. The moment also introduces his optimistic vision of living as a whitened man, a moment auguring an epoch in which millions of blacks try to become whites. On a metaliterary level, it is a movement that changes the generic face of *Black No More*. It suggests the susceptibility of ethnic literary traditions to "textual-color" discrimination and taxonomic segregation. As the characters' color becomes black no more through fantasy and satire, *Black No More*'s textual color also becomes black no more, to the extent that the novel, in a sense, becomes black literature no more. Schuyler's novel demands not merely that we rethink what it means for a person to "pass," but that we also think about how representations of "passing" in literary texts can determine our racialization, classification, and interpretation of African American literature as a whole, that is, as a canon or tradition.

Chapter 5

"A Negro Peoples' Movement in Writing"

In 1937, in room 212-B of the office of the *Daily Worker*'s Harlem Bureau, located at 200 West 135th street, Richard Wright typed a letter to "Prof. Locke," a professor of philosophy at Howard University. The letter came from a man who had been publishing poems for three years in American magazines deemed "radical" for their leftist discussions of the proletariat, Communism, and Marxism. Wright's letter was following up on an earlier request to have Alain Locke review Claude McKay's new fictional autobiography, *A Long Way from Home* (1937). The review would appear in *New Challenge*, a short-lived literary quarterly of which Wright was preparing to be associate editor.

The letter foreshadows Wright's plan to intersect racial realism and radicalism in ways that his black predecessors, Locke included, once resisted but later conceded to be inevitable in the New Negro movement. At the outset of the letter, Wright expresses certainty that Locke should already have received *New Challenge*'s copy of *A Long Way from Home*. Wright confides that, after having discerned the "attitude" of Locke's correspondence with black poet and journalist Frank Marshall Davis, he recommended Locke as a book reviewer to Dorothy West, another editor of *New Challenge*. The correspondence "pleased me so much," Wright admits to Locke, "I thought you would be the ideal one to do justice to MacKay [*sic*] and his whole attitude." Wright goes on to explain the implications of Locke's review in *New Challenge*: "The groups, though moving in a Left direction, are not out and out Communist. We believe that it is too early for such a call. We want to build, if possible, a *Negro peoples' movement in writing*. A more explicit statement will be forthcoming in the first issue of New Challenge. I do hope you will feel free to enter the ring with both hands loaded when you review MacKay. Since you know that Harlem School so thoroughly, we felt that you were the only possible person to handle such a book" (italics mine).[1]

The social, economic, political, intellectual, and ideological backdrop of black culture in the 1930s provides the context for the lore cycle of racial realism in Wright's "Negro peoples' movement in writing." Calling this movement the cultural representation of "New Negro radicalism"—a term Barbara Foley similarly employs as the inverse of "Harlem Renaissance culturalism"—implies that the term "New Negro" remained in discursive currency in Wright's work and elsewhere in black intellectual society and culture.[2] The fact that Wright's literary contemporaries, as well as subsequent writers and scholars, characterized him as a "New Negro" should compel us to take the words of James Edward Smethurst seriously, that we should avoid "obliterating the 1930s as a period of black literary production distinct from that of the New Negro Renaissance, a distinction that many writers and readers of the era certainly felt."[3]

Indeed, in 1939, Locke, perhaps mindful of Wright's rise to prominence, posed a question to the readers of *Opportunity* magazine: "Do we confront today on the cultural front another Negro, either a newer Negro or a maturer 'New Negro'?"[4] Twelve years later, James Baldwin answered Locke's question when he noted that, "[i]n the thirties, swallowing Marx whole, we discovered the Worker and realized . . . that the aims of the Worker and the Negro were one. This theorem . . . became, nevertheless, one of the slogans of the 'class struggle' and the gospel of the New Negro. As for this New Negro, it was Wright who became his most eloquent spokesman."[5] The discursive and cultural continuity of the New Negro across the 1920s and the 1930s belies the specific historical circumstances and ideological perspectives, especially with respect to racial realism, that distinguish it from era to era.

Wright's essay "Blueprint for Negro Writing" (1937), alongside other essays on New Negro radicalism, shows that he envisioned avant-garde African American literature as the revision of New Negro modernism, discussed in Chapter 3. "Blueprint for Negro Writing" served as the literal blueprint of the nature and necessity of this revision in the inaugural fall issue of *New Challenge*. This periodical was the cultural institution primarily responsible for introducing the aesthetic and racial-political importance of New Negro radicalism to African American history. Wright's description of four protocols of New Negro radicalism—namely, New Negro cultural revisionism, Marxism, black nationalism, and the aesthetic reconciliation of Marxism and black nationalism—rhetorically coincides with Locke's essays of the 1930s in a couple of ways. First, both Wright and Locke point out the ideological disjuncture, once exacerbated by the Harlem Renaissance, between the proletariat and the intelligentsia. Second, Wright's demand that the black writer meet the "serious responsibility" of doing "justice to his subject matter, in order to depict Negro life in all its manifold and intricate relationships" (59) echoes Locke's insistence that the black writer should avoid "spiritual truancy and social irresponsibility."[6]

In order to make a case for his "Negro peoples' movement in writing," Wright appropriated the critique of "spiritual truancy" that Locke applied to McKay in that first issue of *New Challenge*. This means that the powerful transfer of cultural ambassadorship from Locke to Wright did not operate through extreme ideological disagreement. Rather, it occurred through their mutual recognition of the "failures" of the Harlem Renaissance,[7] the black cultural opportunities afforded by radicalism, and the importance of pragmatic collaborations between writers and "the people." In sum, Wright and Locke had more in common in the 1930s than the historical and ideological divisions between their respective movements—the Harlem Renaissance and the Chicago Renaissance—lead us to believe. By implication, radicalism and modernism were not utterly irreconcilable or contradictory in New Negro ideology; they were continuous and represented distinct yet overlapping phases of racial realism.

The differences between Wright and Locke lie more in their thematic emphasis and ideological impetus. While not directly criticizing black writers for avoiding racial realism, as Locke did regarding Tanner in 1925, Wright did critique the Harlem Renaissance and, implicitly, Locke for producing or endorsing cultural works lacking in proletarian authenticity. His critique belongs to a larger Marxist-critical demand for authentic proletarian literature, by, about, and for "the worker."[8] Thus, Wright prided himself and other black writers with appropriating radicalism for the sake of devising a kind of cultural pragmatism to engage the "masses." At the same time, he employed Marxist discourse to indict earlier New Negro intellectual discrimination against the proletariat. He used it to swap the central and marginal positions, respectively, of the intelligentsia and the proletariat in New Negro culture. He encouraged black writers to develop class consciousness, to become more sensitive to the psychological disunity of the proletariat, as well as to express the lore of this group through racial realism.

New Negro radicalism was not solely a creation of black culture. By bridging various approaches to the "black radical tradition" of Marxists and studies of interwar American literature and social science, I intend to argue that naturalism and the Chicago School of urban sociology factored into the infrastructure of New Negro radicalism. Contrary to claims that they weakened Wright's relationship with folklore, naturalism and sociology enabled him to elucidate the complexities of race and class in the "Negro Problem." From here he distinguished his own generation's mode of racial realism from what he believed were the romantic approaches of the Harlem Renaissance.[9]

Ultimately, *New Challenge* did for Wright in 1937 what *The Survey Graphic*

Number did for Locke in 1925: it led contemporaries and later scholars to appoint Wright as dean of a black cultural renaissance and to identify the renaissance with the city of Chicago. Many of the contributors to the inaugural issue of *New Challenge* became identified with the Chicago Renaissance, and accordingly Wright became the dean of this movement.[10]

Wright's deanship of the Chicago Renaissance and the impact of this status on his generation of black writers were consummated in several ways. His unparalleled critical and commercial success sheds light on the discursive lore-cycle of racial realism that continued in reviews of his fiction, and on the fact that reviewers spotted the protocols of New Negro radicalism that he defines in "Blueprint for Negro Writing" and "How Bigger Was Born," the appendix to his best-selling novel *Native Son* (1940). But Wright's work created critical, commercial, and canonical consequences that overshadowed the literary complexity and originality of black authors. Complaints that his "school" pigeonholed African American literature dovetailed with emerging critiques of racial consciousness, along with the prevailing insistence that, according to Sterling Brown, Arthur P. Davis, and Ulysses Lee, the "bonds of literary tradition seem to be stronger than race" for black writers.[11]

Out of such literary and critical reactions to Wright's literary work, two critical camps formed with the hope of performing the kind of racial desegregation of American literature that New Negro radicalism, in their eyes, hindered. Instead of appreciating African American literature derived from New Negro radicalism, the first reaction focused on the more universal possibilities of Wright's work and African American literature generally. The second reaction considered racial realism as handicapping black literary progress toward claims to Americanness. Later, it will become clear why and how Frank Yerby entered this second group.

New Negro Radicalism

The 1930s was an eventful decade in Richard Wright's life. The 1929 crash of the stock market precipitated the Great Depression, and the United States suffered unprecedented unemployment, economic weakness, consumer debt, and poverty. Blacks bore the brunt of this misery. No group of farmers was more impoverished than black farm tenants and wage laborers. No group of urban laborers was more unemployed or underpaid than black workers. The Great Depression exacerbated the racial discrimination blacks had historically experienced in social, institutional, and governmental contexts. The New Deal (1933–38) sought to counteract the Great Depression; it established various domestic programs, including the Public

Works Administration and the Works Progress Administration. Nevertheless, the underrepresentation of blacks in Congress, the racially biased legislation and distribution of funds and services for the poor, and the social intimidation of the black poor further burdened the race as it struggled for jobs and means of subsistence. Between 1920 and 1930, more than one million blacks had migrated from the rural South, congesting the urban North and falling victim to the Great Depression.

Such socioeconomic problems affected black culture. The Great Depression undercut the patronage of black performances and the philanthropy of black culture, effectively ending the commercial success of the Harlem Renaissance. The imminent decline of this movement, however, did not cause a long-lived depression in black political and cultural activity. In 1936, the National Negro Congress initiated the "Negro People's Front," "an auxiliary to the Popular Front meant to promote a synthesis of communism and black cultural and political work."[12] The larger Popular Front had already planted in American society a "cultural apparatus" consisting of "the organizations and *milieux* in which artistic, intellectual and scientific work goes on, and of the means by which such work is made available to circles, publics, and masses. In the cultural apparatus art, science, learning, entertainment, malarkey and information are produced and distributed." Despite the threat of its populist integrationism to highlighting specific issues of racial discrimination, prejudice, and oppression in the United States, this "cultural front," this "often unstable alliance of cultural figures with distinct alignments: modernist, émigré, or plebeian," enhanced Wright's literary imagination and productivity.[13]

Indeed, Wright was a prolific writer. In 1935, he published poetry in many periodicals and at an astounding rate. He earned relative celebrity in the black intellectual circles of New York City and Chicago.[14] He added to his fame a year later, when he switched to writing fiction and nonfiction essays, his most productive literary genres for the next decade.[15] Prodigious white social, cultural, and political critic Lewis Mumford selected Wright's work for the edited annual anthology *The New Caravan* (in 1936). The Harlem Bureau section of the *Daily Worker*, a proletarian newspaper, published the bulk of his prose writing, over 220 articles, between June and December 1937, on topics ranging from local Harlem news and the Scottsboro case in Alabama to the Works Projects Administration and the Communist Party, the last of which Wright had been affiliated with for about four years.

Two *Daily Worker* articles in particular capture his approach to African American literature. In "Negro Writers Launch Literary Quarterly" (1937), Wright urges black writers "to render their race in social and realistic terms," with particular attention to "problems such as nationalism in literature, perspective, the relation of the Negro writer to politics and social movements."[16] And in another article, "New Negro Pamphlet Stresses Need for U.S. People's Front" (1937), Wright describes a "penny-pamphlet, 'The Road to Liberation for the Negro People,' . . . a short statement by 16 leading Negro Communists summarizing from a Marxist point of view the Negroes' position in the United States today."[17] Published four months before and one month after the inaugural issue of *New Challenge*, respectively, these two articles symbolize the philosophical nexus of aesthetics and racial politics within which Wright, among other writers, conceived of avant-garde African American literature as a radical revision of New Negro modernism.

The emergence of *New Challenge*, alongside other magazines such as Chicago's *Defender* and *Negro Story*, reflects the impact of radicalism on black literary experimentation with racial realism.[18] The chief editors of *New Challenge*, Dorothy West and Marian Minus, had been in charge of the monthly *Challenge*, which was published from March 1934 until April 1937 and was a major forum for several writers of the Harlem Renaissance, including Langston Hughes, Zora Neale Hurston, and Countée Cullen. The spin-off, *New Challenge*, marketed the newer generation of black writers. The cancellation of *Challenge*, the name change, the transfer of West's and Minus's editorial responsibilities to the new magazine, the addition of Wright as associate editor, the well-publicized mission of the new magazine—all of these factors combined to make the inaugural edition of *New Challenge* a remarkable event in African American history.

The mission of *New Challenge* asserted the aesthetic and racial-political salience of New Negro radicalism. In the magazine's first editorial, West, speaking on behalf of Minus and Wright, states that "the realistic depiction of life . . . should not be *in vacuo* but placed within a definite social context." She goes on to imply a distinction between the symbolism of the new magazine from that of *The Survey Graphic Number* of twelve years earlier, which helped to usher in the Harlem Renaissance: "We are not attempting to re-stage the 'revolt' and 'renaissance' which grew unsteadily and upon false foundations ten years ago. A literary movement among Negroes . . . should . . . be built upon the writer's placing his material in the proper perspective with regard to the life of the Negro masses. For that reason we want to indicate, through examples in our pages, the great fertility of folk material as a source of creative material."[19]

Of all the essays included in the first issue of *New Challenge*, Wright's "Blueprint for Negro Writing" best elaborates the magazine's mission. Wright derived the thesis and logic of the essay mostly from his conversations with members of Chicago's South Side Writers' Group, which he organized in 1936. The members included Marian Minus, Arna Bontemps, Margaret Walker, Frank Marshall Davis, Edward Bland, Russell Marshall, Robert Davis, Theodore Ward, all of whom associated further with Fern Gayden, Dorothy Sutton, Julius Weil, and Fenton Johnson. These writers constituted the avant-garde of New Negro radicalism and the members of the Chicago Renaissance.[20]

"Blueprint for Negro Writing" boils down into four subjects: New Negro cultural history; the class consciousness of Marxism; the racial consciousness of black nationalism; and the aesthetic reconciliation of Marxism and black nationalism. By contemporaneous and subsequent consensus, these were the four protocols of New Negro radicalism, and "Blueprint for Negro Writing" was the blueprint for this genre. In this essay, Wright sounds much like Locke in the 1930s, when he was claiming that the Harlem Renaissance exacerbated the ideological disjuncture between the proletariat and the black intelligentsia. "Blueprint for Negro Writing" reiterates this argument by channeling the progressive voices of the other contributors to *New Challenge* and examining the state of the African American literature.[21]

The revealing first line of "Blueprint for Negro Writing" indicates the direction of Wright's polemic: "Generally speaking, Negro writing in the past has been confined to humble novels, poems, and plays, prim and decorous ambassadors who went a-begging to white America." The "humble" literature and social hierarchy of the Harlem Renaissance supposedly conspired with patrons to spare black artists from "serious criticism." Shocked by the talent and promise of these artists, Wright suggests, white patrons spent more time adoring their work than correcting its flaws. These "conditions" transformed African American literature into "a conspicuous ornamentation, the hallmark of 'achievement'" and "the voice of the educated Negro pleading with white America for justice." "Rarely," he goes on to say, "was the best of this writing addressed to the Negro himself, his needs, his sufferings, his aspirations" (Wright, "Blueprint," 53).

Wright sounds much like Locke in "Harlem: Dark Weather-Vane" (1936), released one year before "Blueprint for Negro Writing." Locke published the essay at a time when the Great Depression was exposing the ideological disconnect between underprivileged black working-class communities and the elite producers and consumers of New Negro modernism, a disconnect hidden by the "bright illusions or a cruelly deceptive mirage" of the Harlem Renaissance.[22] Wright also reiterates several ideas in Locke's "Spiritual Truancy." According to Dorothy West, Locke's essay was included in the inaugural issue of *New Challenge* because it demonstrates remarkable "objectivity."[23] When placed in the context of Locke's relationship to McKay, however, "Spiritual Truancy" is by no means objective. The review critiques the failures of the Harlem Renaissance as exemplified in the work of a writer Locke once celebrated but whose later decline he mourned.

In the essay, Locke claims that McKay's *Banjo* (1929), *Gingertown* (1932), and *Banana Bottom* (1933)—novels set not only in Harlem but also in places ranging from Marseilles to Jamaica—indicate an author led astray. As early as 1933, Locke was grieving "the exile of this great talent from contact with his most promising field of material."[24] When McKay's fictional autobiography, *A Long Way from Home*, appeared, Locke was neither surprised by the title's symbolism nor impressed by the story itself. These reactions (among other personal ones) partially motivated him to write the review. (McKay's ridicule of the dean in *A Long Way from Home* also could have motivated Locke to criticize the younger author so harshly.) To Locke, McKay has become "a bad boy who admits he ought to go to school and then plays truant. It is this spiritual truancy which is the blight of his otherwise splendid talent."[25]

Elsewhere in "Spiritual Truancy" Locke details McKay's shirking of the two responsibilities that black writers should shoulder: "racial spokesmanship," and the demonstration of a racially "representative character." McKay, according to Locke, oscillates between embracing and repudiating the doctrines of radicalism that Locke once disregarded as "quixotic" and potentially detrimental to the Harlem Renaissance.[26] McKay's attention to "the folk"—or the common black lower classes disconnected from the "elite" culture to which Locke belonged—has not comprised the necessary "unalloyed reverence," "high seriousness, deep loyalty, racial reverence of the unspectacular, unmelodramatic sort, and when necessary, sacrificial social devotion." McKay's commitment to "expatriate cosmopolitanism and its irresponsible exoticisms" makes him, in Locke's estimation, "the *enfant terrible* of the Negro Renaissance," indeed guilty of a "spiritual truancy and social irresponsibility."[27] (The topic and tone of Locke's denigration of McKay surely recall those of his bastardization of Henry Ossawa Tanner.) Locke's criticism of McKay concludes with a word of advice for Wright's generation of black writers: avoid the "flippant," "care-free," and "irresponsible" "individualism" of the Harlem Renaissance and aspire to become "truer sons of the people."[28] Such advice demonstrates Locke's unflagging desire to mentor the black liberati, even though his old age, controversial legacy, and racial-political conservatism, to an extent, undermined his credibility during the Chicago Renaissance.

Wright agreed with Locke's characterization of the irresponsible truant by demanding pragmatic collaborations between black writers and "the people." In "Blueprint for Negro Writing," he adds that, until "Negro writers . . . stand shoulder to shoulder with Negro workers in mood and outlook," the cultivation of racial consciousness alone will continue to fail amid socioeconomic crises such as the Great Depression (55). Apparently, Wright and Locke were in some respects fellow ideological travelers in the 1930s. They believed that interwar black writers should address and overcome the failed pragmatism of the Harlem Renaissance.

Wright used Marxism to develop a more pragmatic cultural genre. Central to the philosophical viewpoint of the Communist Party of the United States of America (CPUSA), the class consciousness of Marxism was the lens through which Wright interpreted the New Negro. From 1933 until 1942, he associated with this group, serving as executive secretary of the Chicago John Reed Club before withdrawing from the party. Because Marxism was central to the Communist mobilization of black intellectuals, Wright, unsurprisingly, refers to Lenin in "Blueprint for Negro Writing," a document written at the height of his involvement in CPUSA. Wright's recategorization of earlier New Negro intellectuals as "oppressed petty bourgeoisie"—the people who relied on the bourgeoisie for privileges but did not have the actual power of the bourgeoisie, which owned or controlled the means of production—indicts their classist discrimination against the proletariat. He resituates them according to a specifically Marxist differentiation of people vis-à-vis capitalist modes of production. Through this discourse, he shifts the intelligentsia from the center to the margin of New Negro culture. At the center, now, is the proletariat, commanding "a wide social vision and a deep social consciousness," the result of "organizations [that] show greater strength, adaptability, and efficiency than any other group or class in society" (54).

"Blueprint for Negro Writing" proposes new ways of engaging the masses. Wright insists that black writers develop that socioeconomic or class consciousness, that "awareness" and "perspective," peculiar to the proletariat. Over time, he contends, the class stratification of black communities has caused psychological disunity. The literary imagination must articulate, ameliorate, and mobilize those who have experienced this disunity, especially the proletariat. In short, a special kind of pragmatism must be designed to unite intellectual authors and proletarian readers: "The Negro writer who seeks to function within his race as a purposeful agent has a serious responsibility. In order to do justice to his subject matter, in order to depict Negro life in all of its manifold and intricate relationships, a deep, informed, and complex consciousness is necessary; a consciousness which draws for its strength upon the fluid lore of a great people, and moulds this lore with the concepts that move and direct the forces of history today" (59). Racial realism must be able to express this lore, just as it did in the earlier lore cycles of William Howells and Alain Locke.

Wright's hopeful exploration of the compatibility of Marxism and racialism echoes the philosophical attempts of W. E. B. Du Bois in the 1930s. By viewing American slaves and slavery in world-historical terms—that is, as black laborers operating within global capitalism—Du Bois's *Black Reconstruction in America, 1860–1880* (1935) undermined the theoretical transhistoricity Marxism had acquired by the 1930s for CPUSA. Speaking in 1933 in *The Crisis*, Du Bois racially historicized Marxism for what the doctrine was: "a true diagnosis of the situation in Europe in the middle of the nineteenth century."[29] The American Communist Party might have tried to confront the "Negro Question" by the early 1920s, yet Du Bois dove headlong and deeper into the intellectual process of revising American Marxism to explain African American history.

Wright's attempted philosophical reconciliation of race and class was consistent with the collaborative efforts of CPUSA members and black writers, who sought to produce "a cultural model that attempted to accommodate a revolutionary black nationalism with a sort of working-class integrationism within an internationalist framework."[30] Signs of an analytic struggle for such a model appear in Wright's proposition of an alliance between black and white writers. As he mentions in "Negro Writers Launch Literary Quarterly," *New Challenge* embraced those "white writers dealing definitely with minority themes and depicting conditions of life common to the Negro people," a welcome reiterated in "Blueprint for Negro Writing."[31]

The rhetoric of interracial collectivity corresponds with his involvement in the Popular Front. His article "New Negro Pamphlet Stresses Need for U.S. People's Front" discusses a national movement that started around 1934, the year of various U.S. social and union uprisings, and that ended in the early 1960s, with the rise of New Leftism, black nationalism, and feminism. In the intervening years, especially during the 1930s, the Communist Party and the Congress of Industrial Organizations provided the ideological infrastructure of the Popular Front and developed the strategies behind proletarian unionization. Wright's "Blueprint for Negro Writing" reflects this cultural context.

The interracial, black-white alliances central to the Popular Front, however, conflicted with Wright's demands for black commitment to racial causes and consciousness. At certain points in "Blueprint for Negro Writing," he asks black writers to address the folk in their work. He also wants them to recognize the value of like-minded works by white writers and to view these writers as "allies," with whites involved in the larger Communist schemes for interracial cooperation and progress. On other occasions, and contrary to the class-based goals of the American Communist Party, Wright privileges race over class by contending that racial consciousness could uplift the black proletariat.

Wright's focus on black folklore underscores this point. A literary theme will emerge for Negro writers, he states in the essay, "when they have begun to feel the meaning of the history of their race as though they in one life time had lived it themselves throughout all the long centuries" (63). Wright thus refers to the transplantation of blacks from Africa, the institution of the black church as an "antidote" to "[l]iving under the slave conditions of life, bereft of . . . African heritage," and the production of the blues, spirituals, and orally exchanged folktales "through which the racial wisdom flowed" (55–56).

The rise of the black petite bourgeoisie in the late nineteenth century, however, stratified the folk along lines of class. Racial consciousness, synonymous with an awareness of the folk tradition, consequently declined among black writers. But several books, ranging from Du Bois's *The Souls of Black Folk* (1903) and Jean Toomer's *Cane* (1923) to Sterling Brown's *Southern Road* (1932), among other texts, undermine Wright's argument. His omission of such books permits his contention that a cultural gap had formed within the black community between "the Negro masses, unwritten and unrecognized," and "the sons and daughters of a rising Negro bourgeoisie, parasitic and mannered." And since "the nationalist character of the Negro people is unmistakable [and] reflected in the whole of Negro culture, and especially in folklore," class chasms had posed a remarkable threat to the legacy of the American Negro (56).

Wright's argument mirrors Hughes's in "The Negro Artist and the Racial Mountain" (1926). Hughes's essay not only criticizes black upper-class churches for preferring white hymnals over spirituals, it also takes to task black middle-class homes for inculcating white morals and values. Wright's racial proletarianism, it turns out, is indebted to Hughes precisely because the former immersed himself in the latter's collegial literary and political thought. The thematic similarity between the essays thus is not surprising. By 1937, Wright had given a lecture on Hughes's writings from *The Weary Blues* (1926) to *The Ways of White Folks* (1934), publicly debated with him about the social role of the Negro writer, and judged his plays for contests.[32]

The racial nationalism of "Blueprint for Negro Writing" also recalls Marcus Garvey's African fundamentalism, or Garveyism, the more radical version of Hughes's own early racial nationalism. (I would note that, although Garvey undeniably had a great impact on Hughes, there were philosophical differences between the two men, such as the leader's promotion of racial uplift and the poet's critique of its incompatibility with vernacular black culture.) Garveyism, one of the "quixotic" radicalisms marginalized during the Harlem Renaissance, insisted on black self-interest, self-reliance, and nationhood. Among other programs, the doctrine encouraged the repatriation of blacks to Africa, particularly Liberia, for "the founding of a racial empire, whose only natural, spiritual and political limits shall be God and 'Africa, at home and abroad.'" Garveyism drew on the theory of a racial "union" around the globe.[33] Wright admits in his autobiography, *Black Boy*, and in his addendum to *Native Son* (1940), "How Bigger Was Born," that Garveyism appealed to the African diaspora around the world and galvanized it to act for a solid racial cause. But he also realizes the tenuous bond between this doctrine and Marxism, despite his admiration for Garveyism.[34]

The theoretical tensions between Garveyism and Marxism, racial nationalism and socialist proletarianism, ended up characterizing the organizational politics of American Communism in the 1930s. Garvey's United Negro Improvement Association (UNIA) sometimes collaborated with the African Blood Brotherhood (ABB), a postwar black leftist and pro-Bolshevik-nationalist organization founded in 1919 by Cyril Briggs, in order to anchor nationalist consciousness to the masses. The world historicity of these racial organizations overlapped with the globalism of the Communist Party, which was trying to organize a proletarian socialist movement across national boundaries. The UNIA and the ABB helped to create the political and ideological circumstances under which CPUSA could mobilize both radical black intellectuals and the masses. (Both UNIA and ABB were diminished somewhat in the 1930s, but several core members of these groups, such as Cyril Briggs and Harry Haywood of ABB, still were involved in CPUSA.)

Yet the World Wars revealed that nationalism could overpower socialism in motivating workers to battle on behalf of their respective countries. Racial nationalism fundamentally disagreed with ideologies prioritizing class solidarity over all other forms of ideological collectivity. The either-or scenario caused by this tension between class and race (and nation) was a problem that the Negro Commissions of the Fourth, Fifth, and Sixth Congresses tried to resolve in the 1920s through the American Communist Party.

Wright might have been conceiving New Negro radicalism in the wake of Garvey's decline, but at that time he was still involved in a black radical tradition that was negotiating this tension between class and race. Allyn Keith, in an essay published following "Blueprint for Negro Writing" in

New Challenge, tried to resolve "much discussion lately of nationalism, and whether or not it may be used in connection with the revolutionary movement."[35] More famous contemporary thinkers such as Du Bois, James S. Allen, Haywood Hall, and C. L. R. James participated in this conversation as well.

Black radicalism enabled Wright, in particular, to imagine racial nationalism as a transitional stage prior to proletarian consciousness in the black writer. Theorizing this compatibility was groundbreaking, in light of the previous difficulties in bridging the ideologies of certain black constituencies—the socialism of A. Philip Randolph, Chandler Owen, and Schuyler's *The Messenger*; the racialism of Du Bois's *The Crisis* and Charles S. Johnson's *Opportunity*; and the racial nationalism of Garvey's *The Negro World*. The formation of these institutions birthed factions that fragmented the Harlem Renaissance. (By 1928–29, Du Bois had gravitated toward socialism while Schuyler, arguably, had moved toward Garveyism.)[36]

In "Blueprint for Negro Writing," Wright tries to meld these ideologies, mainstream and radical, with the notion that Marxism had to temper the racial nationalism of folklore and its invigoration of the African American literary imagination and expression. But in doing so, he also tries to have it both ways. He calls for racial consciousness to overcome the cultural gap between the bourgeoisie and the masses, yet this perspective is "limited" and "unrealizable" once it reaches the political extremism of nationalism. A Marxist vocabulary could articulate the experiences of the masses, "[y]et, for the Negro writer, Marxism is but the starting point. No theory of life can take the place of life. After Marxism has laid bare the skeleton of society, there remains the task of the writer to plant the flesh upon those bones out of his will to live" (58, 60). New Negro radicalism required both Marxism and racial nationalism in theory, but they could not coexist in practice.

Perhaps this complication explains Wright's curious statement in the essay that "nationalism is a bewildering and vexing question, the full ramifications of which cannot be dealt with here" (58–59). He excuses his inability to resolve the contradiction between racial and class consciousness, black nationalism and Marxist socialism, by stating that he does not have the space to flesh out the argument. Since this contradiction had encumbered the practical efforts of the American Communist Party since the end of World War I, we can ascertain that "Blueprint for Negro Writing" could not, on its own, bear such a theoretical burden while practicing New Negro radicalism.

Understated as a consequence of this conceptual crisis, the term "realism" thus arises only once in the essay. Midway through, Wright states that a "devious" and "simple literary realism which seeks to depict the lives of these people as devoid of wider social connotations, as devoid of the revolutionary significance of these nationalist tendencies, must of necessity do a rank injustice to the Negro people and alienate their possible allies in the struggle for freedom" (58–59). The short shrift Wright explicitly gives to racial realism belies the degree to which he implicitly tries to build a radical foundation for it. The coherence and structure conveyed by the ten subtitles and subsections of the essay equally belie the highly provisional nature of New Negro radicalism.

How a Dean Was Born

Three years after his blueprint for New Negro radicalism, Wright attained the status of dean of the Chicago Renaissance. His best-selling novel *Native Son* represented the climactic by-product of his attempts, between 1937 and 1946, to integrate racial and class consciousness, black nationalism and Marxism, while drawing on the sociology of American naturalism for literary effect.

Of course, Wright published works of considerable merit before and after *Native Son* that demonstrate or discuss New Negro radicalism. His collection of short stories, *Uncle Tom's Children* (1938), unflinchingly covers such subjects as lynching, black impoverishment, rape, race-related fisticuffs and shootings, domestic violence within the black family, and black flight from the South to the North. Wright's best-selling autobiography is equally merciless on readers. First published in 1945, *Black Boy* is his "record of child and youth" (according to the subtitle). We learn that, while he was in the South, Wright's struggles with racism and the suppression of black intelligence justified the frequently restless, frustrated, racially conscious, and even nationalist disposition of black male protagonists in his fiction. His migration from the Mississippi "black belt" to Chicago made his life the ideal subject for urban sociology. His membership in the American Communist Party provided the professional options, racial-political missions, and world-history perspectives he needed to realize and overcome his dispossessed status in the world.

More remarkable than Wright's fiction, however, *Native Son* portrays Bigger Thomas as the kind of modern-day New Negro called for in "Blueprint for Negro Writing." "How Bigger Was Born," the essay appended to the novel, documents the gestation and birth of *Native Son*. The essay does not delve into the plot of the now-classic novel of Bigger Thomas, a twenty-year-old black chauffeur living in a Chicago ghetto who kills the daughter of his white employer. Rather, we learn about the additional roles of naturalism and sociology in the aesthetic traits of New Negro radicalism. Chicago School sociology, in particular, was an intellectual enterprise he learned outside these academic channels: "[T]he most important discoveries came when I veered from fiction proper into the field of psychology and sociology."[37] Sociology and naturalism, rather than "veering," actually intersected in the works of contemporary American writers and in Wright's fiction, where he modified these fields of intellectual thought for his own purposes.

In the formative years of New Negro radicalism, the Chicago School of urban sociology and American literary naturalism were mutually dependent intellectual institutions. Both interpreted human behavior and culture as a function of environmental conditions. Such writers as James T. Farrell, author of *Young Lonigan: A Boyhood in Chicago Streets* (1932) and *Studs Lonigan: A Trilogy* (1935), and Nelson Algren, writer of *Never Come Morning* (1942), belonged to an era when American writers born, reared, or settled in Chicago were exploring the city's social typologies and environmental dynamics with the detail demanded by such sociologists as W. I. Thomas, Florian Znaniecki, Robert Park, Robert Redfield, Frederic Thrasher, and Louis Wirth.

Similarly, Wright prioritized the environment over the individual in New Negro radicalism. He did not imbue the Chicago masses and migrants with as much agency as Locke did during the Harlem Renaissance. At this time, the flood of blacks from the South to the North was restructuring the social, cultural, and intellectual properties of Harlem. Rather, Wright was following a social-scientific paradigm within which he could express the cultural shock black migrants experienced in the city and the oppression they suffered within this environment.

Sociology and naturalism enabled Wright to elucidate the thematic nuances of race and class in the Negro Problem. They supported his rejection of the Left's attempts to fit the Negro Problem into merely a "class-war frame of reference" and the Right's examination of Negroes as individuals while ignoring "the inevitable race consciousness which three hundred years of Jim Crow living has burned into the Negro's heart."[38] Granted, Wright was writing eight years after "Blueprint for Negro Writing," yet he was still concerned with the inability of class-based doctrines to address African American history. He was not so much rebelling entirely against CPUSA doctrine as foregrounding the arguments within CPUSA that emphasized crucial issues of race.

Interweaving Marxism, sociology, and naturalism positioned Wright to represent the masses. Simultaneously, he remained historically aware of black experiences based in folklore. Accordingly, the characters, settings, social relationships, and cultural institutions in his fiction were so "real" that they could withstand the scrutiny of average readers and social scientists alike. Urban sociology and literary naturalism explained the role of the environment in proletarian thought and behavior, two issues central to Wright's grasp of Marxist theory and American Communist policy between the world wars, according to "Blueprint for Negro Writing" and "How Bigger Was Born."

Thus, Wright's literary work manifests the transition of racial realism from its romantic, peaceful, and idealistic folk origins in the Harlem Renaissance to maturity by the start of World War II as radical, violent, and pessimistic. "How Bigger Was Born" crystallized New Negro radicalism in a way that contemporary readers recognized and discussed in detail. The critical reception of *Native Son* turned into a special recognition, appreciation, and marketing of New Negro radicalism.[39] As defined between 1937 and 1946, Wright's blueprint for it permeated the critical discourse around African American literature.

By the time Harper and Brothers released *Native Son*, on March 1, 1940, Wright was already a critical and commercial success. In 1938, a short story he published in *Uncle Tom's Children*, "Fire and Cloud," won first prize of $500 in a short story competition held by *Story* magazine. The editors of *The Nation* chose *Uncle Tom's Children* as one of the ten best books of 1938. A year later, he received an O. Henry Memorial Award of $200 for the same story and a prestigious Guggenheim Fellowship, handed to him by First Lady Eleanor Roosevelt. Another short story, "Bright and Morning Star," which he would add to the new 1940 edition of *Uncle Tom's Children*, was selected for two notable anthologies edited by Edward O'Brien, *Best Short Stories of 1939* and *Fifty Best American Short Stories (1914–1939)*. *Native Son* was a Book-of-the-Month Club selection, which led to unprecedented circulation of a novel by a black writer. The astronomical sales of Wright's first novel (200,000 copies in the first three weeks) only confirmed that his time had come.

Most reviews of *Native Son* alluded to Wright's preestablished celebrity. Sales might have legitimated him as a great black writer, but the one event critics viewed as the utmost validation of him as a great American writer was his award from *Story* magazine.[40] The internationally renowned Nobel Laureate and American novelist Sinclair Lewis, along with critics Harry Scherman and Lewis Gannett, chose Wright as a finalist from among six hundred contestants. Although Lewis ultimately did not vote to give the award to Wright, the other two judges did.[41]

Less than two months after *Native Son* was first released, critics began to address the initial responses to the novel.[42] That "double review," in a sense, was the sign of what Sterling Brown calls in his review a "literary phenomenon." Wright was a literary and commercial success, and people were interpreting the implications of this success for both the author and his race. So far and wide had word traveled about *Native Son* that "debates on *Native Son* [could] be heard in grills and 'juke-joints' as well as at 'literary' parties, in the deep South as well as in Chicago, among people who have not bothered much to read novels since Ivanhoe was assigned in high school English."[43] If Brown's assertion is true, then Wright indeed had achieved a goal of New Negro radicalism: to engage the masses.

The allusion of the reviewers to Wright's accolades often turned into praise for the racial realism of *Native Son*. A couple of critics described the novel as "uncompromisingly realistic," displaying characters that were "fully realized," or illustrating "an objectivity which is irresistible." A few linked the realism with Wright's racial authenticity: *Native Son* "is a novel only a Negro could have written; whose theme is the mind of the Negro we see every day." The novel is "a performance of great talent—powerful, disturbing, unquestionably authentic." Or, more curiously, Wright "is a Negro and he writes of Negroes." In most cases, other oblique vocabulary was used. Aside from incidental discontent in the reviews with the novel's style, melodrama, romanticism, and violence, *Native Son* was generally a critical success.[44]

A closer inspection of the reviews shows that readers, perhaps unwittingly, decoded the protocols of New Negro radicalism. Multiple reviews published in magazines like *New Masses* and *Sunday Worker* noted the Marxist focus of the novel. One of the reviewers even quotes the lines from "Blueprint for Negro Writing" in which Wright argues that "it is through a Marxist conception of reality and society that the maximum degree of freedom in thought and feeling can be gained for the Negro writer" (60).[45]

As for sociology, *Native Son* applies to what Dorothy Canfield Fisher, in her introduction to the novel, cites: Owen D. Young's National Youth Commission's conclusive report "that large percentages of Negro youth by virtue of their combined handicap of racial barriers and low social position subtly reflect in their personality-traits minor or major distortions or deficiencies which compound their problem of personality adjustment in American society." For a couple of reviewers, who actually refer to and even quote from this introduction, *Native Son* animates the commission's dry report.[46]

The social-scientific character of *Native Son*, critics suggested, also accommodated literary naturalism in remarkable fashion. *Native Son*, in their words, was "generally Dreiserian," a wonderful Negro analogy to *An American Tragedy*. Even more flattering, Wright's novel was called the best American novel since John Steinbeck's *The Grapes of Wrath* (1939) and a work equally harrowing in its realism.[47]

None of these reviewers addressed all the levels of Wright's New Negro radicalism. The critical reception of the novel as a whole, however, commended its force and clarity, hailing the book as the finest novel ever by a black writer. While many black novelists predate Wright, the aesthetic, racial-political, and ideological circumstances of the era dictated the kind of novel that would excite American readers, black and white, intellectual and lay. *Native Son* tapped the constituency waiting for the Great Negro Novel, and some critics even wondered if Wright's book represented the Great American Novel.

During the Second World War, no black novelist could parallel Wright in stature and influence. *Uncle Tom's Children* in 1938, *Native Son* in 1940, and *Black Boy* in 1945 strengthened his foothold in the American cultural marketplace. Several literary awards, wide critical acclaim, and extraordinary sales legitimated him as one of the greatest novelists in the United States. Wright had also assisted other black writers through the composition, editing, publication, and marketing of their work. He helped these writers in much the same way that Locke had helped him. Locke praised Wright's work in his annual reviews of racial realism in American art and wrote one of the recommendations for Wright's Guggenheim fellowship.[48] Similarly generous, Wright mentored the younger James Baldwin so that Baldwin could win a Eugene F. Saxton fellowship. Well in advance, Wright praised Gwendolyn Brooks's first book, *A Street in Bronzeville* (1945), and he advised Ralph Ellison to study certain books and to write book reviews and short stories. Wright's organization of Chicago's South Side Writer's Group further extended his reach.

Several black writers openly acknowledged and embraced Wright's importance to their work and to the tradition as a whole. In the early part of his career, Ellison regarded Wright as a literary adviser and hailed *Native Son* as American literature of the first order and the starkest contrast from the African American fiction of both the 1920s and the 1930s. Baldwin owned a similar early relationship with Wright.[49]

Chester B. Himes, too, appreciated Wright for creating opportunities for black writers in the literary marketplace and for opening lines of access between black writers and the folk. Speaking in 1970, Himes said he "always had great respect for Richard Wright because of the fact that his first works, *Uncle Tom's Children*, *Native Son*, and *Black Boy*, opened up certain fields in the publishing industry for the black writer, more so than anything else that had happened. The Black Renaissance [of the 1920s] was an inward movement; it encouraged people who were familiar with it, who knew about it and were in contact with it, but the legend of Richard Wright reached people all over."[50] In his reviews of *Uncle Tom's Children* and *Native Son*, Locke also recognized the potential of Wright's "stark contemporary realism" in these very terms.[51]

Negative Influence

The response of black writers to Richard Wright's literary work fell into two camps. The first envisioned New Negro radicalism as the representative literary genre for re-creating black experience. The second indicted this genre for celebrating a problematic synecdoche in which the specific version of racial realism endorsed by Wright and his admirers dominated the canonical and commercial blueprint for Negro writing.

In the first instance, black writers became putative Wright's descendants by the end of World War II. Most notably, William Attaway was known for *Blood on the Forge* (1941), Charles Ruthaven Offord for *The White Face* (1943), Chester Himes for *If He Hollers Let Him Go* (1945), and Ann Petry for *The Street* (1946). *If He Hollers Let Him Go*, particularly, excited Wright and other like-minded readers.[52] A reviewer noted that the book "has most of the qualities that assure wide popular appeal," such as "an exciting backdrop, a fast pace, a tight plot, a smoothly fluid and readable style, and a hero who is easy to identify with." In 1946, Langston Hughes identified the book with Wright. He bemoaned, however, its being one of a growing number of good novels about bad Negroes who come to "bad" ends.[53] Hughes's lament foreshadows the stigma of Wright's "school" of New Negro radicalism, identified by the second camp. The dean of the Chicago Renaissance, while opening the doors of opportunity for some, indeed created critical, commercial, and canonical consequences for others.

The fate of Hurston's novel *Their Eyes Were Watching God* (1937) exemplifies the problem with the way Wright's rise to literary stardom in the United States, while spanning merely a decade, overshadowed a generation of black writers. *Their Eyes Were Watching God* earned generally favorable reviews from Alain Locke and Sterling Brown, among others. By contrast, Wright wrote a harsh review in *New Masses* (1937), underscoring, more than in any other extant document, the ideological rift between him and Hurston.[54] Of course, Wright had not yet earned the status of literary dean (that would arrive in 1940). However, his audacity in slamming Hurston—who, by contrast, was already a major figure in the black literati and ready to respond to Wright in kind—was remarkable.[55]

Their Eyes Were Watching God, according to Wright, fails "to move in the direction of serious fiction." "Miss Hurston voluntarily continues in her novel the tradition which was forced upon blacks in the theatre, that is, the minstrel technique that makes the 'white folks' laugh."[56] In an interview three years later, Wright continued his criticism of Hurston, this time not through what he said but through what he did not say. In the interview, he embraces only a handful of Negro writers as part of his "growing movement": a former writer of the Harlem Renaissance (Langston Hughes); a few writers of the 1930s (William Attaway, Arna Bontemps, and Sterling Brown); and a promising writer who would emerge in the late 1940s and the early 1950s (Ralph Ellison). No room is left for Hurston or for any other black woman writer.[57]

In 1950, one decade after Wright's interview about his "growing movement," Nick Aaron Ford, in a rather Wrightean essay, "A Blueprint for Negro Authors" (1950), perpetuated the dean's disregard of Hurston. He classifies *Their Eyes Were Watching God* and Hurston's first novel, *Jonah's Gourd Vine* (1934), as works treating "racial themes with no regard to their deeper social implications."[58] Ironically, not until Hurston's last novel, *Seraph on the Suwanee* (1948), which avoids New Negro radicalism and focuses on Florida "Crackers," did certain critics come to regard her as not just a good writer but as one who had finally come of age.

The commercial and critical prosperity Wright enjoyed did not immunize New Negro radicalism from the reasonable complaint that it restricted black literary expression. As early as 1938, Hurston critiqued *Uncle Tom's Children* not only for its merits and demerits, nor only out of revenge for Wright's scathing review of *Their Eyes Were Watching God* a year earlier. Above all, the book's literary and racial implications for the future concerned her. Some of Wright's sentences "have the shocking power of a forty-four" and represent "some beautiful writing." But the stories of racial hate and murder, usually among men, exhibit such bloody sensationalism that there is "perhaps enough to satisfy all male readers." Hurston proceeds to ponder what Wright "would have done had he dealt with plots that touched the broader and more fundamental phases of Negro life."[59]

This is one among several indications that praise for Wright did not exist across the board. Some readers of *Native Son*, for example, debated the history, nature, application, and limitations of New Negro radicalism. Some in this group treated this kind of racial realism as an example of stasis or even regression in African American literature.

Other readers and writers assumed the even more extreme position of dispensing with New Negro radicalism altogether. This sort of rhetoric had underwritten the well-known critiques of Wright by Ralph Ellison and James Baldwin. Ellison, despite having agreed in the early 1940s with Wright's racial-political and Marxist views, had eventually gone out of his way to distance himself from Wright and even other earlier black writers in order to foreground his own Americanism. Beneath Ellison's frequently reprinted and seemingly favorable review of Wright's *Black Boy* in 1945 lay one of his earliest public critiques of Wright.

Michel Fabre has examined Ellison's early essays and correspondence with Wright and argues convincingly that "Ellison was far more of an ideological writer at the time than he later acknowledged."[60] Indeed, Ellison's reviews of *Native Son* and *Twelve Million Black Voices* (1941) expose him as a leftist ideologue who sympathized with Wright's disillusionment with the American Communist Party. In making this statement, I am not beginning to delve, as Fabre has, into the factual inconsistencies between Ellison's early relationship with Wright and his highly rhetorical portrayal of this relationship in later essays. More important is Ellison's demonstration of what Joseph T. Skerrett Jr. has proven to be the "anxiety of influence" dictating his memory of Wright.[61]

I also place Baldwin within this argument. Like Ellison, Baldwin contended with New Negro radicalism and separated himself from Wright. Yet Baldwin also uniquely dealt with the place of New Negro radicalism in the general history of racial realism in American literature. In "Everybody's Protest Novel," he illustrates how far racial realism had *not* come in American literary history by World War II. Wright's *Native Son*, Baldwin argues, is a modern-day analogue to Harriet Beecher Stowe's *Uncle Tom's Cabin* (1852). New Negro radicalism is minstrel realism with a twist: its subscription to racial myth or stereotype empties New Negro radicalism of its realism. By being one of the first to label Wright's fiction "protest fiction," Baldwin suggests that minstrel realism had repeated itself in *Native Son*, despite Wright's claims to the contrary. The novel thus is African American literature in its most regressive and counterproductive state.[62]

The Racial Desegregation of American Literature

As the 1940s progressed, at least two more distinct camps of black writers emerged to critique the generic limitations and implications of New Negro radicalism. The first tried to redeem Wright's genre with global humanism. The second, while at times pursuing this same goal, reconceived African American literature in terms of American cultural nationalism. The common goal of these approaches, however, was the racial desegregation of American literature.

The first camp focused on what Alain Locke at one time called the "universal particularity" of African American literature, or the way this literature could be, at once, applicable to universal human values yet operate through the particular stories of black experiences.[63] To some critics,

Wright's ironic desire to employ Bigger Thomas to tackle fundamental, long-standing, and widespread human problems redeemed *Native Son*, despite their being wary of the burdens his literary deanship placed on black writers. Certainly, Bigger enabled Wright to address black proletarian circumstances and demands to which "bourgeois" cultural representations of the New Negro during the Harlem Renaissance tended to be insensitive. However, the proletarian polemic of *Native Son* also articulates the oppressions afflicting one socioeconomic class across the globe. "Bigger was not black all the time; he was white, too, and there were millions of him, everywhere," according to Wright. "All Bigger Thomases, white and black, felt tense, afraid, nervous, hysterical, and restless. . . . [C]ertain modern experiences were creating types of personalities whose existences ignored racial and national lines of demarcation, that these personalities carried with them a more universal drama-element than anything I'd ever encountered before."[64]

Bigger's function as a multiracial and multinational figure intersects issues of race and class. In doing so, it creates a complex and almost paradoxical universalism that determines Bigger's status as a "native son." Amid the prevailing critical apprehension over the burden of New Negro radicalism on the postwar black generation, certain literary critics did agree with Wright's claim that New Negro radicalism was not as provincial as its literary style and themes. Wright's vision of Bigger Thomas as at once black and white, "raced" and "classed," national and international, appealed to contemporary intellectual arguments for the universal particularity of African American literature.

Critics in the special winter 1950 issue of *Phylon*, "The Negro in Literature: The Current Scene," valued the universalist potential of *Native Son* and even paraphrased lines from "How Bigger Was Born." In "Toward Unfettered Creativity: A Note on the Negro Novelist's Coming of Age," Thomas D. Jarrett states that "Richard Wright makes it clear that Bigger Thomas is a Negro, but he makes it equally clear that he could be 'white.' His experiences might well have been those of a white youth in the ghettoes of Chicago."[65] And in "Race and the Negro Writer," Hugh M. Gloster agrees but sounds more optimistic about the simultaneously racial and universal meaning of *Native Son*: "*Native Son* illustrates, perhaps more effectively than any other novel by an American Negro, that it is possible to attack racial oppression and at the same time provide truthful implications for all mankind."[66] The "Negro," in whatever guise, was undeniably American. Black folklore informed American culture. Blackness defined or determined Americanness. Ralph Ellison uttered these ideas to Richard Wright, and perhaps Wright did take them to heart.[67] In sum, the "coming of age" of the Negro novelist predetermined the coming of age of the American novelist. As Albert Halper put it in 1929, "out of the negro will come the great American Novel, the epic poem of America."[68] That statement proved correct two decades later.

The wartime and postwar circumstances of racial integration in the United States, which stimulated what Houston Baker Jr. calls the "integrationist poetics" of African American literature, helps to explain this tradition's coming of age.[69] In 1941, after certain black intellectual and political demands, President Franklin D. Roosevelt issued an executive order establishing the Fair Employment Practices Committee. The committee's charge was to indict wartime manufacturers and other governmental industries for evidence of racial discrimination in hiring practices. Seven years later, new president Harry Truman signed a similar executive order barring racial segregation in the armed forces and the civil service. In the intervening years, other federal and judicial policies enforced desegregation in interstate transportation, housing, and schools. Statutes prohibiting interracial marriage and endorsing white primaries and the poll tax were also being overturned. Progress continued in other cultural arenas, such as Major League Baseball, when Jackie Robinson became the first black player in 1947.

From roughly 1946 until 1960, the era of the Cold War, tensions increased between the United States and the Soviet Union, manifested in the ideological struggle between democracy and communism. The witch hunt for Communists in governmental and cultural communities in the United States was coterminous with the black intellectual struggle with Communism. The Senate Subcommittee on Investigations, headed by Sen. Joseph McCarthy, blacklisted Paul Robeson and W. E. B. Du Bois and dubbed civil rights sit-ins as Communist. Wright, Ellison, and McKay, on the other hand, criticized the inability of Communism to solve the Negro Problem. Blacks therefore stood at the center of both national and international political activism.

The racial desegregation of American literature, whereby texts authored by blacks and whites shared the national literary tradition, supposedly reflected the racial desegregation occurring in the living, human world. Racial desegregation, of course, could not totally overcome the social, cultural, political, economic, and institutional entrenchment of antiblack racism in the United States. Nonetheless, the discourse and law of racial desegregation enforced at the federal level and in the courts rippled through society, institutions, and, eventually, black culture.

Northern and liberal southern publishers and periodicals were becoming more progressive by featuring black reporters, writers, and editors, in contrast to the state of the publishing industry in the late nineteenth century. The black publishing industry was coming of age as well. Writing in 1950, Era Bell Thompson, for example, appreciated the great progress in publishing and journalism. Black and white abolitionists had worked side by side in the antebellum years, T. Thomas Fortune became assistant editor of New York's *Evening Sun* in the 1880s, Charles Chesnutt was publishing stories around this same time in the *Atlantic Monthly*, and in the early twentieth century, William Stanley Braithwaite worked as a critic for Boston's *Evening Transcript*. "Today," Thompson exclaimed, "it is quite common in the North for the larger white dailies to employ a Negro reporter and even some of the more liberal Southern papers are following suit. . . . Negro journalism has at last come of age."[70]

Against this contextual backdrop, critics had come to appreciate black authors, ranging from former participants in the Harlem Renaissance to those in Wright's generation, for producing literature that viewed race and racism as incidental in the world of human interaction. Critics described literary works such as Jean Toomer's *Cane*, Langston Hughes's *Not without Laughter* (1930), Countee Cullen's *One Way to Heaven* (1932), Hurston's *Jonah's Gourd Vine* and *Their Eyes Were Watching God*, William Attaway's *Let Me Breathe Thunder* (1939), Adam Clayton Powells's *Picketing Hell* (1942), Lewis Caldwell's *The Policy King* (1945), George Henderson's *Jule* (1946), Alden Bland's *Behold a Cry* (1947), Ann Petry's *The Street*, and Dorothy West's *Living Is Easy* (1948) as examples of black aspiration toward the kinds of acculturation and socioeconomic mobility that appealed to American society as a whole.[71]

The critical insistence on defining Negro writers as American writers and Negro writing as American literature characterizes *The Negro Caravan* (1941), an anthology edited by poet Sterling Brown and critics Arthur P. Davis and Ulysses Lee. Designed to supersede previous anthologies by being "more comprehensive in scope" and "a more accurate and revealing story of the Negro writer than has even been told before," *The Negro Caravan* spans over one thousand pages and includes short stories, novels, poetry, folk literature, drama, speeches, pamphlets, letters, biography, and essays. Wright, obviously, is one of the many authors the editors selected. A poem published in *New Masses*—"I Have Seen Black Hands" (1934)—and two prose pieces that ended up in *Uncle Tom's Children*—a short story, "Bright and Morning Star," and an autobiographical sketch, "The Ethics of Living Jim Crow"—represent Wright's oeuvre. In terms of his books, *Uncle Tom's Children*, the editors say, "penetrat[es] the interior regions of Negro life politely overlooked by the racial idealists and inaccessible to white writers." *Native Son* is "highly successful" and "the best example of the new social realism."[72]

However, *The Negro Caravan* resists the notion that African American literature historically clusters into aesthetic movements or a "unique cultural pattern," such as the kind typifying Wright's era. Rather, "Negro writers have adopted the literary traditions that seemed useful for their purposes," namely, those developed by Anglo-European and -American writers. Thus, the notion of "Negro literature" is at once inaccurate and ambiguous. The "bonds of literary tradition seem to be stronger than race" for the black writer, as do the bonds of American cultural nationalism.[73]

Reorienting the African American literary tradition on a cultural-nationalist map, the editors of *The Negro Caravan* echo almost verbatim Countée Cullen's foreword to *Caroling Dusk: An Anthology of Verse by Negro Poets* (1927). Black writers, Cullen asserts, do not automatically think, feel, or write the same way by virtue of common racial ancestry. By inaccurately classifying black authors and their literary works in terms of race rather than national culture, Cullen continues, "Negro literature" has existed in an aesthetic and cultural "alcove" apart from American literature. The editors of *The Negro Caravan* likewise "consider Negro writers to be American writers, and literature by American Negroes to be a segment of American literature."[74]

As *The Negro Caravan* asserted the cultural nationality of African American literature, other critics emphasized the tradition's commercial popularity as an index of national acceptance. "Five American Negro Authors," a special story in *Salute*, hails Motley, Petry, Yerby, Wright, and Hughes as "authors [who] are showing that they can equal their white colleagues both in prestige and in sales."[75] And "America's Top Negro Authors," another major article published in 1949 in *Color*, boasts that ten million people had read Wright's *Black Boy*; Frank Yerby's *The Foxes of Harrow* (1946), *The Vixens* (1947), and *The Golden Hawk* (1948); Willard Motley's *Knock on Any Door*; Ann Petry's *The Street*; Walter White's *A Man Called White* (1948); and Roi Ottley's *Black Odyssey: The Story of the Negro in America* (1948). Sales served as a crucial barometer of the national acceptance of African American literature.

The second camp of literary critics took the next logical step toward consummating the racial desegregation of American literature: they advocated the utter avoidance of traditional racial realism, which they considered a handicap. To some critics, African American literature of racial realism reflected the immaturity of black authors, who could not think beyond the so-called Negro Problem. The recurrence of this kind of literature, in which protagonists and narrators often sermonized, spewed propaganda and didacticism, and expressed racial hypersensitivity, justified the shortsighted and dangerous expectation among American readers that Negro authors would always write this way, that they could not help but write about race and racism.[76] Petry's *Country Place* (1947), Hurston's *Seraph on the Suwanee*, and Yerby's *The Foxes of Harrow*, *The Vixens*, *The Golden Hawk*, and *Pride's Castle* (1949) demonstrated that the avoidance of racial realism in African American literature could help to make an author's own racial identity incidental. This idea could prove favorable to black aspirations toward the kind of nationality and popularity that could overcome racial stigma.

The relationship between the relative absence of racial realism in literature and a black author's identity as an American or universal writer was the logical converse of the situation that black authors had faced since the nineteenth century, and even most recently, as I mention at the outset of this book. At this time, paratexts such as frontispieces and authenticating documents enclosed stories about black life, culture, and racial politics. By contrast, in the 1940s, some critics perceived racial identification in paratexts and racial realism in texts as the bane of African American literature. E. M. Forster, in his review of *Knock on Any Door*, wonders aloud about the novel's author, Willard Motley: "Is it true that he is a Negro? How incredible, how very nice, for there is no inkling of it in his writing."[77] The novel's avoidance of racial realism made Motley's racial identity a bonus. On theoretical and practical levels, such literature rendered moot the necessity of racially desegregating American literature. There was no need to judge a book by its author's skin.

Not all black writers were willing to avoid racial realism, however. In a 1961 interview published in *December*, Ralph Ellison was asked what seemed to be a straightforward question about the early part of his literary career: "Did you think you might write stories in which Negroes did not appear?" Although beginning as simply as the question ended, Ellison's answer elaborates complex autobiographical and theoretical reasons for this lack of impulse:

No, there was never a time when I thought of writing fiction in which only Negroes appeared, or in which only whites appeared. And yet from the very beginning I wanted to write about American Negro experience and I suspected that what was important, what made the difference, lay in the perspective from which it was viewed. When I learned more and started thinking about this consciously, I realized that it was a source of creative strength as well as a source of wonder. It's also a relatively unexplored area of American experience simply because our knowledge of it has been distorted through the overemphasis of the sociological approach. Unfortunately, many Negroes have been trying to define their own predicament in exclusively sociological terms, a situation I consider quite short-sighted.[78]

Ellison belongs to a wider postwar critique of New Negro radicalism, evident in his criticism of the "overemphasis of the sociological approach," one of the genre's protocols. However, he refused to follow in the footsteps of black writers who worked against this genre by celebrating anomalous writing. Developing "perspectives" and writing on the "American Negro experience," according to Ellison, outweighed committing himself to a genre of African American literature that eliminated this experience in order to demonstrate its Americannness. Rather, the literature should prove its Americanness *through* depictions of the black experience.

Critic Lloyd L. Brown is even blunter than Ellison about the problems of African American literature's avoiding racial realism. In "Which Way for the Negro Writer?" an essay serialized in the March and April 1951 issues of *Masses and Mainstream*, Brown argues that the abandonment of "racial material" for "universal perspectives" and "global points of view" only perpetuates the ideas and values of "the white ruling class," "American imperialism," and the "melting pot" paradigm by which "all so-called inferior cultures must be re-molded to conform to the Anglo-Saxon ideal." The black avoidance of racial realism and gravitation toward aesthetic universalism reflected, he felt, the self-destructive internalization of antiblack racism.[79] By one and a half decades, Brown's complaint that African American literature "has not been Negro enough—that is, it has not fully reflected the real life and character of the people"—anticipated the Black Arts Movement, specifically, its critique of anomalous African American literature and its call for black authors to remain dedicated to racial realism for the political sake of black cultural pragmatism and nationalism.[80]

Nonetheless, there was a postwar intellectual consensus that, if Wright symbolized the first great Negro novelist and black authors of universal particularity stood on the threshold of maturity, then another group had succeeded in actually coming of age by, in a sense, emancipating themselves from these two conditions. More than any other black writer of the postwar 1940s, Frank Yerby dedicated himself to this philosophy by playing truant from Wright's school of New Negro radicalism.

Chapter 6

"The Race Problem Was *Not* a Theme for Me"

Richard Wright and Frank Yerby thrived in similar social, geographic, and intellectual circles. Born in the same month but seven years apart, both came from the American South, Yerby from Augusta, Georgia, and Wright from Roxie, Mississippi.[1] During the Great Depression, poverty forced Yerby to drop out of a doctoral program in English at the University of Chicago, where Wright happened to obtain and read sociological literature during his formative stage as a writer. Toward the latter part of the 1930s, Yerby participated in a Chicago-based New Deal program and probably rubbed elbows with Wright, Margaret Walker, William Attaway, and Arna Bontemps, all affiliated with the Chicago Renaissance. Like Wright, James Baldwin, Chester Himes, and William Gardner Smith, all expatriates in the 1950s, Yerby moved, in 1951, to Paris. In five years, he relocated to Madrid, where he lived until his death on November 29, 1991.

The earliest highlight of both of their literary careers, furthermore, was the O. Henry Award, which Wright won in 1939 for "Fire and Cloud" and Yerby in 1945 for "Health Card." Yerby's story critiques the ideology and practices of racism in the United States in ways Wright, a decade later, found provocative. For Wright, "Health Card" relates "a variation of the same theme, a man subjected to a sort of psychological castration, as it were, directly in front of his wife's eyes . . . This Negro, being further from his roots, weeps tears of innocent rage."[2] Despite the similarities between his work and Wright's, beginning in the mid-1940s, Yerby tried to rid himself of the expectations and responsibilities that came with writing both as a black man and in the wake of Wright's success.

In a letter written to Michel Fabre, who was working on a biography of Wright, Yerby clarifies the extent of his dissociation: "I knew Dick Wright none too well. I admired him immensely as a man. I visited him in Paris circa 1953 or 4, I don't remember which. I was not at all influenced by him as a writer, except perhaps negatively. . . . I liked, admired, enjoyed his earlier books; but if they influenced me at all, it was to confirm my growing suspicion that the race problem was *not* a theme for me."[3] Certain correspondence and literary works (poems, short stories, novels, and criticism) Yerby wrote between 1933 and 1956 could explain that last line, "the race problem was *not* a theme for me." He was referring to the "race problem" as constructed by the genre of New Negro radicalism in African American literature, led by Wright.

Yerby's aversion to this genre, as articulated in his letter to Fabre, did not exist throughout his career. Nor was it the sole reason for his production of thirty novels between 1946 and 1986, with nonblack protagonists and eclectic historical settings, cultural geographies, and political themes. Early in his career, during the early 1930s, Yerby was a poet ambivalent in his employment of outdated atavistic tropes attributable to the Harlem Renaissance and in his experimentation with classical Western verse forms and humanistic themes. In the latter part of the decade, he shifted to writing short stories in the genre of New Negro radicalism, capitalizing with great critical success on the prevailing interest in Wright's fiction.

Around this time, however, Yerby was becoming increasingly aware of the racial politics of American literary criticism and commercialism. Sounding much like the discontents of New Negro radicalism, he was learning that as a black writer he had to deal with the market for racial stereotypes, which appreciated Wright's Bigger Thomas at the expense of other kinds of characterizations, including the uplifted black protagonist featured in the novel he was trying to publish, *This Is My Own*. After several failed attempts to sell this novel to a publisher, Yerby decided that he would never write in a literary market in which racial myths, stereotypes, and other related discourses so constrained his creative options. In this regard, his first *published* novel, *The Foxes of Harrow*, signifies a philosophical turn toward an anomalous aesthetic.

The Foxes of Harrow is quite complex. It is a peculiarly "American" story about Stephen Fox's vision "for endless generations" of Foxes at Harrow, the plantation in Louisiana where Stephen builds a mansion, settles his family, and cultivates his notoriety in the eyes of the local gentry. Stephen forges an individualistic identity as an American by coming from a wayward and almost mythic past and achieving several goals, namely, creating a controversial reputation in local southern towns or cities; founding a dynasty; following an industrious work ethic; and acquiring socioeconomic privilege (alongside the reaffirmation of his own racial privilege) by constructing a plantation of grandiose proportions.

Of course, this story line is not new in American literature. We can turn to William Faulkner's *Absalom, Absalom!* (1936) for a similarly dynastic story about Thomas Sutpen. And the other great novel of 1936, Margaret Mitchell's *Gone with the Wind*, has attracted much scholarly attention to its thematic intersection of race, romance, and southern literary tradition in American culture between the world wars. This is the kind of intersection that generated the master narratives that Yerby operated both within and against. Mitchell's novel has been mentioned in scholarly work that places *The Foxes of Harrow* in the context of twentieth-century American historical romance.[4]

Yet Yerby's philosophical approach to sociocultural respectability and the racial politics of the South works to critique the myths reproduced or perpetuated by Faulkner, Mitchell, and other American writers of the South. Indeed, the range and complexity of *The Foxes of Harrow*'s commentary on dangerous myths about race relations, the folk, and the South demand more sophisticated readings of Yerby's place in American literary history. I propose that his intersection of the conventions of the historical novel and the romance novel in *The Foxes of Harrow* enabled him to explore the kinds of racial reconciliation between individuals and communities that writers like Faulkner had previously depicted as improbable.

Yerby's productivity enhanced the commercial popularity of his novels. From 1946 to 1986, he published thirty-three novels. Three were translated into film, one for television. Twelve were best-sellers, and almost all were selections of the Book-of-the-Month Club. They have been translated into over thirty languages. And, as of this writing, close to sixty million copies have been sold around the world. Yerby's literary ambition and his commercial success are so outstanding that continuing to marginalize him in discussions of African American canon formation and literary criticism defies scholarly sense. Indeed, he is relatively absent from anthologies of African American literature, and even from those of American literature generally. And although he passed away in 1991, still only a handful of studies of him exist.[5] The long-standing stigma applied to his novels as lowbrow pulp fiction, hack writing, and therefore representative of a subliterary genre is problematic and complicit in his absence from the African American canon. This state of affairs oversimplifies the complexity of a black writer who became not just a *national* writer but a *popular* writer as well, despite and because of the fact that Yerby played truant from the Wrightean school of African American literature.

Quietly Burning the Manuscript

To repeat, Frank Yerby did not begin his literary career as a writer of "costume" novels of historical romance. He was a fledgling poet. In 1933, he sent a batch of poems to James Weldon Johnson for the kind of feedback that only an intelligent, influential, and veteran poet-critic could offer.

After reading the poems "carefully," Johnson concluded that Yerby should ditch the atavism. He tried to be tactful. The tendency of writers of the Harlem Renaissance to invoke ancestral African themes in their work, he wrote, did not come out of "genuine emotion" or any "actual physical or spiritual experiences." Yerby's outdated primitivism failed to reach the level of Countée Cullen's poem "Heritage," which Alain Locke had selected for his 1925 Harlem issue in *The Survey Graphic*. Moreover, Yerby's experimentation with imagism, associated with Ezra Pound's "high" modernist poetry, which articulated precise visual objects, was not "well-nigh perfect to justify itself." Only one of the poems, "Old Gardener," pleased Johnson (for reasons undisclosed). Johnson hoped, "Do not let what I have said discourage you. Keep at work."[6]

Johnson's letter had mixed results. Evidently, Yerby stopped writing poems with the kind of atavistic tropes of ancestral Africa that were popular during the Harlem Renaissance. But he continued to write poems until 1938, publishing them in American periodicals ranging from *Challenge* and *Shards* to *Arts Quarterly* and *The Fisk Herald*.[7] Instead of discussing Africa or its diaspora, these poems describe animals, farming, art, love, nature, human life and death, temporality, and God.

In 1934, Yerby's poetry debuted in *Challenge*. Editor Dorothy West introduced the magazine as a search "for the new voice. It is our plan," she writes, "to bring out the prose and poetry of the newer Negroes. We who were the New Negroes challenge them to better our achievements. For we did not altogether live up to our promise."[8] James Weldon Johnson echoed West's optimism. Dubbed by the magazine as "the dean of Negro letters," Johnson similarly lamented the days of the Harlem Renaissance, when the "loud huzzas" about "the Negro literary millennium" proved to be an exaggeration. The "newer voices," the "younger writers," have "serious work to do" in "breaking down and wearing away the stereotyped ideas about the Negro and for creating a higher and more enlightened opinion about the race."[9]

Yerby, a rising poetic talent, belonged to this avant-garde. So invested was *Challenge* in exhibiting Yerby's work that the magazine actually delayed its next issue (September 1934) in order to debut his poems "Miracles" and "Brevity." Over the next couple of years, the magazine would continue to publish his quatrains and sonnets.

In 1937, Yerby changed his literary approach. No longer was he writing poems about the mundane, the secular, the spiritual, and the abstract. He had turned to prose, which in the tumultuous interwar era was becoming more common than poetry in African American literature.[10] Though he had published a couple of short stories in this vein in *The Fisk Herald*, it was not until 1939 that his short story "The Thunder of God" appeared in *The New Anvil*.[11] The title of this story and Yerby's name headlined the magazine's cover, even above the names of authors who had appeared previously in proletarian magazines (e.g., *The New Masses*) and worked for the Federal Writers' Project.[12] This story marks his initial gravitation toward Wright's bestselling brand of racial realism.

Set in 1929 Augusta, Georgia, "The Thunder of God" depicts racist white police rounding up black men during a torrential rainfall to work to fortify a levee buckling against a massive flood. Thunder and lightning distract the men from hoisting sandbags into the stopgap. Despite one section boss's orders for them to resume their labor, "one huge black fellow threw down his shovel," saying, "Listen, whitefolks, dat's God talking out dere now. An' when God talks, I listens!"[13] Through a twist of fate, as the boss wields a shotgun to intimidate the workers, the flood breaks the levee and washes him away. "The Thunder of God" contains almost everything in Wright's *Uncle Tom's Children*: blacks withstanding white racism; patterns of violence; layers of regional dialect; examples of folklore; unwavering fatalism; and the naturalist kind of literary verisimilitude.

The "Notes on Contributors" section of *The New Anvil* provides revealing biographical information about Yerby: "FRANK G. YERBY, Chicago, writes of himself: Age: 22. Race: Negro. Education: A.B., M.A. (English). Been published about seven or eight times in those oh so literary magazines of verse. Slight feeling of nausea whenever I see one now. 'The Thunder of God' will be my first published story—outside of college magazines. Working on Federal Writers' Project of Illinois. My home town, Augusta, Georgia, is the richest mine of story material I know of.'"[14] Yerby capitalized on his personal identity, educational achievements, professional credentials, literary aversions ("nausea"), class and political orientations, and birthplace in order to forge himself as that "newer Negro" which the black writers of the Chicago Renaissance represented. His rhetorical shift from "oh so literary magazines" to "the richest mine of story material" in his southern hometown reflected his embrace of the key doctrine of cultural pragmatism. Yerby saw himself as a conduit between his race (outside the academic setting) and such venues as *The New Anvil*.

After "The Thunder of God" appeared, Yerby stuck to what worked for Richard Wright—radical stories of racial unrest and violence—in order to achieve widespread critical acclaim and commercial success. When his short story "Health Card" (1944) appeared in *Harper's*, the story's themes and the magazine's literary prestige and commercial reach combined to launch Yerby onto the national stage. "Health Card" was the first of five short stories he published in the mid-1940s that reiterate his commitment to literary subjects about black struggles with racial discrimination, especially in the South.[15] Hailed by *Harper's* as "Mr. Yerby's first story in a national magazine," "Health Card" won the O. Henry Memorial Short Story Prize in 1945. It made him the first black writer to win the award since Wright had won it six years earlier for "Fire and Cloud," one of the four short stories included in the 1938 edition of *Uncle Tom's Children*. Benefiting from the expectations shaped by Wright's fiction, Yerby customized his story to address racial and economic oppression, interracial conflict, the derogation of black womanhood, and the expression and sexual redemption of black manhood.

Set in the South, "Health Card" begins with the protagonist, Private John ("Johnny") Green, reading a letter from Lily, his girlfriend. She is living up North and tells him that she has saved enough money to visit him. Living amid unpaved streets and shanties in the "Black Bottom," or "Negro section," he is a black soldier who has hoped in vain for the military to give him a furlough so that he can see Lily more. Since Lily is coming to town, he rents a room in the home of the local Baptist church pastor so that he and—in his dishonest words to the pastor's wife—his "shonuff, honest t'Gawd wife," "married in th Baptist Church in Deetroit," can spend time together.[16]

Soon Johnny encounters two problems. First, the colonel bars black soldiers for a month from entering town, where his apartment is located. The order is in response to an interracial scuffle between black soldiers and white military and civilian police officers who were stopping black women downtown and demanding to inspect their health cards. The women turned out to be the partners of the black soldiers, who resented the police's tendency to associate black women with sexually transmitted diseases. Luckily, Johnny, despite his curfew, tracks down the colonel and convinces him to permit the soldier to go into town each evening for a week. But the next problem, predictably, irks him: Lily does not have a health card.

When she arrives in town and they stroll into Black Bottom, two police officers confront them and, fatefully, request to see her card. Lying to the men, as he did to the pastor's wife, Johnny insists that Lily is his wife, that she "ain't no ho!" Racial epithets fly. Fortunately for Johnny, one officer persuades the more adamant interrogator to loosen up. As they leave, Lily must restrain Johnny from attacking them. He slumps to the ground, crying, "I ain't no man!" To which she responds, "You's a man awright. You's my man!"[17] The couple then heads to the pastor's house to settle in.

"Health Card" interested many American readers on its way to winning the O. Henry Award. It especially intrigued black military men, one of whom wrote Yerby questioning the story's realism and depiction of racial uplift. The 1944 exchange between this soldier and Yerby offers insight into Yerby's growing cynicism about the direction of African American literature in the early 1940s, just before he switched to the costume novel of historical romance.

At a military base in Augusta, Georgia, Private John S. Cousins, in a letter, recounts to Yerby an unresolved dispute he was having with his fellow soldiers over "Health Card." Private Cousins believes that Johnny and Lily faced discrimination, not because of their relatively upstanding and moral character, but because "[c]olor, not character, is the deciding factor." Others at the military base argued that Yerby did not distinguish the protagonists enough from the masses. Johnny and Lily speak in the same kind of dialect that had historically functioned to debase the education and refinement of literary characters. These fellows maintained that "it would have been more true to reality had [Yerby] shown [Johnny and Lily] as average educated members of the Northern Negro group."[18]

In a letter, Yerby responds by stating that, at the outset, Private Cousins, not his fellow soldiers, is correct. Yerby admits that he constructed the characters to be "clean, fine moral people." Yet they are not too educated, because he did not have enough narrative room to account for it while connecting the story line to race. Private Cousins's friends are also right that uplifting portrayals of blacks *are* realistic. To explain this point, Yerby relates the encounter with the publishing world that sparked his cynicism about the commercial mind-set of literary publishers and the necessary conformity of writers to their expectations:

I wrote a novel in which the chief character is a Negro Ph.D. The publishers suggested that I have him quit school in his early high school days and become a prize fighter! They know that there are fine, well educated, clean, intelligent, moral Negroes. But the book buying public—which is 99 percent white doesn't [know] and doesn't care to.

Publishers make money. So unfortunately, must writers.

But before I become too cynical—"Health Card" was written with the high purpose of pure education propaganda to help make things better racially. As such it had to be published, and if I had insisted as I dearly desired to—upon making college graduates out of Johnny Green and Lily I can assure your friends that Harper's or no other white magazine would have touched it. Is it or isn't it better to make a small point than no point at all?

Yerby discloses his personal negotiations with a publishing industry resistant to counternormative racial representations. He participated in an African American literary tradition of racial realism, where the stereotypes of morality, cleanliness, education, and cultural refinement signified racial uplift. To publishers, however, his idea of a "Negro Ph.D." implied a multifaceted antithesis to Wright's Bigger Thomas. Bigger was the popular literary figure with which Yerby had to contend and which, as we shall soon see, would cause him to avoid racial realism almost forever. In sum, Yerby was confiding to Private Cousins the racial politics of the American publishing industry and literary readership by which black writers were abiding in order to succeed in both the critical and the commercial arenas.[19]

Why and how did these military readers recognize the story's racial polemics? In the same letter to Private Cousins, Yerby presumes that they both belong to the same race and thereby share the same racialism: "We, as people (by the way I am assuming that you are colored) are extremely touchy—naturally so, due to the persecution we've undergone. We forget that we do have crooks and general undesirables just as do white peoples. We tend to deny the existence of those Negroes who would do the race a service by going off somewhere and quietly shooting themselves."[20] Yerby's letter articulates one of the major goals of New Negro radicalism: to expose oppression and the lives of those who are oppressed. Yerby was aware of the tension between racial uplift and, from his perspective, the sometimes unwanted and unwarranted brutality in representations of Bigger Thomas. But he conceded that such depictions could—and eventually would—saturate the literary market, at the expense of most other depictions. For this reason, and at least for a brief period in his early career, he chose to write against the grain with stories of racial uplift.

An examination of the correspondence between Yerby and his agent and friend, Muriel Fuller, about his first novel, *This Is My Own,* further reveals the entrenched market resistance to fiction about educated blacks. The resistance was symptomatic of the critical and commercial burden imposed by New Negro radicalism on a generation of black authors. Ultimately, a series of setbacks and experimentation with other literary genres would alter the direction of Yerby's life and work.

Over a span of seven weeks in 1943, Yerby wrote *This Is My Own,* a novel that included all of the "taboos" of African American literature. Yerby tells Fuller in a letter that the protagonist "is intelligent, educated—no 'Bigger Thomas' in any sense of the word. He is myself and thousands of my friends and maybe a little bit of all the persecuted minority peoples all over the world."[21] Fuller also regarded *This Is My Own* as the "opposite" of *Native Son.* When she contacted Edward Aswell, Richard Wright's editor at Harper and Publishers, she presented the novel as the antithesis of *Native Son.* Bigger Thomas "was bad in any language or race," while Yerby's "idea of a decent, well educated colored man and what he is up against hasn't been presented in fiction, so far as I know."[22] Truth be told, this kind of characterization had already appeared in African American literature of racial uplift between the late nineteenth century and the early twentieth century. In Fuller's defense, however, it was less prevalent in the era of New Negro radicalism.

Unsurprisingly, the publisher flatly rejected *This Is My Own*, even though its former editor and currently best-selling author of *The Darker Brother* (1943), Bucklin Moon, partially edited Yerby's novel and delivered it to the press himself.[23] And although Yerby's agent, Fuller, won the O. Henry Award in 1943 and influenced certain members of the judging committee when her client was up for the award two years later, she could not work enough magic to sway the judges of the *Redbook*–Dodd, Mead, and Company Prize Novel Contest to honor *This Is My Own*.[24]

Likewise, no one could convince Wright's editor at Harper and Publishers to accept *This Is My Own*. The chief character of Yerby's novel is as exceptional and interesting as Bigger, but Edward Aswell believed that he was not "a wholly credible character." This problem, in addition to what Aswell considered excessive editorializing and infelicitous prose, compelled him to demand significant revisions before the manuscript could proceed any further in the review process.[25] In response, Yerby eventually followed the advice of his agent: he wrote an "unpopular" story in "superlative" prose to attract "sympathetic" readers.[26]

The period when Yerby was revising *This Is My Own* offers one of the first glimpses into the kind of writing that typified the majority of his career as a novelist. In December 1943 and January 1944, Yerby wrote an experimental short story that, in his estimation, "stunk." He wrote it not because he was wholeheartedly committed to it, but because his wife at the time, Flora, convinced him that "stories about Negroes by Negroes from a Negro's point of view just don't get published anymore."[27]

For a brief while, Yerby played with a story that avoided "the upper middle class Negro," the "richest source of literary material that [he] knew."[28] Disappointed with the end result, Yerby regretted sending a copy of the story to Fuller, scrapped this approach, and decided to return to what he knew best at the time: revising *This Is My Own*. He was also preparing to write *Sweet Land*, a novel about the life of Marian Anderson, the great black opera star. *Sweet Land* avoids the racial "bitterness" Yerby was "forever stumbling into" in his fiction.[29] He tried to reconstruct the life of Anderson, who sang at the Lincoln Memorial in Washington, D.C., on Easter Sunday in 1939, after the Daughters of the American Revolution denied her the right to sing at Constitution Hall because of her race. She performed before over seventy-five thousand and was broadcast on national radio, which, arguably, inaugurated the modern civil rights movement. The novel was never published.

Almost six months after first delivering *This Is My Own* to Harper and Publishers, Yerby suffered a major setback. The revisions to the manuscript did little to satisfy Aswell and the other editors. Everyone complained that the protagonist "never emerges from [the] pages as a flesh and blood real person. He is too much of an idealization—too good to be true. This doesn't have anything to do with the color of his skin."[30] As genuine as Aswell sounds here, his dismissal of race from his assessment of Yerby's novel is suspect. I would contend that Aswell's discrediting of the protagonist's believability has *everything* to do with skin color. How could it not be so for Aswell, who was the editor for what has been called the most anti-idealistic African American novel in history, *Native Son*? And how could it not be so, in light of the traditional appreciation of voguish racial realism in Aswell's phrase, "flesh and blood real person"? What was unrealistic to Aswell and to his colleagues was, arguably, a way of life for Yerby and many others. By clinging to literary renditions of racial uplift, however, Yerby alienated a marketplace enamored with Wright and his New Negro radicalism.

Coincidentally, months before Aswell's rejection letter, Yerby anticipated the generic failure of racial uplift in African American literature and, by implication, the probable failure of his novel:

This Is My Own violated one of the basic tabus [*sic*]: one must never present the Negro as a man and a brother. Even when one is entirely sympathetic toward the cause of justice for all men one must observe this tabu. Richard Wright's immensely successful *Native Son* observed it: the story of Bigger Thomas is the case history of a tortured animal. . . . T. S. Stribling once told me that I shouldn't try to write about the educated Negro, that he was too much like the white man and hence lacked "color." Perhaps he is right . . . And [yet] he [the educated Negro] is so terribly different from the white man. The point is that the white reading public, in common with the public generally, likes to pretend that such Negroes do not exist. This is unrealistic, they say.[31]

Yerby foresaw that the novel was doomed, and his rejection letter from Aswell was the confirmation. Two days after receiving the letter, Yerby sent an apologetic and self-deprecatory note to his agent wondering if he should "quietly burn" the manuscript of *This Is My Own*.[32] (The manuscript has yet to be found.)[33] By early 1946, despite having won the O. Henry Award, Yerby had resigned himself to the fact that stereotypical representations of the folk, framed by conventional discourses on the race problem, monopolized the African American literary marketplace.

This is why Yerby's insistence to Michel Fabre, quoted earlier, that "the race problem was *not* a theme for me" is all the more remarkable, if coun-

ternormative. At the same time, as I explain in Chapter 5, writers and critics were growing more open to African American literature's adhering to
this philosophy as it claimed Americanness. Ironically, the text and context
of Yerby's first published novel, *The Foxes of Harrow*, reveal that the race
problem was always a theme for him, even if the protagonists were not
black. He just wanted to keep his creative options open.

The Foxes of Harrow

The Foxes of Harrow is not a traditional novel of African American literature, in which the protagonist tends to be identifiably black. Rather,
Stephen Fox possesses "coppery red hair," "blue eyes," and "freckles on his
fair face," racial stereotypes of his "whiteness" (31, 58, 176).[34] Fluent in
French and German, the result of his travels through Western epicenters
such as London, Paris, Vienna, and New York, Stephen proclaims himself
an Irishman on the winding road toward becoming an Irish American in
nineteenth-century Louisiana.

As a novel of historical romance, *The Foxes of Harrow* embodies both the
historical novel and the romance novel. The literary interplay of supposedly contradictory elements, fact and fiction, allowed Yerby to tell the clas-
sically "American" story that individualism can overcome the burden of
environment. Thus, he resisted the naturalistic protocol of New Negro radicalism, which argues that the environment sacrifices personal individuality and agency.

Set roughly between 1825 and 1865 in New Orleans and its outlying
plantation suburbs, *The Foxes of Harrow* is the first of several novels by
Yerby, published mostly between 1946 and the 1960s, about America in the
context of slavery, the Civil War, and the postbellum aftermath.[35] *The Foxes
of Harrow* traces the development of Stephen into an Irish American citizen through an entrepreneurial ethic of self-help and industry. The historical period, cultural geography, and theme of rugged individualism in *The
Foxes of Harrow* recall, simultaneously, mythic and historical visions of the
antebellum South and its politics of race, culture, and nation. A close reading of Stephen's character in *The Foxes of Harrow* reveals the range and
focus of Yerby's critique of these visions.

A pivotal theme in the novel is the importance of "Creoles" to Louisiana
and the sense of American identity. Yerby distinguishes Creole society from
white society primarily in cultural terms, but he leaves Creole identity
vague enough to invite racial distinction. Gavin Jones notes that "*creole* as a
language and *creolization* as a wider cultural force were explicitly made in
the Louisiana context. *Creole* referred to the 'patois' of Louisiana, yet Cre-

ole could also refer to the French-speaking descendants of French and Spanish settlers in the region, *and* to the many inhabitants of Louisiana— the so-called quadroon or mulattoes—born of mixed racial heritage."[36]

Textual evidence in *The Foxes of Harrow* suggests that Yerby was aware of the initial cultural and historical meaning of "Creole" to which Jones refers. Stephen Fox tends to interchange "Creole" with "Frenchman," to characterize "Creole" as the stylistic "hauteur" found on the edifices of New Orleans, to recognize its suggestion of a generational and ideological conflict between "older Frenchmen" and "modern youth" in Louisiana, and to suggest a comparable societal conflict between "Creoles" and "Americans."

At moments, however, the narrator ascribes racial significance to "Creole." The "dark" skin color of Creoles contrasts with Stephen's skin color. Andre Le Blanc, a Creole whom Stephen befriends, acknowledges this contrast but subtly tries to empty it of racial meaning when he "rebukes" a stranger for failing to address him courteously as a member of "the [white] race whose courtesy is celebrated throughout the world."[37]

The lack of courtesy that Andre senses resembles the level of mistreatment that a Creole could face in Louisiana. Again according to Jones, such misidentification was not uncommon in American society during the mid-to-late nineteenth century, the setting of *The Foxes of Harrow*: "[T]he white creoles of Louisiana became unnerved by this double meaning for the name of their racial group—the fact that, instead of signifying only a line of pure Latin descent, the word *Creole* had somehow come to signify a person of mixed blood."[38] In *The Foxes of Harrow*, this degree of racial nervousness hovers around "Creole," which the narrator calls a "much abused term" (46).

In order to thrive in Louisiana, Stephen must overcome the unfamiliarity, insularity, and skepticism of outsiders that Creoles, in his eyes, have come to express. One strategy includes holding a ball in his newly built house at Harrow and inviting many "ancient" Creole aristocratic families as part of his "formal assault" on their prejudices against Americans and him, in particular (32, 35). The older Creole generation, believing that Louisiana should still belong to the French, tends to despise the influx of ruthless Americans, whose businesses and families displace Creole gentry into undesirable sections of New Orleans. Stephen's friend, Andre, describes this prevalent anti-Americanism succinctly: "And perhaps they hate the devil himself worse than they do an American, but, frankly, I doubt it." "To a Creole," Andre continues, "all Americans are . . . bad" (183–43).

Creole anti-Americanism stems from the cultural differences native Creoles recognize between themselves and someone like Stephen. They detest the "gentleman" who tries to speak French when, in fact, his engagement with the language goes no further than necessary for international tourism and local opportunism. Stephen's conduct, however well-intentioned, makes a mockery of the French cultural ideals and affiliations that the older Creole generations hold so dear. The resistance of Creole-predominated city councils, even to their own detriment, to American entrepreneurs seeking to improve the impoverished conditions of New Orleans also reveals the depth of the sociogenerational rift between Creoles and Americans. Stephen hopes to overcome this rift by committing to his vision of what a successful American should be (a prosperous landowner) and do (work hard to till the soil and acquire more property) to benefit society (support technological innovation and capitalism based on sugar and cotton).

The roots and routes of Stephen's rationale for cultivating land to build a mansion and a plantation, while tied to a desire to become respectable, can be traced back to long-standing and deep-seated desires to establish himself as an entrepreneur and, later, to create a dynasty of Foxes at Harrow. In our first encounter with Stephen's plans, he is boarding the *Prairie Belle*, a ship set to sail the Mississippi River and on which fellow passengers, sore over losing to him at cards, curse at him. A flatboat intersects the ship, and Stephen convinces the smaller boat's captain, Mike, to transport him to New Orleans. In a conversation between the two, Stephen discloses his desire to overcome his tendency toward international transience and to settle in Louisiana: "I'm through with the river. A place of my own, that's what I want. . . . A country place—a plantation. A big one" (13).

Stephen's construction of Harrow does not hinder his connection to surrounding communities. Instead, it unites him with the Louisiana aristocracy, who welcome his aspiration to American citizenship. Stephen articulates his private self and such public relations through the dream of Harrow: "That was it, Stephen thought. To live like this—graciously, with leisure to cultivate the tastes and to indulge every pleasure—a man must be free of labor. Leave the work for the blacks. Breed a new generation of aristocrats. Yes, there was no doubt about it. . . . He knew what he wanted now: freedom for himself and his sons; mastery over this earth; a dynasty of men who could stride this American soil unafraid, never needing to cheat and lie and steal" (30). For Stephen, cheating, lying, and stealing were counterproductive ways of excelling as an American. Gambling was initially what determined his cultural activity and was his primary source of income. New Orleans, Stephen realizes at one point, "was a gambler's paradise," and "the Americans played poker" (44).

On first setting foot in New Orleans, he meanders over to The Swamp, a venue for poker games, and observes cheaters, sore losers wielding guns, and ensuing bloody violence. Here, Stephen still acknowledges the role of poker in his self-Americanization in New Orleans. However, he begins to admit that the rampant unfairness and incivility of the sport threaten his survival in Louisiana, not to mention the design of Harrow.

Certainly, Harrow is not Stephen's first entrepreneurial consideration. He first imagines investing in the construction of "two palatial gaming houses" that an Englishman is planning for New Orleans. But this project turns out not to have been respectable. The social chasm between Creoles and Americans would have hindered the ability of the houses to earn sufficient revenue—that is, a combination of Creole and American money—to remain profitable. Thus, Stephen considers another option: a fifteen hundred–acre strip of land next to the residence owned by Hugo Waguespack, a German gambler. Stephen outwits him in a game of poker and kills him in a duel.

With the help of a scandalous man named Tom Warren, Stephen purchases the fifteen hundred–acre strip of land for $30,000. He also buys many "good," "well-trained" "blacks" from the West Indies in order to plant and grow sugarcane and, in some newly cleared backlands, cotton (58, 102). This land—along with Hugo's, which Stephen secures after killing him—becomes Harrow, where generations of Foxes, he imagines, will reside and forge their identity in Louisiana.

Despite the initially poor condition of the land, Stephen "worked in the fields like a Negro," just as industriously as his own Negroes. As a result, the crop grows and sells for a good price (102). Business expands, along with slave labor. By 1831, after about six years of development,[39] Harrow becomes the most successful of the prosperous plantations of Bayou County. Between 1840 and 1853, thanks to Stephen's adoption of revolutionary technology for processing sugar, the plantation nearly triples its production (207, 330–31). This kind of "respectable" business earns Stephen the name "gentleman planter" (113).

Yet Stephen is more than a planter. On the plantation, he builds a majestic mansion, signaling his arrival in the southern aristocracy, with its entrepreneurial success and personal wealth. Stephen's neighbors travel to Harrow again and again to observe the construction of a house that, even while unfinished, they admire as "Fox's Lair" (118).

The most complete description of Harrow comes in the novel's preface. There the mansion is portrayed at the turn of the twentieth century—close to eighty years after its construction—as a shell of its former self. Traces of its grandiosity remain, despite the ravages of time:

It is better to see Harrow at night. The moonlight is kinder. The North Wing has no roof and through the eyeless sockets of the windows the stars shine. Yet at night when the moon is at the full, Harrow is still magnificent. By day you can see that the white paint has peeled off and that all the doors are gone, and through them and the windows you can see the mud and the dust over everything. But at night the moon brings back the white again and the shadows hide the weeds between the flagstones. The Corinthian columns stand up slim and silver and the great veranda sweeps on endlessly across the front, and the red flagstone swings in perfect curves through the weed-choked garden where once the cape jasmine grew, past the mud-filled birdbath and the broken crystal ball on the column to the smokehouse and the kitchen house and the sugar mill and the slave quarters.

You walk very fast over the flagstones and resist the impulse to whirl suddenly in your tracks and look back at Harrow. The lights are *not* on. The crystal chandeliers are *not* ablaze. There are no dancers in the great hall. And in the garden the smell of the pinks and the lavenders and the white crepe myrtle and red oleanders and the mimosas and the feathery green and gold acacia and the magnolia fuscatas and the cape jasmines and the roses and lilies and the honeysuckle are ghosts too and figments of the imagination, but so real that at last you turn and scratch the flesh of your palms and your fingers with the harsh and rank reality of the weeds. (vii–viii)

In this beautiful excerpt from a larger description, the shift in narration from second-person ("you") at the outset of the novel to third-person thereafter ("he," "she," "they," etc.) works to establish the tangibility of Harrow, despite and because of the reader's historical displacement. The images still vividly tell a story about the two communities that lived on Harrow— the Foxes in the mansion, and the slaves in the quarters—as well as the events that took place on the plantation to forge the identity of Stephen, his family, and his residence in Louisiana.

The image of Harrow's desolation and dilapidation in the preface does suggest that the dynasty of Harrow failed, as Sutpen's does in *Absalom, Absalom!* But whereas Faulkner thoroughly depicts the demise of Sutpen's Hundred, we do not know why the narrator of *The Foxes of Harrow* informs the reader at the outset that "it is no good to stay" at a deserted and deteriorating Harrow, that when you leave the vicinity "you don't look back" (viii). For the answer, we must first realize that the house, decimated during the Civil War, signifies the complexity and problem of Stephen's vision of a dynasty. Standing beside his son, Etienne, Stephen observes Harrow in all its misery after the Civil War:

Now I must begin again, Stephen thought, and I am old. It must be left to the young men—'Tienne and the rest. And I fear that they will look forever backward to what was. Ye can't turn the world back again, ye must go forward. If they try to shape the world again in the image of the past, they'll waste generations and mountains of blood and treasure in something that cannot succeed because of its very nature. If there is any one thing upon the face of the earth that is unconquerable 'tis human freedom. And if they try to take it away again from the blacks they will end by losing it themselves.

He looked out over the cypress grove, and the oak alley which had now come into sight. Beyond them, through the trailing streamers of Spanish moss, the house gleamed whitely—all except the blackened ruin of the North Wing.

"We must rebuild it," he said.

"No, Father," Etienne said. "We must never rebuild it. Leave it as it is so that never in a generation will any man of our blood forget. We'll build a new house—out on the old Waguespack place—but let Harrow stand as a reminder of what we suffered and what we will never forget or forgive!" (530–31)

Located at the end of *The Foxes of Harrow*, this conversation between Stephen and Etienne explains why and how the narrator, at the novel's outset, portrays Harrow as decrepit in the 1900s. Coincidentally, in *Absalom, Absalom!* Clytemnestra (Clytie) Sutpen, the illegitimate daughter of Thomas Sutpen and one of his slaves, sets ablaze the manor on Sutpen's Hundred in 1909. Around the same time, in other words, the mansions of both Sutpen's Hundred and Stephen's Harrow symbolize a traumatic or eventful past. In the former case, Clytie relieves local townspeople of the desire or the need to explore the myth of Sutpen's peculiarly American individuality and freedom. But *The Foxes of Harrow* does not provide its readers such a luxury. Stephen's deserted house, even eighty years after its erection, expresses poignantly the tragedy of the Civil War.

A compelling thematic and narrative schema defines race in Yerby's novel. While married to Creole royalty, Odalie Arceneaux, Stephen enjoys Desiree, a Creole quadroon. And after Odalie dies while delivering their second child as a stillborn and Desiree leaves him because she cannot have him all to herself, he marries a woman he realizes he has loved all along, Odalie's sister, Aurore. Several other interconnected relationships, successful and failed, fill the novel and justify its claims to the romance genre. For example, Etienne tries to seduce his father's mistress, Desiree, to no avail, then marries Ceclie Cloutier. Ceclie's father, Phillippe, has always been infatuated with Stephen's first wife, Odalie. Stephen's best friend, Andre, marries an American, Amelia. And Stephen facilitates the courtship of two of his slaves, La Belle Sauvage and Achille, who wed and have a child. These relationships allow Yerby to discuss the interracial, cultural, and sexual contact that persisted in the antebellum nineteenth century, the setting of the novel, and the mid-twentieth century, when the novel was published and being read.

Despite being a Creole, Odalie is by no means "incidental" in Stephen's design. The idea of her living at Harrow factors centrally into Stephen's dreams of a dynasty. He designs the mansion to house a family of Foxes who enhance his presence in the local community. "Always I've had the dream of it—the great white house of which I would be master," Stephen says to Odalie. "But 'twas ye that shaped it into reality. When I first saw ye . . . the dream became more than a dream—it became a need, a necessity—an obsession. And for the first time it was a means toward an end rather than an end in itself. Ye were the end, Odalie. Harrow was no longer important then—it was the mistress of Harrow that mattered" (151). Symbolically, Odalie turns the house into Harrow, into something like an American institution that can extend its influence through the generations.

Later, Odalie reiterates Stephen's dream by offering to give him "a son for Harrow," who will be called Etienne. Patrilinearity in the family tree appeals to Stephen's patriarchal senses: "Strange how right the phrasing was: not his son, nor hers, but Harrow's—a son to be shaped by the house into the finely tempered image of a gentleman, who would grow with it until at last he became master of it, until his son came, too, to manhood" (179). Driven by the idea that Harrow should accommodate and nurture a son, he realizes that "now he must work harder." He must erase all debt so that future generations of his family will not inherit it. He must also secure the best educational and cultural training to ensure their qualifications to thrive in the world—"to lead it, rule it, leave their mark upon it." And since Stephen has no "ancestors," "I am become one" (182).

Thus, at the outset of constructing Harrow, Stephen's monomaniacal diligence, much like Thomas Sutpen's monomania in Faulkner's *Absalom, Absalom!* is commensurate with the enforced industry of his slaves. Harrow represents not the reconstruction of history but the beginning of it. It is the origin of morals and values where later Foxes can be proud descendants and torch bearers.

Until the last third of the novel, which concentrates on the exploits of Stephen's son and daughter, Etienne and Julie, *The Foxes of Harrow* focuses primarily on Stephen Fox's pursuit of the kinds of cultural citizenship and leadership in Louisiana that will benefit his wife and children. Eventually, residents of New Orleans begin to rave about his "taste in attire" and self-transformation into "one of the best known gentlemen of the city" (52, 76). By achieving this status, Stephen becomes the stereotypical American—characterized by "enterprise, push, boorishness" and even as "barbarian"—but with "better manners" (190). Uttered by Phillippe Cloutier, a jealous man always friendly toward and infatuated with Stephen's first wife, Odalie, these words capture the specific role of Stephen's sexual reputation in his American identity.

Put another way, Stephen's American style evolves not only from a traditional individualism, but also from his sexual relations with Creole quadroons. In the narrative bulk of *The Foxes of Harrow*, which focuses on Stephen, there are interrelated themes of his entrepreneurship at Harrow and his sociocultural citizenship in Louisiana, the latter of which pivots on his relationships with Creole women. The intersection of these two themes determines the figuration of Harrow as the spatial and palatial epitome of Americanness, on behalf of his Creole wives and his Irish-Creole progeny of Foxes.

As he enjoys sexual relations with a Creole quadroon, Stephen coincidentally gravitates away from degrading people of ostensible African ancestry. His feelings evolve in the context of prevailing debates over the antidemocratic principles of slavery, and over the ongoing tension between blacks and whites that caused the Civil War. Here, Yerby is committed to plotlines focused on slaves, especially Stephen's. He portrays the evolution of the master-slave relationship from Stephen's racist stage of mistreating blacks to the remarkable moment when he becomes a knowledgeable sympathizer opposed to their oppression. At this time, Stephen begins to grapple with the very abolitionist questions that foretell the national-cum-racial crisis of the Civil War.

At the outset of *The Foxes of Harrow*, Stephen's racial discourse is binary, employing mainly the words "black" and "white" to distinguish racial groups. He goes as far as to complain to his friend Andre, as they distinguish Creoles from slaves, "To me there is nothing on earth so repulsive as a black. To sleep with that old monkey—ugh!" (33). And on another occasion, he calls "blacks" "evil," "apes," and "demons" (38). Aside, perhaps, from sleeping with a quadroon—who is black, according to the one-drop rule—certain incidents and interactions with his slaves alter Stephen's worldview. His slaves always respect his industry on the plantation. Whenever he falls ill, slaves such as Tante Caleen, a long-living conjure woman he owns, take care of him and create potions to revive him to full health. Tante Caleen continues to care for him even when, as a married man, his wife becomes his primary caregiver during his occasional bouts of sickness. Over time, as he acquires slaves, Stephen begins to distinguish them by African or Caribbean ancestry, to learn their histories of insurrection, and to recognize the fallacy of certain racial myths that preserve their inferior status in America.[40]

A sign of Stephen's eventual ideological crisis—that is, his confusion about whether he is a protagonist or an antagonist of slavery—occurs halfway through *The Foxes of Harrow*, in March 1836, after approximately a decade of building Harrow. Proverbially, he meets Andre "at the fork of the river road" prior to riding at a gallop into New Orleans (229). Here they commence a discussion about the propriety and political implications of slavery. Against Andre's claim that "[e]verybody knows that slavery is the natural order of things, ordained by God," that "blacks themselves have benefited by it" in being brought "out of ignorance and savagery" and given "useful work," Stephen laments his friend's "Louisiana faculty for self-delusion." "Slavery is a very convenient and pleasant system—for us," Stephen admits. "But I've often had qualms over the rightness of a system which permits me to sell a man as though he were a mule" (230).

Stephen's ideological change of course from racist to would-be abolitionist should jar the reader. Great narrative distance exists between instances of his racism or lack thereof. His progression to black sympathizer, in other words, is not consistent. After making the above statement, Stephen humiliates the brother of his mistress, Desiree, when the young man, despite appearing "white," too slowly accords a Louisiana gentleman and aristocrat the proper or entitled respect (273). (Desiree does rebuke Stephen for his conduct.) This reinscription of racial hierarchy in Stephen's relationship with a Creole quadroon complicates the novel's discernible progression toward deconstructing this hierarchy. Even if we grant such ideological complexity to Stephen, Yerby fails to connect the character's mood swings to the larger dynastic context of *The Foxes of Harrow*.[41]

While sometimes failing in thematic coherence, *The Foxes of Harrow* does refer to compelling debates about the role of race in antebellum American society, especially in relation to democracy, slavery, politics, and the Civil War. By the time of his successful entrepreneurship, Stephen's "philosophy of democracy had become a thing very real to him, for which he was willing to brave the ill-concealed sneers of his fellow planters" (238). This philosophy envisions democracy extending to slaves and recognizes the inherently antidemocratic principles of racial prejudice and oppression intrinsic to slavery. Stephen's revolutionary political stance against the flawed moral theories and national practices of slavery threaten to alienate him from the very local community to which he has been selling himself for decades as an "American." In his mind, however, this freedom to voice political opinion constitutes as much of his Americanness as did his previous complicity in the practices of enslavement that accorded American cultural and legal citizenship to a preselected few.[42]

If *The Foxes of Harrow* begins by defining Stephen's Americanness in terms of his consent to southern values, the novel ends by redefining it as a product of his ideological dissent on the race problem. Yerby's novel does not adhere to the long-standing southern literary vision of the insolubility of the race problem. Rather, it warns, to repeat Stephen's words to his son, if "the young men—'Tienne and the rest" try to "take [freedom] away again from the blacks they will end by losing it themselves" (530). Stephen's house at Harrow remains standing as a historical reminder of the meaning and impact of the Civil War, but also of the dynasty that Stephen can no longer sustain in the postbellum era.

"Something Entirely New in Fiction Sold to the Millions"

The Foxes of Harrow achieved remarkable commercial popularity and distinguished Yerby from his black literary peers. Beginning in 1946, he became a regular on the survey "What America Is Reading," published in the *New York Herald Tribune Weekly Book Review*. (Yerby's first appearance in the magazine was on March 17, 1946.) According to Louis Michaux, manager of the National Memorial Book Store, "the largest Negro book-selling establishment in the United States," *The Foxes of Harrow* was among the top-three books of 1946 sold in Harlem, listed alongside Ann Petry's *The Street* and Fannie Cook's *Mrs. Palmer's Honey*. The Frederick Douglass Center in Harlem also ranked Yerby's novel as a top-three book in 1946, alongside Petry's *The Street* and Oscar Micheaux's *The Case of Mrs. Wingate* (1944), which was still selling well.[43] Within three years, *The Foxes of Harrow* had sold over two million copies.[44]

In 1949, C. L. R. James began writing a book of Marxist cultural criticism and history, *Notes on American Civilization*, reflecting on the commercial success of *The Foxes of Harrow* and Yerby's next three best-selling novels, *The Vixens* (1947), *The Golden Hawk* (1948), and *Pride's Castle* (1949). James underscores Yerby's importance: "The popular writer who in his books has most expressed the modern American feeling for violent, uninhibited direct action and individualistic self-expression is Frank Yerby, a Negro writer." Ironically, James does not refer to Richard Wright, whom he commends earlier in the book for attacking Russian Communism and its satellite parties on the Left for their betrayal of black revolutions surging in the post–World War II era. In a sense, Wright was a "popular writer," having initially sold 250,000 copies of *Native Son* (1940).[45] But Yerby deserves the "climax" of James's *Notes on American Civilization*, for several reasons:

The success of Frank Yerby's novels completes the general picture of the "entertainment" world. . . . Yerby is characteristic of something entirely new in fiction sold to the millions. His characters break every accepted rule of society. They are out for what they want and get it how they can. They cheat, lie, scheme, plot, are brutal, cruel, lustful, expressing their free individuality. They are also successful. It is true that there are powerful elements of sentimentality and society is not in the end destroyed. But the difference between these and previous popular novels of the same genre is immense. The novels are eagerly read by millions who find in them the same satisfaction that is found in the gangster film. . . . Yerby's books are a primitive elemental response to some of the deepest needs of the American people in their reaction to society.[46]

James attributes the success of Yerby's novels to their accomplished depiction of free individualism and their commercial appeal to a large and diverse American readership. Their particular representations of individualism reflect certain ideological trends in the production and consumption of American popular culture. These representations, according to James, enable escapist alternatives for early twentieth-century readers negotiating the crises of interpersonal alienation in modernity.

By communicating at an "elementary" level, James argues, Yerby's novels undermine the notion that literature cannot achieve the instantaneous aesthetic effect of film. Granted, a semiological distinction exists between the two cultural media. Film requires its viewers to synthesize language and create meaning in much the same way that a literary work does, but it does not necessarily or always entail literature's extra cognitive step of reading printed text.

Nonetheless, Yerby's novels were transformed into commercially successful as films. 20th Century Fox released *The Foxes of Harrow* in 1951, Columbia Pictures released *The Golden Hawk* and *The Saracen Blade* (published in 1952) in 1954, and *Pride's Castle* eventually appeared as a television movie. Yet Hollywood's consideration of such novel-to-film adaptations materialized only after a book attracted numerous readers. For C. L. R. James, individualism lay at the heart of that attraction.

Despite the thematic importance of Yerby's "costume novel," however, it did not come close to achieving literary greatness.[47] "I have to stop here and make myself clear," James asserts. "I believe that the novels of Frank Yerby, particularly the last one, are as bad, as writing, as they can possibly be. *Pride's Castle* (the latest) in fact sets a landmark for illiteracy."[48] James's later distinction of Yerby from "high modernist" writers such as T. S. Eliot and James Joyce reveals the extent of the Trinidadian's education in the literary classics of Western civilization. This training embedded in his literary criticism a discernible elitism that at once legitimated him as a classicist yet, ironically, empowered his radical interpretations of popular culture. James's criticism of Yerby's novels thus should not, from our current perspective, discredit James's critical sophistication. Rather, it shows how he could distinguish and assess separately the form from the content of Yerby's novels.

James's denunciation of Yerby's first four novels echoes those of book reviewers. One reviewer said that *The Foxes of Harrow* "never catches the faintest flutter of the breath of life" and "is badly proofread and replete with unorthodox punctuation." Another critic said that "literary standards are irrelevant to [*The Vixens'*] high sheen and jet propulsion." For another critic, *The Golden Hawk*'s "roaring prose belongs in a cartoon balloon, rather than between the corners of a full-price novel." Yet another critic lamented that "an appropriate, albeit probably characteristic, vulgarity pervades [*Pride's Castle's*] expression of nineteenth-century tastelessness."[49]

What does it mean, however, that *The Foxes of Harrow* still enjoyed commercial popularity, despite its (at best) lukewarm critical reception? Yerby never denied that bad writing was an initial phase of his first published novel. In a 1982 interview, he stated that he "remembered that nobody ever went broke underestimating the taste of the American public, so I set out to write the worst possible novel it was humanly possible to write and still get published but it sort of got hold of me, and about half way through, I started revising and improving it."[50] By contrast, when he was not writing the "worst possible" novels, such as when he wrote "seriously" in his nineteenth and twentieth novels, *The Old Gods Laugh* (1964) and *An Odor of Sanctity* (1965), Yerby was apprehensive, if not scared. He believed that the novels resembled—alas!—*literature* of the high-culture sort. He knew they would not sell well and would mark his decline. He was half-correct: while the novels failed to sell as many copies as his early novels, his career survived the literary turn.

Yerby believed that an author's intention to amuse and entertain should have a central place in contemporary American letters. His pursuit of entertainment, he knew, would short-circuit the possibility of his costume novels' achieving canonical status. A formal resistance to high literariness, Yerby's costume novels were admittedly a "genre of light, pleasant fiction." This does not mean, however, that we can or should dismiss them as dishonorably formulaic, predictable, trendy, and thus unliterary, despite the fact that Yerby's discussion of them in his notorious 1959 essay, "How and Why I Write the Costume Novel," might tempt us to do so. According to Walter Nash, "All narratives employ conventions." Yet "in popular fiction the conventions are simplified and more or less fixed, whereas in writing of more advanced pretension the conventional game is free, diverse, endlessly modified."[51] If we take this statement, as many literary critics would, at face value and then characterize Yerby's novels as popular fiction, what are we to make of the fact that he infused them with some of the same literary conventions that most of these critics would, without hesitation, deem canonical?

Yerby's "How and Why I Write the Costume Novel" raises this question as it blurs the canonical and the popular, the classic and the modern. "The classics of today are very nearly always the bestsellers of the past," Yerby writes. "Thackeray, Dickens, Defoe, Byron, Pope, Fielding—the list is endless—enjoyed fabulous popularity in their day. And, crossing the channel, what can one say of Balzac, Hugo, Maupassant, Dumas?"[52] Confessing that he refused to read contemporary novels for literary inspiration, Yerby referred in his early career only to the classics, whose canonicity he tested in two ways: first, they must have been successful (widely read) upon publication; and, second, they must have remained so thereafter.

Of course, this simple test ignores the historical volatility of literary-commercial markets, even of those regarded as canonical today. Nonetheless, Yerby's point is clear: should not his conventional derivations of theme, character, and plot from Henry Fielding's *Joseph Andrews* (1742) and *Tom Jones* (1749), William Makepeace Thackeray's *Vanity Fair* (1847–48), Daniel Defoe's *Moll Flanders* (1722), Emily Brontë's *Wuthering Heights* (1847), and Charlotte Brontë's *Jane Eyre* (1857) qualify his costume novel as a legitimate literary artifact?[53] Perhaps. But in all honesty, Yerby's talents as a writer do not come close to those demonstrated by these novels. Yet his artistic exploration and attempted replication of how they "were read then" and "are being read now" are intellectual causes that at least should earn him a look in current scholarship on African American literary history.

The fact that Yerby resisted contemporary novels and, for that matter, contemporary African American novels, also testifies to his resistance to a generic affiliation with an African American literary tradition whose aesthetics and racial politics he considered provincial and counterproductive. For Yerby, if a novel tried to "instruct" or "preach" propaganda, which characteristic critics often assigned to African American literature of the 1940s, it devalued itself as a form of entertainment. Propaganda here refers to "religion, race, politics, and economics," any of which might transform the novel into a "tract basket," similar to the kind of novels Yerby considered writing earlier in his career. Once he came to his commercial senses, he avoided propaganda "like the plague."[54]

Things changed in 1969, however, when he published *Speak Now: A Modern Novel*. Marking a turning point in Yerby's career, the novel was not a historical romance, a genre that he had applied or modified for his previous twenty-two novels. That earlier work tended to focus on white protagonists and antagonists in settings as far apart as the Unites States, (pre)modern Europe, and the West Indies. *Speak Now* was the first of only three novels he wrote that focused on the African diaspora and featured black main characters in stories about African villages, the slave trade, slavery, miscegenation, or racial oppression in the United States.[55]

Of course, Yerby had published several short stories about race and with black protagonists prior to his career as a novelist. But he refused to return to this traditional genre of African American literature until what turned out to be well into his expatriate years in Spain. He abandoned the costume novel formula after 1964 in order to talk about more serious social issues. Unfortunately for Yerby, however, his change of heart would not endear him to members of the Black Arts Movement, who especially valued both racial realism and political activism in African American literature.

Chapter 7

"A-World-in-Which-Race-Does-*Not*-Matter"

In June 1969, *Negro Digest* ran an advertisement entitled "Literature and the Black Aesthetic in Future Issues of Negro Digest." It announced that an emerging black writer, Amiri Baraka (formerly LeRoi Jones), would "define" the "Black Aesthetic" for readers. Indeed, three months later, Baraka made one of his first entrées into the discussion over the Black Aesthetic in the essay "The Black Aesthetic."

At the outset, Baraka tackles the notion "What does aesthetic mean? A theory in the ether. Shdn't it mean for us Feelings about reality! The degrees of in to self registration Intuit. About REality. In to selves. Many levels of feeling comprehension. About reality."[1] Such a statement, according to Phillip Brian Harper, "coin[s] alternate etymologies and manipulating typography to assert the essential groundedness of the Black Aesthetic."[2] Baraka turned out to be one of the most influential figures in the Black Arts Movement and clung to the idea that the groundedness, or the pragmatism, of the Black Aesthetic was a core principle of African American literature. He held this belief despite the evolution of his aesthetic and racial-political opinions over the two decades of the Black Arts Movement, the 1960s and the 1970s.

Toni Morrison's only short story, "Recitatif," illustrates best an anomalous if postmodern defiance of racial-realist ideologies central to the Black Aesthetic. At the same time, it highlights for us the importance of gender and sexuality to constructions of black identity. It first appeared in *Confirmation: An Anthology of AfricanAmerican Women* (1983), which Amiri Baraka coedited with his wife, Amina Baraka (formerly Sylvia Jones). The anthology proves that Baraka's vision of African American literature remained relatively intact, despite the decline of the Black Arts Movement. The collection also represents a belated and failed attempt at gender-political diplomacy by the movement's former arbiter.[3]

The editorial categorization of black women writers in *Confirmation* as pan-Africanist, anticolonialist, and racially and politically activist cannot account for the nature and implications of Morrison's story.[4] "Recitatif" unsettles the idea that race can be fixed in identity politics and that this so-lution should constitute the sole protocol for reading, writing, and defining African American literature. The story's probing of the strong relation-ships between women also recalls Morrison's long-standing literary effort to accentuate the mutual interests and dependency of women in the face of masculinist, patriarchal, and heterosexual circumstances in American society.

Although Morrison belongs to the generation of black women writing against the Black Aesthetic, "Recitatif" also raises issues about an aca-demic field emerging at that historical juncture, namely, African American literary theory. Practitioners in this field alleged that the Black Arts Move-ment perpetuated certain counterproductive assumptions about racial au-thenticity, essentialism, and realism. In particular, Henry Louis Gates Jr.'s notion of a "hermeneutical circle" of blackness had influenced the study of African American literature in both academic and public settings. Briefly, Gates suggested that the aesthetic or ethical "value" of African American literature corresponded with the degree to which the actual text approached or deviated from readers' initial imagination of the text's intel-lectual authenticity or the author's racial authenticity. Gates's hermeneuti-cal circle of blackness thus described the tendency among critics to perpetuate this correspondence between text and what Gérard Genette has called paratexts, but which Gates calls "pretexts."[5]

Ironically, Gates's formulation reinscribes and exploits the assumptions that it pins to the Black Arts Movement. What is more, it suppresses cru-cial information about the hermeneutical circle's eighteenth-century ori-gins in German philology and its modern-day development in American literary theory. The hermeneutical circle, it turns out, has customarily re-ferred to the circular, variable, and almost paradoxical way in which un-derstanding one part of a text presupposes understanding the whole text, and vice versa. Against this backdrop, I would argue not that all of us are drawn into the hermeneutical circle of African American literature. Rather, Morrison demonstrates a most sophisticated attempt to break out of this circle, even if, at times, she is complicit in reinscribing it.

In this chapter I intend to contribute to recent studies of the Black Arts Movement, which have come a long way since the early 1990s. At that time, David Lionel Smith published a visionary essay, "The Black Arts Movement and Its Critics," in which he bemoans the "paucity" of scholar-ship on the efflorescence of black culture, intellectualism, and politics that spanned the 1960s and the 1970s. In the essay he complains that "the most rudimentary work" remains incomplete and that the recent scholarship tends to be "openly hostile" and "deeply partisan." Consequently, the

movement comes across as an "unappealing" and counterproductive confusion of social theory, aesthetics, nationalism, ethnic chauvinism, and sexism, a negative portrayal that oversimplifies the era's ideological and
historical circumstances. Thus, Smith calls for "careful and balanced scholarship" to set the record straight.[6]

Since David Lionel Smith's clarion call for scholars in 1991, "careful and
balanced scholarship" has slowly but surely emerged. William L. Van De-
burg, Madhu Dubey, Eddie S. Glaude, Adolph Reed Jr., James C. Hall,
Jerry Watts, Wahneema Lubiano, Phillip Brian Harper, Winston Napier,
James Smethurst, and Cheryl Clarke have researched the ways in which
aesthetics, race, gender, sexuality, and class have intersected in the movement. Aside from Dubey and Harper, though, these scholars do not limn
the ideological circumstances under which ideas such as the Black Aesthetic became a synecdoche of the Black Arts Movement. Indeed, people
associated with the movement—and those writing about it afterward—
constantly referred to the "Black Aesthetic." The concept exerts such a
gravitational pull on the discourses informing the movement that it has become a catchall philosophy of cultural expression and racial-political activism. In the analysis of the Black Aesthetic one must also connect gender
politics to the forms of interpersonal relations and cultural expression in
black intellectual communities. Beneath an overarching emphasis on deans
and truants, racial realism and anomalies, in this chapter I seek to make
such connections.

The Black Aesthetic

There are three anthologies of African American literary criticism and the-
ory that best represent the principles of the Black Arts Movement: *Black
Fire: An Anthology of Afro-American Writing* (1968), edited by Baraka and Larry
Neal; and *Black Expression: Essays by and about Black Americans in the Creative
Arts* (1969) and *The Black Aesthetic* (1971), both edited by Addison Gayle Jr.
These collections articulate most clearly the importance of racial self-
pride, collectivity, and nationalism to auguring the Black Aesthetic. By
printing original essays about African American literature, or by reprinting
those that first appeared in *Negro Digest* and *Phylon*, among other black periodicals associated with the Black Arts Movement, *Black Fire, Black Expression*, and *The Black Aesthetic* helped to consolidate aesthetic and
racial-political discussions of the Black Arts Movement.[7] The essays in
these volumes often insist that the art and criticism of black culture has to
be racially authentic, designed, as noted by the subtitle of *Black Expression*,
"by and about Black Americans."

Aside from advocating an authentically black art and criticism, the Black Aesthetic demanded racial and political loyalty from black critics. More specifically, it sought to expose two problems: the antiblack racism of white academics; and the impact of this doctrine on American cultural institutions and practices. The purported scientific objectivity of whites in the academy was believed to be incompatible with black culture. By contrast, black scholars were perceived as having a common racial identity, history, ideology, and political interest. They were believed to be more qualified than white scholars to incorporate racial sensitivity and insight into cultural analysis of Africa and its diaspora.

The impact of black critical ability remained minimal, however. Black Aestheticians believed that the academy refused to acknowledge or help establish the criteria for the study of African American literature and culture. Black critics, furthermore, remained invisible as more and more white critics of black culture dominated academic attention and resources. For these reasons, certain black critics decided to turn their backs on the academy and head toward the "black university," an institution supposedly resistant to academic tendencies to perpetuate white and Western hegemony.[8]

Implicit in this movement from historically white to historically black academic institutions was an equation of the visible presence of black bodies with the assumed presence of certain racially specific experiences and ideological values, including loyalty to the interests of black communities. This dynamic, it was hoped, would diversify academic intellectualism and thereby foster a critical subjectivity capable of improving the way black art and artists were classified, interpreted, and appreciated.

Many of these issues pertain to the cultural politics of racial realism. The academy, it was said, not only resorted to ahistorical formalisms that failed to connect art with lived reality, it also favored white cultural and academic renditions of black people over black renditions of black people. Cultural representations of the race thus returned to the lamentable days of stereotypical enterprises like blackface minstrelsy. In order to combat this problem, black artists bore the burden of rendering life experience realistically—of "telling it like it is."

The approaches of the Black Arts Movement, consistent with the cultural genealogy of racial realism that I have so far examined, had to be pragmatic. They had to enhance the ideological relationships between artists and critics within the race, heighten collective racial self-awareness, develop unique racial perspectives of the world, and encourage racial-political activism. Deplorable were those black authors and critics who, prior to the Black Arts Movement, had promoted Americanism, Westernism, universalism, or whiteness.[9]

In *Black Expression* and *The Black Aesthetic*, Addison Gayle Jr. captures this rather harsh and reductive criticism of truant black writers. Gayle argues that three of Paul Laurence Dunbar's novels and most of his poetry suggest that the nineteenth-century author "would not have written about the black experience at all" if he were not compelled to do so by critical and commercial influence. Dunbar "internalized the definitions handed him by the American society," especially those of one of his "white liberal mentors," William Dean Howells.[10] Other black writers, furthermore, had "traveled the road of Phillis Wheatley." Ann Petry, Zora Neale Hurston, William Attaway, Willard Motley, and Frank Yerby "negated or falsified their racial experiences in an attempt to transform the pragmatics of their everyday lives into abstract formulas and theorems."[11] Gayle accuses even Alain Locke, who, ironically, at times was ideologically aligned with the Black Arts Movement, of leading the charge, championed later by Albert Barnes and Ralph Ellison, that "the New Negro [should] turn inward to self expression" and forgo attempts "to make white men listen."[12] Gayle's language typifies the writing of other protagonists of the Black Arts Movement.[13] Coincidentally, the number of anomalous texts declined markedly during this period, after the abundance produced in the 1950s.

Baraka, one of the leaders of the Black Arts Movement, argued for the proper kind of African American literature, one that reflected the pragmatic ethos and aesthetics of racial realism. In "The Myth of a 'Negro Literature,'" first delivered as an address at the American Society for African Culture on March 14, 1962, then printed in *Black Expression* in 1969, Baraka is consistent with the aforementioned edicts of the Black Aesthetic. His essay adheres to the principles that the art and criticism of black culture should not cater to white mainstream commercialism, should remain in touch with the folk to assure the racial authenticity of the literary work, and should represent this constituency as "realistically" as possible. A Marxist, Baraka indicts black writers, notably those belonging to the middle class, for having lost sight of these goals. They must take the blame for the long-standing "mediocrity" of "Negro literature."[14]

Baraka's class-based argument echoes almost verbatim the writings of Langston Hughes's "The Negro Artist and the Racial Mountain" (1926) and Richard Wright's "Blueprint for Negro Writing" (1937). The ideological imprints of Hughes and Wright are discernible in Baraka's contention that the desire of a black middle-class to "gain . . . prestige in the white world" has grave consequences: "The abandonment of one's local (i.e., place or group) emotional attachments in favor of the abstract emotional response of what is called the general public (which is notoriously white and middle class) has always been the great diluter of any Negro culture."[15] The writers who fall into this category include Phillis Wheatley, Charles Chesnutt, Jean Toomer, Richard Wright, Ralph Ellison, and James Baldwin.

Baraka also maintains that literary constructions of "reality" should not belong to the vision held by a predominantly white audience, to whom "mediocre" writers of "Negro literature" try to appeal. Rather, they should evolve from a black society capable of distinguishing between the "real" America and the "invented" one. "High art . . . must issue from *real* categories of human activity, *truthful* accounts of human life . . . And aside from Negro music, it is only in the 'popular traditions' of the so-called lower class Negro that these conditions are fulfilled as a basis for human life." What is more, "even most of those who tried to rebel against that invented American were trapped because they had lost all touch with the reality of their experience within the *real* America, either because of the hidden emotional allegiance to the white middle class, or because they did not realize where the reality of their experience lay."[16] Baraka clearly states that literary pragmatism can succeed only in proportion to an author's class status, which, at a lower level, validates her or his racial identity.

One decade later, in the introduction to *Confirmation*, Baraka further inquires into the relationship between art and reality. This focus marks the rhetorical climax of the essay: "[W]hat remains clear is how important history is to seeing and understanding what is real. At another lower level of occurrence is the work meant to elevate perception itself, of experience, of life, and of one's own life, as constant revelation. What is real? What is relevant? What is life for? What is meaning? What is the use of the constant registration given us by our senses?" These questions about realism capture Baraka's major aesthetic philosophy as he ascended to influence during the Black Arts Movement and as coeditor of *Black Fire*.[17]

The goal of *Black Fire*, Baraka reminds us, was to introduce "a new generation of black writers" who represented "clearly, in most cases, the most militant and progressive tradition of AfricanAmerican letters." By contrast, *Confirmation* serves as a multigenerational representation of fifty black women writers and draws attention to their "existence and excellence." By dint of its own existence, the anthology seeks to alert readers to the "white male bourgeois world" of the American canon, which, at that time, featured only "a smattering of black men."[18]

Baraka's claims, to an extent, ring true. The rise of the Black Arts Movement and black studies occurred simultaneously, if not reciprocally, during the political atmosphere of the 1960s.[19] Thus, the collection sought to help bring black women writers into the canonical fold by recognizing their importance to American literature.

The gender politics of *Confirmation*, however, fails to account for the intraracial complicity of the Black Arts Movement and of black men, in particular, in "the injustice of black women's low profile in the world of literature."[20] During this movement, the collective drive of black writers to combat racism sprang, in part, from an indigenous patriarchy that infused the political and literary discourses of black nationalism with sexist, if not also misogynistic, expressions against or about women. As Madhu Dubey points out, "the gender identity of black women complicated their position as the racial subjects of black nationalist discourse."[21] Black men, it turns out, represented the main subject of this discourse and, to repeat Baraka's words, of that "most militant and progressive tradition of AfricanAmerican letters." Women, by contrast, were cast or envisioned within the Black Arts Movement, and mostly by black men, as the kind of matriarchal caricatures found in American literature since the decline of slavery. They became symbolic of an oppressive past of racial stereotyping that threatened to derail the prospective mission of the Black Aesthetic.[22]

In *Confirmation*, Baraka's description of women as "triple losers"—that is, as victims of classism, racism, and sexism—works admirably to indict white men for exploiting black women in the service of capitalist labor and patriarchy. He also confronts both white men and white women, even feminists, for their mutual agreement on white supremacy. Written in 1983, Baraka's arguments were in sync with scholars—namely, Barbara Smith, Sherley Ann Williams, Hazel Carby, Mae Gwendolyn Henderson, Valerie Smith, Barbara Christian, and Mary Helen Washington—who were similarly indicting the racism of white feminists directed toward black feminists during and in the aftermath of the Black Arts Movement. These scholars were examining how literary art and criticism enabled black women to inject race into traditional feminist models of gender and sexuality.

However, Baraka discounts the patriarchal alignment of black men and white men as well as their collusion in the denigration of black women. "While liberating an oppositional racial consciousness," to quote Dubey again, "black nationalist ideologues defined black feminine identity within a heterosexual and reproductive frame that reinscribed the white U.S. bourgeois ideology they set out to subvert." An example of this kind of ideology includes the Moynihan Report, "The Negro Family," which identifies patriarchy as more likely than matriarchy to strengthen the black family.[23] Black women had made great strides in correcting such misperceptions and myths. Baraka had not.

The Hermeneutical Circle

Writing in the early 1990s, Henry Louis Gates Jr. recognized black feminist progress. He declared that Americans were witnessing a fourth "efflorescence," or renaissance, of "cutting-edge" "black creativity," beginning with "the literature and criticism by black women published in the early '80s." "These women, and those who came later," Gates would go on to say, "were able to reach both the traditional large readership, which is middle class, white and female, and a new black female audience that had been largely untapped and unaddressed."[24]

Gates has always played a prominent role in recovering, celebrating, or promoting the gender-political interests of black women authors. He has written about, reprinted texts by, or edited critical editions of authors such as Phillis Wheatley, Harriet E. Wilson, Zora Neale Hurston, Gloria Naylor, Alice Walker, and Toni Morrison. His scholarship invaluably highlights how black women writers have negotiated and counteracted what Claudia Tate calls "male texts," or texts asserting a "male narratology in which masculine values and patriarchal ambitions govern the characters' development and in which there is no critique of patriarchal values." In such works, "male expectations, privilege, and proprietary authority" determine stereotypical portrayals of female protagonists and gender discourses.[25] Black women writers have constituted a literary tradition of revising such portrayals and discourses, especially those crystallized during the Black Arts Movement.

The historical difference between black men's literature and black women's literature cannot be stressed enough. The tropes of domesticity in the influential civil rhetoric of Booker T. Washington's *Up from Slavery* (1901) and W. E. B. Du Bois's *The Souls of Black Folk* (1903), for example, define racial freedom in terms of black manhood. By contrast, such "female texts" as Anna Julia Cooper's *A Voice from the South* (1892) and Gertrude B. Mossell's *The Work of the Afro-American Woman* (1894) subvert these male texts by describing racial freedom in terms of black womanhood and feminine citizenship.[26]

Certainly, "female texts" and "male texts" are not without their limitations. They can be essentialist and simplistic, and their mutual exclusivity can belie their moments of confusion. Marlon Ross has reiterated this theoretical point. He is reluctant "to segregate the experiences, writing, structures, and practices of African American men from those of black women," since there can be great ideological overlap. The literature of the Black Arts Movement supports this idea. Nikki Giovanni, in *Black Feeling, Black Talk, Black Judgment* (1968, 1970), subscribes to some of the stereotypes of gender difference and sexuality found in "male texts," even as she attempts to accentuate black female agency. However, Ross does agree that "black manhood should be understood as a peculiarly instituted identity formation with a particular history of its own."[27]

While addressing this history, Gates called into question the limitations of African American literary criticism born out of the Black Arts Movement. Gates was defining himself and the field of African American literary theory against the movement and Baraka, whom he once called its "founder." In the process he derived methodologies that would become commonplace in African American literary studies.

In "Preface to Blackness: Text and Pretext" (1979), for example, Gates sketches "an ironic circular thread of interpretation that commences in the eighteenth century but does not reach its fullest philosophical form until the decade between 1965 and 1975: the movement from blackness as a physical concept to blackness as a metaphysical concept. Indeed, this movement becomes the very text and pretext of the 'blackness' of the recent Black Arts movement, a solidly traced hermeneutical circle into which all of us are drawn." By "physical blackness," Gates is referring to the interconnections between the African "species" and "cranial capacity, regional variation, skin color, and intelligence" found in authenticating documents either prefacing or appended to African American literature in the eighteenth and nineteenth centuries. By "metaphysical blackness," he is referring to the decisive transition of African American literary criticism, beginning in the late nineteenth century, from discussing what was perceptible to the physical senses to what was not, namely, the more abstract thoughts and feelings that critics would essentialize as "black." It is this correlation between external "characteristics" and internal "character," between the physical and the metaphysical, that Gates believes distinguishes the criticism of black-authored texts and determines their ethical and aesthetic values. The irony lies in how critics so "unalike," separated by centuries, ideologies, and even color lines, could operate as "blind men" tracing this hermeneutical circle. By the time of the Black Arts Movement, these men still made aesthetic judgments on "how readily a text yields its secrets or is made to confess falsely on the rack of 'black reality.'"[28]

Ever since "Preface to Blackness," Gates has reiterated the principle of the hermeneutical circle of blackness by reprinting the essay in full or with modifications and by authoring or editing books (literary and scholarly) that employ this idea as a theoretical frame. (The influence of the essay on

African American literary studies goes without saying.) From this work it is apparent that Gates himself has benefited from the hermeneutical circle of blackness, even when he does not call it by name. For example, he has admirably recovered and released Harriet E. Wilson's *Our Nig* (1983) and Hannah Crafts's *The Bondwoman's Narrative* (2002), but only after appending authenticating documents written by himself and, for the latter book, a handwriting expert. Even more recently, he has reintroduced the concept of this circle not only in an essay on Phillis Wheatley published in *The New Yorker* but also in his introduction (cowritten with Nellie McKay) to *The Norton Anthology of African American Literature*.[29]

The very notion of the hermeneutical circle recalls a series of lectures Friedrich Schleiermacher delivered in 1819, entitled "Hermeneutics." Here, Schleiermacher outlines the rules for examining the linguistic and psychological properties and implications of literary texts. In the introduction, he claims that "with summaries like those publishers authorize for prefaces one comes under the influence of their interpretations."[30] Such prefaces, by extension, can help dictate our expectations and our actual reading of a text. Put another way, prefaces could factor into the moment when readers imagine what a text says or means before even seeing it.

However, Gates's notion of the hermeneutical circle, which, indeed, centers on prefaces, does not exactly coincide with Schleiermacher's notion of the hermeneutical circle. Just before the section on prefaces in his lectures, Schleiermacher asserts that interpretations of literary texts "must depend on a knowledge of the whole literary circle a work belongs to, and the whole development of an author himself. . . . An individual element can only be understood in light of its place in the whole text; and therefore, a cursory reading for an overview of the whole must precede the exact exposition."[31] Schleiermacher is identifying not a contradiction between how to interpret one part and the entirety of a text at the same time. Indeed, the preliminary or "cursory reading" resolves that issue. Rather, he is suggesting that the mutual determinacy and dependency of textual parts and wholes involve a sustained critical and circular process. Any understanding of one part is constantly being shaped by an understanding of the whole, and vice versa, until some sort of cognitive resolution is achieved.

The hermeneutical circle fascinated American literary theorists in the 1960s and the early 1970s. Debates included defenses or challenges of the theories put forth by Schleiermacher and, later on, in revised form, by Wilhelm Dilthey, Martin Heidegger, Hans-Georg Gadamer, Leo Spitzer, Murray Krieger, and E. D. Hirsch Jr. According to Wallace Martin, the most recent theorists agreed that what critics "ultimately see" and what they (in literary criticism) "would reveal as existing" are implicit in their "assumptions."[32] He goes on to state another major shared principle at the time: not only "the existential assertion that a critic's being determines what he [or she] sees," but also an extra layer of analytic circularity, namely, the idea that "interpretation proceeds from assumptions about literature as a whole and the world as a whole, but not simply from assumptions about the work itself."[33] How can one escape this hermeneutical circle? Is it possible that the understanding of one part can actually complicate, undermine, or contradict the understanding of another, such that cognitive resolution is *never* achieved?

A close reading of Toni Morrison's "Recitatif" enables us to answer these questions. It is a postmodern-cum-hermeneutical story that forces us, more precisely, to rephrase Wallace Martin's words, to explain how a critic's racial being determines what she or he sees. Morrison explores this idea by complicating the reader's relationship with assumptions about African American literature and the world of racial and cultural difference. In doing so, she breaks out of the hermeneutical circle of African American literature while avoiding the ideological pitfalls of the Black Aesthetic detectible in Baraka's *Confirmation*.

"Recitatif"

"Recitatif" tracks the relationship between the main characters, Twyla (the narrator) and Roberta, for a span of about thirty years, beginning with their first encounter as girls at a shelter (St. Bonaventure). Twyla and Roberta have no fathers. The only father mentioned in the story is Twyla's father-in-law, whom she admires for his longevity, for caring for his family (which includes five children, one of whom is James, her husband), and for his recollection, in detail, of the geocultural traditions unique to Newburgh Hall, the town in which James and his ancestors have always lived.

We do know about Twyla's and Roberta's mothers, however. The women's shared inability to parent their daughters explains why the two girls meet in the first place. Twyla characterizes her mother as such a dancing socialite, and Roberta's as so sick, that the two girls stay at St. Bonaventure for about twenty-eight days until their mothers are ready to retrieve them. Yet by this time, the girls are so absorbed by each other's company that, initially, they do not miss their parents. When their mothers arrive, the girls are reluctant to leave one another. The bond between Twyla and Roberta forms and strengthens during the period when they are separated from their mothers and despite the absence of their fathers.

By the time Morrison published "Recitatif," she had already released novels in which the relationships between women grow in resolve and spirituality due to the absence, violence, or abuse attributable to their parents, particularly their fathers. In her first novel, *The Bluest Eye* (1970), Claudia and Frieda MacTeer form a united front against their mother's constant verbal abuse. They also accept into their "stable" home and ultimately learn to care a great deal about Pecola Breedlove. Pecola comes from a seemingly dysfunctional family, exists in the temporary custody of the county of Lorain, Ohio, and gets raped and impregnated by her father.

In Morrison's second novel, *Sula* (1973), Nel Wright and Sula Peace become intimate friends despite coming from contradictory family histories and households in "Bottom," Ohio. Nel is born into a middle-class and monogamous home with "values." Sula lives in an unstable home and is abandoned by her father. The home is visited by multiple men with whom her domineering mother enjoys sexual relations and is populated by generations of family and various boarders passing through.

These two novels, respectively, interrogate the "masculine will to power" and the "heterosexual cliché of men and women" imagined and endorsed during the Black Arts Movement.[34] They also examine the demands masculinity, patriarchy, and heterosexuality often place on women's minds and bodies and how these demands motivate women to find strength and sustenance in one another rather than in the opposite sex.

At the same time, such a homosocial paradigm is rather deconstructive, in the postmodernist sense of the word. Morrison tends to begin her stories by creating expectations of figures residing on opposite sides of the spectrum—such as Claudia/Frieda and Pecola, Sula and Nel—only to show that these figures are two sides of the same coin. In the process, she breaks down the extreme categories into which we first put these figures. She forces us to rethink the very presumptions or assumptions by which we develop our expectations and understandings of human difference.

With "Recitatif," Morrison began her professional career as a fiction writer with an interest in postmodern relationships between reading and race. Madhu Dubey notes that scholars have long noted the tension between "the idea of authentic racial tradition" and "postmodern ideals of interpretive indeterminacy," public "demands for racial representation" and the "aesthetic subversion of totality, unity, and purity," "racial essentialism" and "self-conscious textuality."[35] But that a literary text's replication of these binaries satisfies the criteria of postmodernism—as in the case of Ishmael Reed's *Mumbo Jumbo* (1972)—does not necessarily mean that it completely disavows all claims to racial realism. "Recitatif," in disrupting the hermeneutical circle, demonstrates the postmodernist ability of African American literature to reify certain aspects of racial difference even as it tries, on various levels, to disrupt the conventions of reading and writing racial identity.

For much of "Recitatif" we encounter details about the differences be-

tween Twyla and Roberta. The climax of the story highlights their differences—particularly how they view each other, their families, and themselves as mothers—and occurs during their public disagreement over
whether "nicer looking" schools should be more integrated and should bus
in kids from underprivileged schools so they can take advantage of the
schools' exceptional educational facilities and resources. As Twyla drives
past a school officials are trying to integrate, she notices Roberta involved
in a public demonstration against bussing. Twyla eventually drives up to
the protest to speak with Roberta, who complains that her children, as a
consequence of the integration, might be shipped out to another, less prestigious school. Twyla responds:

"So what if they go to another school? My boy's being bussed too, and I don't
mind. Why should you?"
   "It's not about us, Twyla. Me and you. It's about our kids."
   "What's more *us* than that?"
   "Well, it is a free country."
   "Not yet, but it will be."
   "What the hell does that mean? I'm not doing anything to you."
   "You really think that?"
   "I know it."
   "I wonder what made me think you were different."
   "I wonder what made me think you were different."

Against the backdrop of the story, Twyla's and Roberta's assertions of
maternal responsibility to their children contrast with the context in which
the women met at St. Bonaventure. The shelter was a place where they
bonded precisely because their own mothers were unavailable for close to
a month. Obviously, this bond was magical, because it ends up lasting three
decades and, if the end of "Recitatif" is any indication, perhaps even
longer. Twyla marries and gives birth to a son, and Roberta becomes the
parent of four stepchildren. Their subsequent commitments to their children build on an early lesson about the problems and implications of
mothers who abandon their children or who cannot meet their every need.
In the argument quoted above, they actually believe the same thing, something that has figured prominently in all of Morrison's novels: the children
are the center of their lives as mothers, and they reflect the women's
choices in life, just as the two women reflect their mothers' choices.
   The discord between Twyla and Roberta lies in how one person disrupts
the expectations of the other. Each person utters the same words ("I wonder what made me think you were different") because she believes that her
friend has defied certain ideological norms, which, as I shall soon elucidate,
are racialized. But the possibility that friendship was only a distraction, that

these norms required only a precise set of circumstances for them to become manifest, disturbs the two women and sheds light on an ideological chasm that probably has always existed between them. That chasm, it turns out, represents the symbolic "color line" that separates blacks and whites. After all, Twyla calls the protest against bussing the product of "racial strife" (255).[36] But Morrison complicates this color line by confusing who stands on either side of it, that is, which of the two main characters is black and which is white.

The racial politics of "Recitatif" begins with that first encounter between Twyla and Roberta and ends with their simultaneous realization that racial differences account as much for the cultural individuality that, at times, has strengthened their relationship as for the ideological disagreements that, at times, have weakened it. The complexity of "Recitatif" arises if we, as readers, try to determine the racial identity of Twyla or Roberta and then align this identity with the array of contextual information or codes Morrison assigns to each protagonist.

We know for a fact that, from Twyla's perspective as narrator, Roberta belongs to "a whole other race" (243). We also know that one is "black" and the other is "white" (253, 255). The overriding theme of "Recitatif" is that neither Twyla's nor Roberta's nor anyone else's racial identification is objective, accurate, or reliable. The ability to identify someone's race is as imprecise as any sort of human perspective is subjective.

When we are compelled to agree with either protagonist's racial identification of the other, when we feel comfortable or confident in putting one of the main characters into a racial box, Morrison confuses the information or codes supporting or undermining this process. Consider these examples that play to black stereotypes: Twyla states that Roberta "sure did . . . smell funny" (243); Twyla's mother "likes to dance all night" (244); Roberta's mother brought "chicken legs and ham sandwiches and oranges and a whole box of chocolate-covered grahams" for her daughter and Twyla, to which Twyla responds that the "wrong food is always with the wrong people" (248). Roberta appreciated the guitarist and songwriter Jimi Hendrix, while Twyla knew little of him (253). Eventually, Twyla supported the bussing of inner-city children to suburban schools while Roberta was against it (255–59). Morrison, in order to subvert the consistency of our racial identifications of Twyla and Roberta, constantly invokes words, situations, and events that, historically, have been associated with—or, more problematically, have stereotyped—a particular race or set of races. At best, this process of identification is premature or provisional, at worst, inaccurate, since identity is always changing according to one's perspective. "Recitatif" prohibits us from advancing beyond this premature or provisional mode of classification. *How* Twyla and Roberta interact and read race compels us to ask *why* they do so. The answer, to repeat, inevitably comes down to which woman is black and which one is white.

Elizabeth Abel has hitherto explored the various possibilities of racial identity in "Recitatif."[37] In arguing that Roberta is black, one could point to her skepticism over "racial harmony." One could look at her "distrust of white intervention and impulse toward a separatist Black Power movement," the result of an "insider's perspective on power and race relations." One could notice her "sophisticated read[ing] of the social scene." One could listen to her telling of "better (although not necessarily more truthful) stories." One could observe her appreciation of Jimi Hendrix. Finally, one could detect, through psychoanalysis, Twyla's "fantasy" as a white person of Roberta's "potency" as a black woman.

In arguing that Twyla is black, however, one can point to an interpretation "emphasizing cultural practices more historically nuanced." The codes include the racial heritage of Twyla's name and the crossover appeal of Hendrix to both races (which undermines the alleged blackness of Roberta). Perhaps most important, the hypothesis about Twyla's racial identity could focus on the climax of the story. Here "Twyla's support of bussing, and of social change generally, and Roberta's self-interested resistance to them" turn out to "position the women along the bitter racial lines that split the fraying fabric of feminism in the late 1970s and early 1980s."

Even these categories of social psychology and cultural history, however, cannot account for all the complexities of characterization that enable Morrison to disrupt the hermeneutical circle. Abel's correspondence with Toni Morrison about "Recitatif" reveals that the historical category of class can further complicate our racial identification of Twyla and Roberta. For example, Roberta's residence in the gentrified Annandale, Newburgh, where rich doctors and IBM executives (including her husband) moved from the suburbs, could imply her whiteness. And Twyla's residence in the ungentrified section of Newburgh, where her husband and his family are working class and where the majority of the town's welfare recipients live, could further imply that she is black. But historically, the firefighters' union to which Twyla's husband belongs in upstate New York was exclusively white, while IBM in the 1960s and the 1970s recruited blacks to work for the company as executives.[38] Given the improbability of interracial marriage in the context of the story, these situations could imply that Twyla is white working class and Roberta, black middle to upper middle class.

In each of these scenarios, the historical fact that racial differentiation has consistently accompanied class differentiation forces us to speculate on whether substituting class for race is a reliable method of human classification. Morrison's hermeneutical concerns—or her concerns about theories of interpretation—drive her confusing of racial and class codes at the expense of historical reality. "Recitatif" is faithful to the historical and contemporary realities of race, yet it does not consistently align these realities with the figures, locales, artifacts, and events in the story. In the process, racial identity remains narratively disrupted and disruptive.

The plethora of historical information that both settles and unsettles our reading of "Recitatif" is further complicated by Twyla and Roberta's disagreement over the racial identity of a mute "old and sandy-colored" "kitchen woman with legs like parentheses" named Maggie (244, 245). She worked at the shelter where the two first met as girls. We know that Maggie plays an important role in the story because, on a couple of occasions, Twyla remembers the moment at St. Bonaventure when Maggie fell in the shelter's orchard. Conflicting memories of this incident eventually drive a wedge between Twyla and Roberta. When the two meet again after a long hiatus and reminisce over their time at St. Bonaventure, Twyla asks Roberta to remember Maggie's accident in the orchard and, afterward, the "gar" (or big) girls laughing at her. Roberta does not remember the fall as an accident at all. Instead, she accuses the girls, along with Twyla, of knocking Maggie down and kicking her.

Later, at the bussing protest, a disagreement between Twyla and Roberta about this charged issue, and the depth of their ideological differences, pivots again on their deviating recollections of the Maggie incident. Roberta's words put it best: "Maybe I am different now, Twyla. But you're not. You're the same little state kid who kicked a poor old black lady when she was down on the ground. You kicked a black lady and you have the nerve to call me a bigot" (257). We can infer, at this instant, that Twyla is a white bigot. However, Maggie's racial identity, the basis of the accusation and of our image of Twyla, turns out to be uncertain. Twyla insists, instead, that Maggie "wasn't black" (258). Eventually, Twyla concentrates on the incident and expresses certainty that she did not abuse and could not have physically abused Maggie. What is more, the worker "wasn't pitch-black" (259).

The racial code of human phenotype is not the only deciding factor in the story, however. Twyla admits to herself that she indeed held a vague desire at that time to knock Maggie down. This desire could make her as culpable as the girls who actually committed the deed: "I tried to reassure myself about the race thing for a long time until it dawned on me that the truth was already there, and Roberta knew it. I didn't kick her; I didn't join in with the gar girls and kick that lady, but I sure did want to. We watched and never tried to help her and never called for help" (259).

Can the desire to commit an act be morally tantamount to actually committing it? Is Twyla, in this sense, no different from the abusive girls? Is Roberta correct, then, in calling Twyla a bigot? Does this mean that Twyla is white? These questions, and their answers, presume the confirmation of Maggie's blackness. But by the end of the story, it becomes clear that we cannot even grant Maggie, much less Twyla and Roberta, a certain racial identity.

When the two women meet again, we learn that Roberta admits her confusion about Maggie: "I really did think she was black. I didn't make that up. I really thought so. But now I can't be sure" (261). Roberta also realizes that Twyla should not bear the burden of being the racial "bigot." Roberta tells her that she, too, wanted to hurt Maggie: "We didn't kick her. It was the gar girls. Only them. But, well, I wanted to. I really wanted them to hurt her. I said we did it, too. You and me, but that's not true. And I don't want you to carry that around. It was just that I wanted to do it so bad that day—wanting to is doing it" (261).

Yet Roberta's confession now casts doubt on whether or not "bigot" is even the appropriate word to describe the private desires and the complicity of both women in Maggie's abuse. We do not know—because the end of "Recitatif" leaves open—the reasons behind Twyla's and Roberta's animosity toward Maggie. The evidence in the story points as much to their racism and classism concerning the "kitchen woman" as to their childish ageism and their prejudice about Maggie's muteness. In the latter case, Twyla has denigrated Maggie as being "deaf" and "dumb," and Roberta has done the same by calling the worker "crazy," a symptom of being "brought up in an institution like [Roberta's] mother was" (259). Roberta feared that this was her destiny, and thus projected her anxiety onto Maggie (261).

Since either Twyla or Roberta may be black, the animosity toward Maggie could also be intraracial, not the product of interracial or interclass difference. This possibility adds another level of complexity, namely, that the confusion about Maggie's racial identity occurs irrespective of Twyla's or Roberta's own racial subjectivity. The circle of racial essentialism, purity, or authenticity surrounding the "black community" is a fiction, if only because one should never be so certain, as is the case with Maggie, of who belongs within or outside it. That community is never as ideologically consistent as its rhetorical service to racial unity has suggested.

One moral of "Recitatif" lies in the story's last line: "What the hell happened to Maggie?" Indeed, the quibbling between Twyla and Roberta over Maggie's racial identity, and our fixation, as readers, on determining with certainty the racial identities of the two main characters and their locus of associations, is not the sole theme of the story, though it is a most important one. Just as significant is the girls' trampling on Maggie and her human rights, which is an ethical problem. Maggie's is the story of how prejudices about a person's disability can lead to the improper transgression of that person's private space, sense of security, and effort to coexist peacefully with others. "Recitatif" suggests that such issues of moral difference tend to be an afterthought of the politics of racial, social, cultural, psychological, emotional, and class difference. However, as the last line of the story suggests, this pattern of prioritization can lead to problematic readings of human experience, past and present.

How does race, then, factor into the argument between Twyla and Roberta excerpted above? When Twyla asks "What's more *us* than [our kids]?" she is suggesting how children reflect their parents, manifest their strengths and weaknesses. She is also implying that race, just as much as, if not more than, any other index of identity (e.g., class), has determined how children have been treated and located within an educational system supposedly built according to demographics.

The role of race in the distribution and quality of education is, of course, historical. It ranges from the legal denial of formal education to blacks, to a separate-but-equal racial paradigm for education, to the de jure abolition but de facto maintenance of this paradigm under the pretext of demographically determined education. Twyla indicts Roberta's role in this history—and, indirectly, her racial identity—when she accuses her of being complicit in preserving the status quo of keeping certain kinds of children (presumably white) in certain kinds of schools ("nicer looking").

Twyla also accuses Roberta of indirectly and regrettably "doing something" to her. From this perspective, the signs the women carry make sense. Roberta's sign during the demonstration—"MOTHERS HAVE RIGHTS TOO!" (256)—implies a direct response to an argument for recognizing those rights that might have been compromised during this "racial strife." Could Roberta's sign be a response to the sign, "WE HAVE RIGHTS," held by a black person? Could Twyla's own sign—"AND SO DO CHILDREN****" (258)—signify race through the trope of offspring? (By the way, Twyla's last sign—"HOW WOULD YOU KNOW?"—makes fun of Roberta's sense of motherhood, which is based not on "authentic" childbirth but on the acquisition and rearing of stepchildren.)

Before we can identify Twyla as black, however, Morrison again confuses racial codes. She returns us to Twyla's anxiety over Roberta's accusation that Twyla is a (white) racist for kicking a (black) woman, Maggie, while she was down. Such strategies of characterization keep us and the hermeneutical circle unstable. They never entirely allow us to oversimplify a protagonist according to certain predetermined beliefs about racial tendencies. As a result, we must refer to various other indices of identity that constitute the multifaceted humanity and history of Twyla and Roberta.

A-World-in-Which-Race-Does-*Not*-Matter

When she wrote "Recitatif," Morrison was resisting the conventional literary overdetermination of race. She would return to that project a decade and a half later in her seventh novel, *Paradise* (1998). *Paradise* tempts readers to determine who, among a group of women in a convent, is the "white girl" shot by a gun, according to the novel's opening sentence. Not only is the girl's identity forever undisclosed, but, as Kathryn Nicol has argued, "this search is ultimately and deliberately frustrated by the omission of positive proof of identity in the text. The question that should be asked is not the question of the identity of the white girl, but the question of who identifies her as white, and why."[39]

A hermeneutical novel of race, *Paradise* belongs to the same mode of literary experimentation Morrison began in "Recitatif." According to Morrison's book of essays, *Playing in the Dark* (1992), the short story and, by implication, the novel represent her attempt to "free up the language from its sometimes sinister, frequently lazy, almost always predictable employment of racially informed and determined chains." The short story "was an experiment in the removal of all racial codes from a narrative about two characters of different races for whom racial identity is crucial."[40] Despite this statement, Morrison does not—indeed, could not—"remove" all racial codes from "Recitatif." The codes always exist in some form in the story. Because we live in a racialized society and bring our own subjective impressions to literary texts, an author can *never* remove racial codes from a text, even if she or he intends to do so. They are almost always projected into it, either consciously or subconsciously, by either the reader or the writer. "Recitatif" exploits the very fact of the indelibility of race by confusing racial codes in order to draw greater attention to them and to the hermeneutical circle itself.

Morrison's vision of African American literature resonates in special ways today. Twenty years after its appearance in *Confirmation*, "Recitatif" appeared in *The Norton Anthology of American Literature* (2003). This was the first time the editors selected Morrison for the anthology. Given that she had been winning nationally and internationally prestigious literary awards since the publication of *Song of Solomon* in 1977, the belatedness of this inclusion is inexcusable and embarrassing. The anthology's introduction mentions the new selections of Latino and Latina writers as well as an excerpt from the posthumous publication of Ralph Ellison's *Juneteenth* (2000), signaling an effort to continue diversifying the anthology. But it does not mention the new inclusion of Morrison.[41]

Nonetheless, the selection of "Recitatif" is welcome and significant. Neither the first nor the second edition of *The Norton Anthology of African American Literature* even mentions the existence of "Recitatif," despite the headnote for Morrison's being one of the most detailed in the book. Ironically, the essay by Morrison that *is* included in the second edition of this anthology, "Unspeakable Things Unspoken: The Afro-American Presence in American Literature" (1989), interrogates the assumptions and definition of African American literature. The essay raises the kind of questions provoked by "Recitatif": "The question of what constitutes the art of a black writer, for whom that modifier is more search than fact, has some urgency. In other words, other than melanin and subject matter, what, in fact, may make me a black writer? Other than my own ethnicity—what is going on in my work that makes me believe it is demonstrably inseparable from a cultural specificity that is Afro-American?"[42]

Such questions underpin Morrison's essay "Home" (1997). A reprint of the keynote lecture she delivered at the 1994 "Race Matters" Conference held at Princeton University, the essay rearticulates her ideas about African American literature in terms of a tradition that is at once "race-specific," free of "racial hierarchy," and a celebration of American cultural nationality: "I have never lived, nor have any of us, in a world in which race did not matter. Such a world, one free of racial hierarchy, is usually imagined or described as dreamscape—Edenesque, utopian, so remote are the possibilities of its achievement. . . . I prefer to think of a-world-in-which-race-does-*not*-matter as something other than a theme park, or a failed and always-failing dream, or as the father's house of many rooms. I am thinking of it as home."[43]

For Morrison, "a-world-in-which-race-does-*not*-matter" means that race does not overdetermine the concepts of human identity, relations, and culture. This does not mean that she desires to "get beyond race" or to deny the fact that "race matters." It goes without saying that Morrison's novels and essays have always asserted the significance of race. But as "Recitatif" shows, her effort to imagine a complex world that allows her to interrogate racial hierarchy and celebrate inclusive Americanism, yet remain attentive to the history of race and racism in the United States, implies a more sophisticated way of thinking about the connection of racial history to the canons or traditions of African American literature. She encourages us to acknowledge, if not also respect, the political intention behind these canons or traditions, even as we attempt to expose their problems for the sake of critique, scholarship, and intellectual progress.

Notes

Introduction

1. In the preface to the second edition of *The Norton Anthology of African American Literature*, the editors indicate that "the trade edition was purchased in great numbers by nonacademics, often members of the growing African American reading public, hungry for texts about themselves" (xxx). Henry Louis Gates Jr. and Nellie Y. McKay, eds., *The Norton Anthology of African American Literature*, 2nd ed. (New York: W. W. Norton, 2004).

2. Toni Morrison has stated: "The question of what constitutes the art of a black writer, for whom that modifier is more search than fact, has some urgency. In other words, other than melanin and subject matter, what, in fact, may make me a black writer? Other than my own ethnicity—what is going on in my work that makes me believe it is demonstrably inseparable from a cultural specificity that is Afro-American?" ("Unspeakable Things Unspoken: The Afro-American Presence in American Literature," *Michigan Quarterly Review* 28.1 [1989]: 1–34, quotation on 19). Rafia Zafar declares that "[c]ritics of African American literature must at some point wrestle with the question of what makes a writer, or her texts, black. Can African descent alone establish a writer's membership in the canon of African American writers?" (*We Wear the Mask: African Americans Write American Literature, 1760–1870* [New York: Columbia University Press, 1977], 6). Claudia Tate has posed the question: "What constitutes a black literary text in the United States? Must it be written by, about, and/or for African Americans?" (*Psychoanalysis and Black Novels: Desire and the Protocols of Race* [New York: Oxford University Press, 1998], 3). Finally, J. Martin Favor has pursued this idea from another angle: "Does a person's racial categorization, the classification of the subject as black, white, or other, necessarily lend a 'racial' character to that person's cultural work?" (*Authentic Blackness: The Folk in the New Negro Renaissance* [Durham, N.C.: Duke University Press, 1999], 5).

3. Mosley has asserted that now is the time for black writers to consider "branch[ing] out past the realism of racism and race," supported previously by "their own desire to document the crimes of America" and by "the white literary establishment's desire for blacks to write about being black in a white world, limitation imposed upon a limitation." Indeed, this process, of "break[ing] the chains of reality and go[ing] beyond into a world of [one's] own creation" is the "hardest thing to do" ("Black to the Future: Science Fiction May Have a Special Allure for African Americans," *New York Times Magazine* [November 1, 1998], 34).

4. Ward Connerly, "Where 'Separate but Equal' Still Rules," *New York Times* (May 8, 2000), sec. A, p. 23.

5. Gérard Genette, *Paratexts* (New York: Cambridge University Press, 1997), 1.

6. Katya Gibel Azoulay, "Outside Our Parents' House: Race, Culture, and Identity," *Research in African Literatures* 27.1 (Spring 1996): 129–42, quotations on 134.

7. Kwame Anthony Appiah, "Reconstructing Racial Identities," *Research in African Literatures* 27.3 (Fall 1996): 68–72, quotations on 68, 69.

8. "Obituary of Frank Yerby," *Daily Telegraph* (London) (January 13, 1992).

9. Cynthia Earl Kerman and Richard Eldridge, *The Lives of Jean Toomer: A Hunger for Wholeness* (Baton Rouge: Louisiana State University Press, 1987), 110–11.

10. "What Do We Need to Teach: Introduction," *American Literature* 65.2 (1993): 325–61, quotation on 326. "What Do We Need to Teach" is a forum in which scholars discuss the academic and cultural politics of the anthologization or canonization of American literature.

11. The complication in this argument, however, is that the meaning of anomalies does not remain constant across ethnic lines, racial formations, and literary history. Indeed, I am disagreeing with Robert Fikes Jr.'s incautious incorporation of black authors and their texts into an African Americanist critical paradigm designed for "white-life" novels. Designed primarily for black authors, his critical model does not guarantee literacy in the various codes governing Asian American and Chicano literary aesthetics and anomalies. For an overview of what he calls the "raceless" fiction of Asian American and Chicano writers, see Robert Fikes Jr., "Suppression of Ethnicity: The 'Raceless' Fiction of Asian American and Chicano Writers," *Connecticut Review* 18.2 (1996): 95–101.

12. See Gene Andrew Jarrett, "Introduction: 'Not Necessarily Race Matter,'" in *African American Literature beyond Race: An Alternative Reader*, ed. Jarrett (New York: New York University Press), 1–22.

13. My literary-critical use of "racial realism" differs in kind and intention from Charles W. Mills's philosophical use and Derrick Bell's legal critiques. See Charles W. Mills, *Blackness Visible: Essays on Philosophy and Race* (Ithaca, N.Y.: Cornell University Press, 1998), 45–48, 56–57, 59; and Derrick Bell, *Faces at the Bottom of the Well: The Permanence of Racism* (New York: Basic Books, 1992), 47, 98–99.

14. Scholarly examples include Tate, *Psychoanalysis and Black Novels;* Favor, *Authentic Blackness*; Robert Reid-Pharr, *Conjugal Union* (New York: Oxford University Press, 1999); James Smethurst, *The New Red Negro* (New York: Oxford University Press, 1999); Madhu Dubey, *Signs and Cities: Black Literary Postmodernism* (Chicago: University of Chicago Press, 2003); and Michelle Wright, *Becoming Black* (Durham, N.C.: Duke University Press, 2004). In popular-culture studies we can point to Phillip Brian Harper, *Are We Not Men?* (New York: Oxford University Press, 1996); John McWhorter, *Authentically Black* (New York: Gotham Books, 2003); and Debra Dickerson, *The End of Blackness* (New York: Pantheon Books, 2004).

15. Raymond Williams, *Keywords: A Vocabulary of Culture and Society* (New York: Oxford University Press, 1983), 261.

16. Louis A. Montrose, "New Historicisms," in *Redrawing the Boundaries: The Transformation of English and American Literary Studies*, ed. Stephen Greenblatt and Giles Gunn (New York: Modern Language Association, 1992), 392–418, quotation on 396.

17. Amy Kaplan, *The Social Construction of American Realism* (Chicago: University of Chicago Press, 1988), 8.

18. W. T. Lhamon Jr., *Raising Cain: Blackface Performance from Jim Crow to Hip Hop* (Cambridge, Mass.: Harvard University Press, 1998), 70–71, 218.

19. Dubey, *Signs and Cities*, 44.

20. John Guillory, quoted in Winfried Siemerling, "Democratic Blues: Houston Baker and the Representation of Culture," in *Cultural Difference and the Literary Text: Plu-*

ralism and the Limits of Authenticity in North American Literatures, ed. Siemerling and Katrin Schwenk (Iowa City: University of Iowa Press, 1996), 40–68, quotation on 41.

21. Peter MacLaren, "Decentering Culture: Postmodernism, Resistance, and Critical Pedagogy," in *Current Perspectives on the Culture of Schools*, ed. N. B. Wyner (Boston: Brookline, 1991), 231–57, quotation on 244.

22. See David R. Roediger, *The Wages of Whiteness* (London: Verso, 1991); Vron Ware, *Beyond the Pale: White Women, Racism, and History* (New York: Verso, 1992); Mike Hill, ed., *Whiteness: A Critical Reader* (New York: New York University Press, 1997); Birgit Brander Rasmussen, *The Making and Unmaking of Whiteness* (Durham, N.C.: Duke University Press, 2001); Richard Delgado and Jean Stefancic, eds., *Critical White Studies: Looking behind the Mirror* (Philadelphia: Temple University Press, 1997); Matt Wray and Annalee Newitz, eds., *White Trash: Race and Class in America* (New York: Routledge, 1997); Ruth Frankenberg, *Displacing Whiteness: Essays in Social and Cultural Criticism* (Durham, N.C.: Duke University Press, 1997); and Clyde Taylor, *The Mask of Art* (Bloomington: Indiana University Press, 1998).

23. Examples include David R. Roediger, ed., *Black on White: Black Writers on What It Means to Be White* (New York: Schocken Books, 1998); Jane Davis, *The White Image in the Black Mind: A Study of African American Literature* (Westport, Conn.: Greenwood Press, 2000); Mia Bay, *The White Image in the Black Mind: African-American Ideas about White People, 1830–1925* (New York: Oxford University Press, 2000); Taylor, *The Mask of Art*; and Tate, *Psychoanalysis and Black Novels*.

24. Bruce Lincoln, *Discourse and the Construction of Society: Comparative Studies of Myth, Ritual, and Classification* (New York: Oxford University Press, 1989), 165–66.

25. Shelley Fisher Fishkin, "Desegregating American Literary Studies," in *Aesthetics in a Multicultural Age*, ed. Emory Elliott, Louis Freitas Caton, and Jeffrey Rhyne (New York: Oxford University Press, 2002), 121–34, quotations on 122, 125.

26. Quoted in ibid., 124–25.

27. Tate, *Psychoanalysis and Black Novels*, 7–8.

28. Ibid., 3.

29. Ibid., 5.

30. Ibid., 9, 10.

31. See ibid., 16, 179, for Tate's discourse of "us."

32. Ibid., 16, 192n6.

33. Michael E. Nowlin, review of *Psychoanalysis and Black Novels*, *Studies in the Novel* 31.2 (Summer 1999): 255–57, quotation on 256.

34. Kenneth W. Warren, *Black and White Strangers: Race and American Literary Realism* (Chicago: University of Chicago Press, 1993), 6, 7.

35. Wahneema Lubiano, "Constructing and Reconstructing Afro-American Texts: The Critic as Ambassador and Referee," *American Literary History* 1.2 (Summer 1989): 432–47, quotations on 432–33.

36. Adolph L. Reed Jr., *W. E. B. Du Bois and American Political Thought: Fabianism and the Color Line* (New York: Oxford University Press, 1997), 130.

37. For more information about characterology, see Gene Andrew Jarrett, "'This Expression Shall Not Be Changed': Irrelevant Episodes, Jim's Humanity Revisited, and Retracing Mark Twain's Evasion in *Adventures of Huckleberry Finn*," *American Literary Realism* 35.1 (Fall 2002): 1–28.

38. Thomas S. Kuhn, *The Structure of Scientific Revolutions*, 3rd ed. (Chicago: University of Chicago Press, 1996), 64–65.

39. According to Toll: "To further distinguish themselves from blackfaced whites, most early black minstrels did not use burnt cork, except for the endmen who used it as

a comic mask" (Robert C. Toll, *Blacking Up: The Minstrel Show in Nineteenth Century America* [New York: Oxford University Press, 1974], 200).

40. Claudia Tate, "Laying the Floor, or the History of the Formation of the Afro-American Canon," *Book Research Quarterly* 3.2 (1987): 60–78, quotation on 63.

41. David Levering Lewis, *When Harlem Was in Vogue* (New York: Oxford University Press, 1989), 183.

42. For Wright's revisiting of these figures in 1940 and other existentialists while an expatriate, see Michel Fabre, *The Unfinished Quest of Richard Wright*, 2nd ed. (Urbana: University of Illinois Press, 1993), 299, 320.

43. A hypothetical connection exists between expatriate novelists and what I would call "expatriate novels," a connection between individual expatriation from a nation and aesthetic expatriation from a national literary tradition. Other examples from the 1950s that support this idea include novels by William Demby, James Baldwin, Chester B. Himes, William Gardner Smith, and Frank Yerby. Wright's expatriate life has largely been ignored by the scholarly community in favor of his pre-expatriate activities. (Admittedly, this book, despite this last-ditch effort to acknowledge counterargument, has evidently perpetuated this neglect.)

44. For an interesting analysis of the methodological tension between studies of popular fiction and the canon, see Scott McCracken, *Pulp: Reading Popular Fiction* (Manchester: Manchester University Press; distributed in the United States by St. Martin's Press, 1998).

45. Susanne B. Dietzel, "The African American Novel and Popular Culture," in *The Cambridge Companion to the African American Novel*, ed. Maryemma Graham (New York: Cambridge University Press, 2004), 156–70.

46. I am not going so far as to categorize Gates as a dean who has encouraged schools of racial realism. In fact, Gates, as I mention earlier, has disparaged scholarly one-to-one mappings of literature and life. However, as I show in the final chapter, there are ways in which he has perpetuated the very principles he has refuted and ascribed to the Black Arts Movement.

47. Wahneema Lubiano, "'But Compared to What?' Reading Realism, Representation, and Essentialism in *School Daze*, *Do the Right Thing*, and Spike Lee Discourse," *Black American Literature Forum* 25.2 (Summer 1992): 253–82, quotations on 262, 268.

48. Claudia Tate, *Domestic Allegories of Political Desire: The Black Heroine's Text at the Turn of the Century* (New York: Oxford University Press, 1992), 8.

49. Hazel Carby, "Foreword," in *Seraph on the Suwanee*, by Zora Neale Hurston (New York: Harper Perennial, 1991), x; Hurston in ibid., xiv.

50. Mae G. Henderson, "James Baldwin: Expatriation, Homosexual Panic, and Man's Estate," *Callaloo* 23.1 (Winter 2000): 313–27, quotation on 313.

Chapter 1

1. Paul Laurence Dunbar, *Majors and Minors* (Toledo, Ohio: Hadley & Hadley, 1896). *Majors and Minors* was published in early 1896, not in 1895, which the uncorrected original copyright page states.

2. William Roscoe Thayer, quoted in Donald Pizer, "Introduction," in *Documents of American Realism and Naturalism*, ed. Pizer (Carbondale: Southern Illinois University Press, 1998), 3–17, quotation on 12.

3. James A. Herne, letter to Paul Laurence Dunbar, quoted in Virginia Cunningham, *Paul Laurence Dunbar and His Song* (New York: Dodd, Mead, 1947), 142.

4. William Dean Howells, "Life and Letters," *Harper's Weekly: A Journal of Civilization* 40 (1896): 630, quotation on 630.

5. Thomas Millard Henry, "Old School of Negro 'Critics' Hard on Paul Laurence Dunbar" (1924), reprinted in *The Messenger Reader: Stories, Poetry, and Essays from* The Messenger *Magazine*, ed. Sondra Kathryn Wilson (New York: Modern Library, 2000), 277–81, on 278.

6. Dunbar's dedication reads: "As my first faint pipings were inscribed to her, I deem it fitting, as a further recognition of my love and obligation, that I should also dedicate these later songs to . . . . . MY MOTHER . . . . . "

7. William Dean Howells, Letter to Ripley Hitchcock, Rare Book and Manuscript Library, Columbia University, New York City; emphasis in original.

8. See Elizabeth Ammons, "Expanding the Canon of American Realism," in Pizer, *Documents of American Realism*, 435–52, quotations on 442.

9. The well-known scholarship on theatrical minstrelsy includes Eric Lott, *Love and Theft: Blackface Minstrelsy and the American Working Class* (New York: Oxford University Press, 1995); and Toll, *Blacking Up*. In relation to poetry, see Gavin Jones, *Strange Talk: The Politics of Dialect Literature in Gilded Age America* (Berkeley and Los Angeles: University of California Press, 1999); and Jean Wagner, *Black Poets of the United States: From Paul Laurence Dunbar to Langston Hughes*, trans. Kenneth Douglas (Urbana: University of Illinois Press, 1973).

10. Lhamon tries to overcome this scholarly impasse: "One does not approve the abhorrent racism in most minstrelsy by emphasizing its presence, then moving on to discuss the form's other—even its counter—aspects. I analyze the multiple aspects in blackface performance because it was not a fixed thing, but slippery in its uses and effects" (Lhamon, *Raising Cain*, 6). At another point, regarding blackface performance, Lhamon writes: "Whether [blackface minstrels'] songs were inaccurate pictures of African-American culture is not the point. Until the cows come home, we might debate how well or ill minstrels copied black culture. But that is a fruitless task and always to be followed by such further imponderables as, What is authentic black culture? Is any authenticity there? What is 'black'?" (44–45).

11. See George Fredrickson, *The Black Image in the White Mind: The Debate on Afro-American Character and Destiny, 1817–1914* (New York: Harper and Row, 1972), 101–2.

12. Dale Cockrell, *Demons of Disorder: Early Blackface Minstrels and Their World* (New York: Cambridge University Press, 1997), 141.

13. Daniel H. Foster, "From Minstrel Shows to Radio Shows: Racism and Representation in Blackface and Blackvoice," paper presented at Modern Language Association Convention (Philadelphia, December 30, 2004), 7.

14. For an analysis of the full range of black stereotypes, see Francis P. Gaines, *The Southern Plantation: A Study in the Development and the Accuracy of a Tradition* (New York: Columbia University Press, 1924); Fredrickson, *Black Image*; Catherine Juanita Starke, *Black Portraiture in American Fiction: Stock Characters, Archetypes, and Individuals* (New York: Basic Books, 1971); and Jean Fagan Yellin, *The Intricate Knot: Black Figures in American Literature, 1776–1863* (New York: New York University Press, 1972). For the relationship of these stereotypes to those of white southern women and men, see Susan J. Tracy, *In the Master's Eye: Representations of Women, Blacks, and Poor Whites in Antebellum Southern Literature* (Amherst: University of Massachusetts Press, 1995).

15. Jean Wagner notes that caricatures were "faithful representations of reality" (*Black Poets*, 47). In "the minds of many," Lott agrees, "blackface singers and dancers became, simply, 'negroes' [and] white theatergoers [were] mistaking blackface performers for blacks" (*Love and Theft*, 20). Gavin Jones puts it another way: blackface minstrelsy

"worked by blurring the line between memory and reality; nostalgic stereotypes were politically powerful because they were so often taken as truths" (*Strange Talk*, 195).

16. Toll talks specifically about black minstrels in two chapters of *Blacking Up*: chap. 7, "Black Men Take the Stage" (195–233); and chap. 8, "Puttin' on the Mask: The Content of Black Minstrelsy" (234–69). The book also includes an invaluable appendix, "Chronological List of Black Minstrel Troupes, 1855–1890" (275–80). The thesis of Toll's work on black minstrels has yet to be refuted. Indeed, in *Love and Theft*, Eric Lott, for example, has rightfully led the contemporary scholarly movement to expose "the historical contradictions and social conflicts the minstrel show opened up." This approach complicates the general revisionist approach of Toll, among others, which sees "minstrelsy as racial domination" and, problematically, as "univocal" (*Love and Theft*, 7, 8). But Lott absolutely agrees with Toll on the subject of black minstrels: "Robert Toll makes it clear that blacks in blackface, far from providing an immediate corrective to minstrel types, actually reinforced them, lent them credibility, no doubt because the newcomers had to fit the ideological forms the minstrel show had itself helped to generate, but also because of the impact of racial ideology on even black performers" (*Love and Theft*, 104).

17. Toll, *Blacking Up*, 201–2.

18. Henry B. Wonham, *Playing the Races: Ethnic Caricature and American Literary Realism* (New York: Oxford University Press, 2004), 30.

19. Lott has already shown this idea with respect to George Washington Cable's lectures to postbellum middle-class audiences (see *Love and Theft*, 31).

20. David W. Blight, *Race and Reunion: The Civil War in American Memory* (Cambridge, Mass.: Belknap Press of Harvard University Press, 2001), 211.

21. On the lack of homogeneity in the plantation tradition, see Wayne Mixon, *Southern Writers and the New South Movement, 1865–1913* (Chapel Hill: University of North Carolina Press, 1980), 76. Mixon shows that Joel Chandler Harris was not entirely proslavery. Mixon (*Southern Writers*, 98) and Gavin Jones (*Strange Talk*, 122–33) have also revealed the complexity of George Washington Cable, who occasionally has been placed in the plantation tradition. For more general discussions of the imagery of the plantation tradition, see Gaines, *The Southern Plantation*; Wagner, *Black Poets*; Tracy, *In the Master's Eye*; and Blight, *Race and Reunion*.

22. Howells, quoted in Alan Trachtenberg, *The Incorporation of America: Culture and Society in the Gilded Age* (New York: Hill and Wang, 1982), 185. Trachtenberg does not give a source for the quotation.

23. Van Wyck Brooks, *The Confident Years: 1885–1915* (New York: Dutton, 1952), 142n.

24. William Dean Howells, letter to Henry B. Fuller, November 10, 1901, in Howells, *Selected Letters, Volume 4: 1892–1901*, ed. Thomas Wortham with Christoph K. Lohmann, David J. Nordloh, and Jerry Herron (Boston: Twayne Publishers, 1981), 274.

25. Michael North points out that C. Alphonso Smith, in his essay on "Negro dialect" in the 1918 *Cambridge History of American Literature*, "dismisses Booker T. Washington and W. E. B. Du Bois not because they did not write in dialect but because they were not of 'unmixed negro blood,' and he ignores Charles W. Chesnutt altogether" (*The Dialect of Modernism: Race, Language, and Twentieth-Century Literature* [New York: Oxford University Press, 1994], 22).

26. This is not to say, however, that a black writer such as Chesnutt did not regard himself as a racial insider. See Joseph R. McElrath Jr., "W. D. Howells and Race: Charles W. Chesnutt's Disappointment of the Dean," *Nineteenth-Century Literature* 51.4 (March 1997): 474–99, on 493n, which discusses Chesnutt's unpublished essays, "An Inside View of the Negro Question" and "The Negro's Answer to the Negro Question,"

along with Howells's praise of Chesnutt's racial insiderness in the essay, "Mr. Charles W. Chesnutt's Stories" (1900). Chesnutt, however, was reluctant to disclose his racial identity at the outset of his career.

27. William Dean Howells, "Introduction to *Lyrics of Lowly Life*," in *The Complete Poems of Paul Laurence Dunbar*, ed. Dunbar (1895; rpt. New York: Dodd Mead, 1970), vii–x, quotation on viii.

28. Ibid., vii–ix.

29. For more definitions of "interracialism," which includes ideas about sexual relations and marriage between blacks and whites and descent, see Werner Sollors, ed., *Interracialism: Black-White Intermarriage in American History, Literature, and Law* (New York: Oxford University Press, 2000).

30. For documents covering the responses in the press and by black intellectuals after the case, see *Plessy v. Ferguson: A Brief History with Documents*, ed. Brook Thomas (Boston: Bedford Books, 1997), 127–67.

31. John Stauffer, *The Black Hearts of Men: Radical Abolitionists and the Transformation of Race* (Cambridge, Mass.: Harvard University Press, 2002), 50. E. W. Metcalf Jr. lists nearly sixty articles published in over forty newspapers and magazines between 1892, when Dunbar first attracted interest by reading poems at the Western Association of Writers in Dayton, Ohio, and 1906, when the poet passed away. See *Paul Laurence Dunbar: A Bibliography* (Metuchen, N.J.: Scarecrow Press, 1975), 106–12. These critics often emphasize Dunbar's literary accomplishments in light of the review of *Majors and Minors*; his other books of poetry, songs, and fiction; his lectures across the nation and abroad; and other biographical information shedding light on the privileges and troubles the poet experienced due to his African ancestry.

32. Dunbar, *Majors and Minors*, 44.

33. Hildegard Hoeller, *Edith Wharton's Dialogue with Realism and Sentimental Fiction* (Gainesville: University Press of Florida, 2000), 13.

34. For incisive analyses of the ways in which sentimentalism is described—romantic, melodramatic, bizarrely plotted, and sensationalist—and of how these descriptions have historically contradicted the descriptions of realism, see Hildegard Hoeller, "Economy and Excess: An Introduction," in ibid., 13; and Elissa Greenwald, *Realism and the Romance: Nathaniel Hawthorne, Henry James, and American Fiction* (Ann Arbor, Mich.: UMI Research Press, 1989), 3–7.

35. According to Myron Simon, Dunbar "derived from his mother some indication of black speech in Kentucky," where she and Dunbar's father were plantation slaves. The poet also "had direct knowledge of the speech of black communities in Ohio, Kentucky, Maryland, and the District of Columbia" ("Dunbar and Dialect Poetry," in *A Singer in the Dawn: Reinterpretations of Paul Laurence Dunbar*, ed. Jay Martin [New York: Dodd, Mead, and Co., 1975], 114–34, quotation on 123).

36. In their collection, Harry R. Warfel and G. Harrison Orians introduce the aesthetics of local color in terms of regional authenticity: "Merit depends upon an author's knowledge, insight, and artistry" (see *American Local-Color Stories*, ed. Warfel and Orians [New York: American Book Co., 1941], x). Warfel and Orians reiterate the long-standing definitions of local color ("*la couleur locale*") established in early nineteenth-century France and refashioned, toward the end of the century, by such American authors as James Lane Allen and Hamlin Garland.

37. Jones, *Strange Talk*, 177–81.

38. Several poems in the "Humor and Dialect" section do not represent such racial expression, however. Dunbar did not write all of the poems in that section in dialect: some appear in formal English, falling solely into the humorous category, including

"The Corn-Stalk Fiddle" (*Majors and Minors*, 116–18), "Curtain" (118), "The Made to Order Smile" (126–27), and "The Dilettante: A Modern Type" (134).

39. Henry B. Wonham, "'I Want a Real Coon': Mark Twain and Late-Nineteenth-century Ethnic Caricature," *American Literature* 72.1 (2000): 117–52, quotation on 120.

40. William Andrews writes: "Through his reviews of Dunbar's poetry, Chesnutt's first stories, and Washington's autobiography, Howells developed a fairly consistent psychological profile of the Afro-American consciousness, one which emphasized the black man's 'conservative' temperament, his positive outlook, his 'patience' in the face of injustice, his 'unfailing sense of humor,' and his freedom from 'bitterness' and subversive impulses" ("William Dean Howells and Charles W. Chesnutt: Criticism and Race Fiction in the Age of Booker T. Washington, *American Literature* 48 [1976]: 327–39, quotation on 335). See also W. D. Howells, "Mr. Charles W. Chesnutt's Stories," *Atlantic Monthly* 85 (1900): 699–701; and idem, "A Psychological Counter-Current in Recent Fiction," *North American Review* 173 (1901): 872–88.

41. William Dean Howells, "An Exemplary Citizen," *North American Review* 173 (1901): 280–88, quotation on 280.

42. See Elizabeth McHenry, *Forgotten Readers: Recovering the Lost History of African American Literary Societies* (Durham, N.C.: Duke University Press, 2002), 234, where McHenry discusses an article in the September 1896 issue of *Woman's Era* (a black periodical) that hails the importance of the review to black communities across the country.

43. For these reviews, see Metcalf, *Paul Laurence Dunbar*, 127–29.

44. Robert B. Stepto, *From Behind the Veil: A Study of Afro-American Narrative* (Urbana: University of Illinois Press, 1979), 17.

45. Walter Hines Page became editor of the *Atlantic Monthly* in 1898 and cofounder in 1899 of Doubleday, Page, and Company. Richard Watson Gilder served (circa 1870) on the editorial board of *Scribner's Monthly*. For the restrictions that Howells, Page, and Gilder imposed on Chesnutt, see Henry B. Wonham, "'The Curious Psychological Spectacle of a Mind Enslaved': Charles W. Chesnutt and Dialect Fiction," *Mississippi Quarterly* 51.1 (Winter 1997–98): 55–69; McElrath, "W. D. Howells and Race"; Andrews, "William Dean Howells"; idem, *The Literary Career of Charles W. Chesnutt* (Baton Rouge: Louisiana State University Press, 1980); Helen M. Chesnutt, *Charles Waddell Chesnutt: Pioneer of the Color Line* (Chapel Hill: University of North Carolina Press, 1952); and Richard H. Brodhead, ed., *The Journals of Charles W. Chesnutt* (Durham, N.C.: Duke University Press, 1993).

46. William Stanley Braithwaite, letter to William Dean Howells, October 7, 1899, in *The William Stanley Braithwaite Reader*, ed. Philip Butcher (Ann Arbor: University of Michigan Press, 1972), 238. As for Braithwaite's poems, however, written mostly in formal English, Howells wrote to Braithwaite: "I do not think your verse always runs clear"—certainly not as "clear" as Dunbar's poems in black dialect (Howells, letter to William S. Braithwaite, October, 12 1908, in W. D. Howells, *Selected Letters, Volume 5: 1902–1911*, ed. William C. Fischer with Christoph K. Lohmann [Boston: Twayne, 1983], 260).

47. Paul Laurence Dunbar, letter to W. D. Howells, July, 13 1896, in *Life in Letters of William Dean Howells*, ed. Mildred Howells, 2 vols. (Garden City, N.Y.: Doubleday, Doran, 1928), vol. 2, 67.

48. Paul Laurence Dunbar, March 15, 1897, letter, reprinted in "Unpublished Letters of Paul Laurence Dunbar to a Friend," *Crisis* 20 (1920): 73–76, quotation on 73.

49. Paul Laurence Dunbar, quoted in Michael Flusche, "Paul Laurence Dunbar and the Burden of Race," *Southern Humanities Review* 11.1 (Winter 1977): 49–61, quotation on 52. In his 1922 preface to *The Book of American Negro Poetry*, James Weldon Johnson argues that Dunbar's dialect poems tended to assign the stereotypical temperaments of

"humor" and "pathos" to blacks (see "Preface to the First Edition," in *The Book of American Negro Poetry*, rev. ed., ed. Johnson [New York: Harcourt Brace and World, 1959], 9–48). For summaries of arguments about whether Dunbar was progressive or retrograde in the African American poetic tradition, see Joanne M. Braxton, "Introduction: The Poetry of Paul Laurence Dunbar," in *The Collected Poetry of Paul Laurence Dunbar*, ed. Braxton (Charlottesville: University Press of Virginia, 1993), ix–xxxvi, on xxix; Jones, *Strange Talk*, 185; Simon, "Dunbar and Dialect Poetry," 118; Ralph Story, "Paul Laurence Dunbar: Master Player in a Fixed Game," *CLA Journal* 27 (1983): 54; Nettels, *Language, Race, and Social Class in Howells's America* (Lexington: University Press of Kentucky, 1988), 83–85; and *Paul Laurence Dunbar* (Boston: Twayne Publishers, 1979), 162–75.

50. For observations about Dunbar's poetic protest and counterdiscourse, see Braxton, "Introduction," xxv; Jones, *Strange Talk*, 187, 190–94; Dickson D. Bruce, "On Dunbar's 'Jingles in a Broken Tongue': Dunbar's Dialect Poetry and the Afro-American Folk Tradition," in Martin, *A Singer in the Dawn*, 94–113, on 111; John Keeling, "Paul Dunbar and the Mask of Dialect," *Southern Literary Journal* 25.2 (Spring 1993): 24–38, on 29; Marcellus Blount, "The Preacherly Text: African American Poetry and Vernacular Performance," *PMLA* 107.3 (May 1992): 582–93, on 586; Darwin Turner, "Paul Laurence Dunbar: The Rejected Symbol," *Journal of Negro History* 52.1 (January 1967): 1–13, on 2; James A. Emanuel, "Racial Fire in the Poetry of Paul Laurence Dunbar," in Martin, *A Singer in the Dawn*, 75–93, on 76.

51. For more information about the inability of audiences to detect racial polemics in black minstrelsy, see Lisa Anderson, "From Blackface to 'Genuine Negroes': Nineteenth-century Minstrelsy and the Icon of the 'Negro,'" *Theatre Research International* 21.1 (Spring 1996): 17–23, esp. 20–23. Regarding readers' misinterpretations of racial polemics in the work of Chesnutt, see Robert C. Nowatzki, "'Passing' in a White Genre: Charles W. Chesnutt's Negotiations of the Plantation Tradition in *The Conjure Woman*," *American Literary Realism* 27.2 (Winter 1995): 20–36, esp. 30, 34n23, 35n27.

52. Paul Laurence Dunbar, letter to Alice Ruth Moore, April 17, 1895, reprinted in Herbert Woodward Martin and Ronald Primeau, eds., *In His Own Voice: The Dramatic and Other Uncollected Works of Paul Laurence Dunbar* (Athens: Ohio University Press), 428. For other examples, see Dunbar's letter to James Matthews dated February 7, 1893, in ibid., 417, and to Dr. Toby, in ibid., 431.

Chapter 2

1. The traditional date of the interview, February 12, 1899, comes from Benjamin Griffith Brawley, *Paul Laurence Dunbar, Poet of His People* (Port Washington, N.Y.: Kennikat Press, 1967), 69, 76. The interview is found in the Paul Laurence Dunbar Collection, Reel IV, Box 16, in the Ohio Historical Society, Columbus.

2. Revell, *Paul Laurence Dunbar*, 139.

3. Kenny J. Williams, "The Masking of the Novelist," in Martin, *A Singer in the Dawn*, 152–207, quotation on 171.

4. Jennifer L. Fleissner, *Women, Compulsion, Modernity: The Moment of American Naturalism* (Chicago: University of Chicago Press, 2004), 6, 13–15.

5. Patrick Rael, *Black Identity and Black Protest in the Antebellum North*, The John Hope Franklin Series in African American History and Culture (Chapel Hill: University of North Carolina Press, 2002), 27–44; McHenry, *Forgotten Readers*, 50.

6. Paul Laurence Dunbar, "England as Seen by a Black Man," *Independent* 48 (September 16, 1897): 4, quotation on 4.

7. Paul Laurence Dunbar, "Recession Never," in *The Paul Laurence Dunbar Reader*, ed. Jay Martin and Gossie H. Hudson (New York: Dodd Mead, 1975), 36–39, quotation on 39.

8. Paul Laurence Dunbar, "The Negroes of the Tenderloin," in ibid., 42.

9. Kevin Gaines, *Uplifting the Race: Black Leadership, Politics, and Culture in the Twentieth Century* (Chapel Hill: University of North Carolina Press, 1996), 193.

10. McHenry, *Forgotten Readers*, 85.

11. Marlon B. Ross, "Trespassing the Colorline: Aggressive Mobility and Sexual Transgression in the Construction of New Negro Modernity," in *Modernism, Inc.*, ed. Jani Scandura and Michael Thurston (New York: New York University Press, 2001), 48–47, quotation on 49.

12. I borrow the phrase "trope of a New Negro" from Henry Louis Gates Jr., "The Trope of a New Negro and the Reconstruction of the Image of the Black," *Representations* 24 (Fall 1988): 129–55. For information about the many contexts of New Negro versus Old Negro in the nineteenth and twentieth centuries, see Wilson J. Moses, "The Lost World of the Negro, 1895–1919: Black Literary and Intellectual Life before the 'Renaissance,'" *Black American Literature Forum* 21.1–2 (Spring–Summer 1987): 61–84, on 71–72; Eric J. Sundquist, *To Wake the Nations: Race in the Making of American Literature* (Cambridge, Mass.: Belknap Press of Harvard University Press, 1993), 333–36; Henry B. Wonham, "Plenty of Room for Us All? Participation and Prejudice in Charles Chesnutt's Dialect Tales," *Studies in American Fiction* 26.2 (Autumn 1998): 131–46, on 138; Gates, "The Trope of the New Negro," 136–47. For more information about literacy as a sign of citizenship and the fact that blacks had to write sophisticated prose, see McHenry, *Forgotten Readers*, 42–49.

13. Richard Watson Gilder disregarded the New Negro protagonists of Chesnutt's *The Marrow of Tradition* (1901) as "amorphous" (quoted in Wonham, "'The Curious Psychological Spectacle,'" 55). Howells criticized non-dialect-speaking black characters as "artificial" (Henry B. Wonham, "Writing Realism, Policing Consciousness: Howells and the Black Body," *American Literature* 67.4 [December 1995]: 701–24, quotation on 708). For more information about the way caricatures afford a "fixed," as opposed to an "amorphous," racial identity according to essentialist logic, see idem, "'I Want a Real Coon,'" 119–20. For an example of Howells's critique of the "bitterness" of Chesnutt's *The Marrow of Tradition*, see "A Psychological Counter-Current in Recent Fiction," *North American Review* 173 (December 1901): 872–88, on 881–83. Howells's critique is examined by McElrath, "W. D. Howells and Race," 498–99.

14. For more information about the failures of racial uplift to temper white prejudice, see McHenry, *Forgotten Readers*, 83, 248, and Rael, *Black Identity*, 43, 55.

15. *Woman's Era*, quoted in McHenry, *Forgotten Readers*, 234.

16. H. T. Kealing, review of *Majors and Minors*, *A.M.E. Church Review* 13 (October 1896): 256–59.

17. Quoted in McHenry, *Forgotten Readers*, 116–17.

18. Quoted in ibid., 235.

19. Quoted in ibid., 120.

20. For more information about the antebellum African American literary objectives in the black press, see ibid., 114–29.

21. For a more detailed analysis of Matthews's essay in the context of the contemporary woman's era, see McHenry, *Forgotten Readers*, 193; and Tate, *Domestic Allegories*, 83.

22. Victoria Earle Matthews, "The Value of Race Literature," *The Massachusetts Review* (Summer 1986): 169–85, on 172–73 (emphasis added). Matthews found Mark Twain culpable of outright "Negro-hating." Howells's "tortuous jugglery of words" could not conceal his racial prejudice (quoted in Fred Miller Robinson, "Afterword,"

The Massachusetts Review [Summer 1986]: 186). For an exceptional analysis of late nineteenth-century works by Twain and Howells in which constructions of black vernacular and culture could conceivably have run counter to Matthews's imagination of racial uplift, see Wonham, "Writing Realism."

23. Paul Laurence Dunbar, letter to Mrs. A. S. Lanahan, in Martin and Hudson, *The Paul Laurence Dunbar Reader*, 450; Paul Laurence Dunbar, letter to Alice Ruth Moore, in ibid., 442.

24. Quoted in Cunningham, *Paul Laurence Dunbar*, 183.

25. The one exception is a reference late in the novel to Fred's encounter with blacks when he tours the streets of Cincinnati ("A quartet of young negroes were singing on the pavement in front of a house") (Paul Laurence Dunbar, *The Uncalled* [New York: Dodd Mead and Company, 1899], 207. All references to the nnovel's pages henceforth appear parenthetically in the main text).

26. For more information about the regional breadth of Dunbar's poetry, see Jones, *Strange Talk*, 197; Revell, *Paul Laurence Dunbar*, 75–83; Braxton, "Introduction," xxiii; Simon, "Dunbar and Dialect Poetry," 123.

27. Howells's *Criticism and Fiction* captures this democratic idealism. "[L]ocal flavor of diction gives me courage and pleasure," Howells smiles in his book (*Criticism and Fiction* [New York: Harper and Brothers, 1892], 135). In cheering the special national vernacular of America while shunning the British preference for "priggish" and "artificial" English, Howells stresses the importance of national and regional authenticity in the construction of character: "For our novelists to try to write Americanly, from any motive, would be a dismal error, but being born Americans, I would have them use 'Americanisms' whenever these serve their turn; and when their characters speak, I should like to hear them speak true American, with all the varying Tennesseean, Philadelphian, Bostonian, and New York accents" (ibid., 137).

28. Donna M. Campbell argues that, due to the scarcity of "the spectacle of men in groups acting against each other for reasons of ideological differences," local-color works "frequently disregard the usual fictional staples: current politics, violence, youth, romantic love, cities, wealth, fashionable society, world travel, and action-filled, intricate plots" (*Resisting Regionalism: Gender and Naturalism in American Fiction, 1885–1915* [Athens: Ohio University Press, 1997], 21). *The Uncalled* addresses quite a few of these themes.

29. Elizabeth Ammons and Valerie Rohy, "Introduction," in *American Local Color Writing, 1880–1920*, ed. Ammons and Rohy (New York: Penguin, 1998), vii–xxx, esp. ix.

30. David A. Gerber, *Black Ohio and the Color Line, 1860–1915* (Urbana: University of Illinois Press, 1976), 281.

31. See the chapter entitled "Migration, Urbanization, and the City" in ibid., 279–96, for the relationship between black inner cities, residential housing, morality, crime, and flight from these neighborhoods.

32. Reprinted in Williams, "The Masking of the Novelist," 171.

33. Stephen Crane, "Fears Realists Must Wait," in *Stephen Crane: Uncollected Writings*, ed. Olov W. Frychstedt (Uppsala, Sweden: Uppsala Universitet, 1963), 79–82, quotation on 82.

34. Frank Norris, "Zola as a Romantic Writer," in Pizer, *Documents of American Realism and Naturalism*, 168–69, on 168; Frank Norris, "A Plea for Romantic Fiction," in ibid., 171–74, on 172.

35. Howells, *Criticism and Fiction*, 6, 15–16.

36. Norris, "A Plea for Romantic Fiction," 174.

37. Fleissner, *Women, Compulsion, Modernity*, 16.

38. William J. Scheick, *The Ethos of Romance at the Turn of the Century* (Austin: University of Texas Press, 1994), provides such examples as H. Rider Haggard's romanticism,

Henry James's aesthetic romanticism, and the ethical romanticism of C. J. Cutcliffe Hyne and H. G. Wells.

39. Frank Norris, "Frank Norris' Weekly Letter," in Pizer, *Documents of American Realism*, 169–71, quotation on 171.

40. Norris, "Zola as a Romantic Writer," 169.

41. William Dean Howells, quoted in Crane, "Fears Realists Must Wait," 80.

42. Howells defines the realist against such earlier romantic writers as Sir Walter Scott, who wrote in a "cumbrous" and "diffuse" style, tended toward extreme description and analysis, and distrusted the reader's intuition (*Criticism and Fiction*, 21–22).

43. One reviewer laments that "[w]here the narrative is unobstructed it moves swiftly, but the reader is now and then landed in a morass of the author's philosophy. This is, for the most part, so commonplace as to be fairly naïve." The review goes on to say, however, that Dunbar is perfectly naturalist in "his presentation of a soul's struggle with cramping conditions." (Review of *The Uncalled*, *The Nation* 67 [December 29, 1898]: 491.)

44. Reprinted in Martin and Primeau, *In His Own Voice*, 429.

45. William Dean Howells, quoted in J. C. Levenson, "*The Red Badge of Courage* and *McTeague*: Passage to Modernity," in *The Cambridge Companion to American Realism*, ed. Pizer (Cambridge, New York: Cambridge University Press, 1995), 154–77, quotations on 156.

46. The excerpt of Arnold's "Mycerinus" in *The Uncalled* (stanza 9, lines 49–54) reads as follows: "Oh, wherefore cheat our youth, if thus it be, / Of one short joy, one lust, one pleasant dream, / Stringing vain words of powers we cannot see, / Blind divinations of a will supreme? / Lost labour! when the circumambient gloom / But holds, if gods, gods careless of our doom!" (Dunbar, *The Uncalled*, 230).

47. Richard Lehan, "The European Background," in Pizer, *The Cambridge Companion to American Realism*, 47–73, on 62.

48. In order, the reviews of *The Uncalled* are excerpted from *Bookman* 8 (December 1898): 338; *Manchester Guardian* (May 18, 1899): 4; *Tacoma (Washington) Ledger* (April 16, 1899); *New York Times* (October 22, 1898); *New York Observer* (January 19, 1899); *Philadelphia Press* (December 24, 1898); and *New York Evangelist* (December 8, 1898).

49. Review of *The Uncalled*, *New York Times* (October 22, 1898). The laudatory British reviews come from *London Church Gazette* (May 20, 1899); *Liverpool Mercury* (June 7, 1899); *Bristol Mercury* (August 28, 1899); and *Birmingham Post* (September 30, 1899).

50. Winston Napier, "Affirming Critical Conceptualism: Harlem Renaissance Aesthetics and the Formation of Alain Locke's Social Philosophy," *Massachusetts Review* 39.1 (Spring 1998): 93–112, esp. 104.

Chapter 3

1. Alain Locke, letter to Langston Hughes, no date; quoted in George Hutchinson, *The Harlem Renaissance in Black and White* (Cambridge, Mass.: Belknap Press of Harvard University Press, 1995), 390.

2. Charles Johnson, quoted in ibid.

3. "Midwife" was a loaded term that was more often assigned to men (Locke, Carl Van Vechten, Charles S. Johnson, James Weldon Johnson, and Walter White) than to women (Jessie Fauset) during this period. See Marlon Ross, *Manning the Race: Reforming Black Men in the Jim Crow Era* (New York: New York University Press, 2004), 264.

4. In "Youth Speaks," an obvious discrepancy exists between the numbers of men and women Locke canonizes. He puts women poets "in another file" of classification:

Though still in their prime, as veterans of a hard struggle, they must have the praise and grati-
tude that is due them. We have had, in fiction, Chestnutt [*sic*] and Burghardt Du Bois; in drama,
Du Bois again and Angelina Grimke; in poetry Dunbar, James Weldon Johnson, Fenton and
Charles Bertram Johnson, Everett Hawkins, Lucien Watkins, Cotter, Jameson, and in another file
of poets, Miss Grimke, Anne Spencer, and Georgia Douglas Johnson; in criticism and *belles lettres*,
Braithwaite and Dr. Du Bois; in painting, Tanner and Scott; in sculpture Meta Warrick and May
Jackson; in acting Gilpin and Robeson; in music, Burleigh. . . . Then, rich in this legacy, but richer
still, I think, in their own endowment of talent, comes the youngest generation of our Afro-
American culture: in music, Diton, Dett, Grant Still, and Roland Hayes; in fiction, Jessie Fauset,
Walter White, Claude McKay . . . ; in drama Willis Richardson, in the field of the short story, Jean
Toomer, Eric Walrond, Rudolf Fisher; and finally a vivid galaxy of young Negro poets, McKay,
Jean Toomer, Langston Hughes and Countée Cullen. (Alain Locke, "Youth Speaks," *The Survey
Graphic Number* [March 1, 1925]: 659–60, quotation on 659)

5. Alain Locke, "Negro Youth Speaks," in *The New Negro*, ed. Locke (New York:
Simon and Schuster, 1997), 47–53, quotation on 50.

6. Alain Locke, "The Legacy of the Ancestral Arts," in ibid., 254–67, quotation on
264.

7. Most recent scholarly notions of African American modernism are defined as such
interracial appropriations. Hutchinson argues that we must read comparatively the
Harlem Renaissance and American modernism, and American cultural nationalism
and pragmatism, in order to limn the "interracial dynamics" of the Renaissance (*The
Harlem Renaissance*, 14–28). Conversely, Michael North (*The Dialect of Modernism*), Aldon
Lynn Nielsen (*Black Chant: Languages of African-American Postmodernism* [New York: Cambridge University Press, 1997]), and Sieglinde Lemke (*Primitivist Modernism: Black Culture
and the Origins of Transatlantic Modernism* [New York: Oxford University Press, 1998]) have
spearheaded the investigation of the white literary appropriation of black "exotic" or
"primitive" tropes and language in order to achieve the status of "high" modernism.

8. Focusing on intraracial dynamics, Marc Sanders has shown that Sterling Brown
rejected the polarization of New Negro aesthetics and high modernism: Brown's "poetic project unleashes from the blues, folk balladry, and their like their self-consciously
modernist sensibilities and subjectivities," creating a sort of "Afro-modernism" that celebrated the intraracial diversity of the black community. See Sanders, *Afro-Modernist
Aesthetics and the Poetry of Sterling A. Brown* (Athens: University of Georgia Press, 1999),
10, 23.

9. See Smethurst, *The New Red Negro*, 6–76; and Brannon Costello, "Richard Wright's
Lawd Today! and the Political Uses of Modernism," *African American Review* 37.1 (Spring
2003): 39–52, esp. 40.

10. Alain Locke, "The Beauty Instead of Ashes," in Jeffrey C. Stewart, *The Critical
Temper of Alain Locke* (New York: Garland Pub., 1983), 24; Alain Locke, "The Negro's
Contribution to Art and Literature," in Stewart, *The Critical Temper*, 440.

11. Elisa F. Glick, "Harlem's Queer Dandy: African-American Modernism and the
Artifice of Blackness," *Modern Fiction Studies* 49.3 (Fall 2003): 414–42, quotation on 417.

12. For more information about these theoretical differences, see Seth Moglen,
"Modernism in the Black Diaspora: Langston Hughes and the Broken Cubes of Pi-
casso," *Callaloo* 25.4 (2002): 1189–205, esp. 1190–91, 1202n7.

13. Ross, "Trespassing the Colorline," 53.

14. Interracial criticism of the Harlem Renaissance characterizes the work of
Hutchinson, *The Harlem Renaissance*; Ross Posnock, *Color and Culture: Black Writers and the
Making of the Modern Intellectual* (Cambridge, Mass.: Harvard University Press, 1998);
Ann Douglas, *Terrible Honesty: Mongrel Manhattan in the 1920s* (New York: Farrar Straus
and Giroux, 1995); and Mark Helbling, *The Harlem Renaissance: The One and the Many*

(Westport, Conn.: Greenwood Press, 1999). Intraracial criticism characterizes the work of J. Martin Favor, *Authentic Blackness*; William J. Maxwell, *New Negro, Old Left: African-American Writing and Communism between the Wars* (New York: Columbia University Press, 1999); and Wilson Jeremiah Moses, *The Golden Age of Black Nationalism, 1850–1925* (New York: Oxford University Press, 1988).

Interracial criticism focuses on debunking the racial exceptionalism of the New Negro movement, which helped to give rise to the rhetoric of black authenticity. Referring to such principles as American cultural nationalism, pluralism, and pragmatism, this field looks at the importance of interracial and intercultural contact between blacks and whites in the formation of this movement.

By contrast, intraracial criticism centers black identity politics and agency in the discussion of the New Negro movement, foregrounding a theme that interracial criticism has understated. Intraracial criticism prompts us to look at the centrality of racialism during the Harlem Renaissance, because it generated elastic social, cultural, and biological metaphors of race to define the African diaspora. The methodological marriage of interracial and intraracial contexts of criticism is crucial in order to read the Renaissance, especially Locke's writings, which describe New Negro realism first in interracial and interethnic terms in order to achieve an intraracial effect.

15. The Potomac, located in the east central United States, is about 285 miles long, and forms southeast of Cumberland, Maryland, from the confluence of its north and south branches. It flows mostly southeast toward Chesapeake Bay. It constitutes part of the boundary between Maryland and West Virginia and disjoins Virginia from both Maryland and the District of Columbia. During the Civil War, Robert E. Lee's Confederate Army was stationed in Virginia, and the Potomac River represented, for his troops and his southern constituency, an important military and geographical boundary between the Confederacy and the Union. For the notion of the color line, see W. E. B. Du Bois, *The Souls of Black Folk* (New York: Penguin Books, 1989), 1.

16. Ross, *Manning the Race*, 42.

17. For more information about how blacks tried to control the cultural politics of racial representation through artistic forms more intellectually accessible and directly emotive than literary art, see Anne Elizabeth Carroll, *Word, Image, and the New Negro: Representation and Identity in the Harlem Renaissance* (Bloomington: Indiana University Press, 2005); and Martha Jane Nadell, *Enter the New Negroes: Images of Race in American Culture* (Cambridge, Mass.: Harvard University Press, 2004).

18. I am disagreeing with Posnock, *Color and Culture*, and with Paul Gilroy, *Against Race: Imagining Political Culture Beyond the Color Line* (Cambridge, Mass.: Belknap Press of Harvard University Press, 2000), which Simon Gikandi has also critiqued for its universalist appreciation of cosmopolitanism (Gikandi, "Race and Cosmopolitanism," *American Literary History* 14.3 [2002]: 593–615, esp. 599–600).

19. Locke, "The Beauty Instead of Ashes," 24.

20. Locke, "Negro Youth Speaks," 50.

21. Alain Locke, "The American Negro as Artist," in Stewart, *The Critical Temper*, 176.

22. Alain Locke, "Sterling Brown: The New Negro Folk Poet," in *Negro*, ed. Nancy Cunard (London: Wishart and Company, 1934), 88–92, quotations on 89, 90, 92.

23. Howells, "Life and Letters," 630.

24. Locke, "The Legacy of the Ancestral Arts," 256.

25. Alain Locke, "Harlem," *The Survey Graphic Number* (March 1, 1925), 629–30, quotation on 629.

26. Alain Locke, "Enter the New Negro," *The Survey Graphic Number* (March 1, 1925), quotation on 630.

27. Alain Locke, "The New Negro," in Locke, *The New Negro*, 6.

28. Locke, "Enter the New Negro," 631.

29. Johnson, "Preface," in *The Book of American Negro Poetry*, 51.

30. Locke, "The Negro Poets of the United States," in Stewart, *The Critical Temper*, 44.

31. Locke, "The Negro's Contribution," 444.

32. Quotations appear in both Locke, "Youth Speaks," 659; and idem, "Negro Youth Speaks," 47–48.

33. Alain Locke, *The Critical Pragmatism of Alain Locke*, ed. Leonard Harris (Lanham, Md.: Rowman and Littlefield, 1999), 127–40, quoted in Richard Keaveny, "Aesthetics and the Issue of Identity," in *The Critical Pragmatism*, ed. Harris, 133–34.

34. Quotation appears in both Locke, "Youth Speaks," 659; and idem, "Negro Youth Speaks," 50.

35. Glick, "Harlem's Queer Dandy," 416.

36. Locke, "The Beauty Instead of Ashes," 24.

37. Locke, "Negro Youth Speaks," 50.

38. Ibid., 51.

39. See Brent Edwards, *The Practice of Diaspora: Literature, Translation, and the Rise of Black Internationalism* (Cambridge, Mass.: Harvard University Press, 2003), for a critical elaboration of the theoretical meaning of internationalism in the context of the African diaspora. Locke appreciated Maran, and Maran appreciated him, in various ways. The two men had been in correspondence since Maran criticized French colonialism and the pro-French stance of Locke's essay "The Black Watch on the Rhine" (*Opportunity* [January 1924]). The two men met in Paris and became friends. According to Michel Fabre, they "shared an interest in rehabilitating the race and in keeping up aesthetic standards." Maran even published an essay by Locke, "New African-American Poetry," in the newspaper Maran founded, *Les Continents* (September 1924), making it "the first mention of the incipient New Negro movement to appear in France" (Michel Fabre, *From Harlem to Paris: Black American Writers in France, 1840–1980* [Urbana: University of Illinois Press, 1991], 70).

40. Locke, "Youth Speaks," 659–60, quotation on 660; idem, "Negro Youth Speaks," 47–48, 53.

41. Paul Allen Anderson, *Deep River: Music and Memory in Harlem Renaissance Thought* (Durham, N.C.: Duke University Press, 2001), 120.

42. Dewey F. Mosby, in *Henry Ossawa Tanner: Catalogue* (Philadelphia: Philadelphia Museum of Art; New York: Rizzoli International Publications, 1991), 11.

43. Locke, "The Legacy of the Ancestral Arts," 266–67.

44. Mosby, *Henry Ossawa Tanner*, 91.

45. Tanner's genre paintings include *The Banjo Lesson* (1893) and *The Thankful Poor* (1894)

46. For more information about the coon era and its complex iconographic relationship with realism, see Wonham, "'I Want a Real Coon,'" 119, and idem, "'An Art to Be Cultivated': Ethnic Caricature and American Literary Realism," *American Literary Realism* 32.3 (Spring 2000): 185–219, esp. 193.

47. Albert Boime, "Henry Ossawa Tanner's Subversion of Genre," *The Art Bulletin* 75.3 (September 1993): 415–42, quotations on 418–19.

48. Henry Ossawa Tanner, quoted in ibid., 419.

49. For more information about genre in relation to French painters, see Jennifer J. Harper, "The Early Religious Paintings of Henry Ossawa Tanner: A Study of the Influences of Church, Family, and Era," *American Art* 6.4 (Fall 1992): 69–85, esp. 80–81;

for those who missed Tanner's critique of genre, see Boime, "Henry Ossawa Tanner's Subversion," 423.

50. Locke, "The Legacy of the Ancestral Arts," 264, 266.

51. Locke, "The American Negro as Artist," 173.

52. Ibid., 171–72.

53. According to Hutchinson, Locke's pragmatist aesthetics developed from an immersion in James's writings and his theory of value resembles that of Dewey, James, and Royce (*The Harlem Renaissance*, 41); his cultural pluralism embodied a philosophical mixture of Kallen's and Boas's writings (ibid., 69, 84); and he even borrowed his conception of African aesthetics "wholesale" from Albert C. Barnes (ibid., 45).

54. Jesse Tanner, "Introduction," in *Henry Ossawa Tanner: American Artist*, by Marcia M. Matthews (Chicago: University of Chicago Press, 1969), xi–xiv, quotation on xi.

55. Henry Ossawa Tanner, quoted in Boime, "Henry Ossawa Tanner's Subversion," 417–18.

56. For more information about the distinctions in critical ideology between the media of both countries, see Mosby, *Henry Ossawa Tanner*, 12–14; and J. Harper, "The Early Religious Paintings," 84, the latter of which also discusses the public disappointment surrounding Tanner's switch to biblical portraiture.

57. The landscape paintings Tanner submitted include *Horse and Two Dogs in a Landscape* (1891), and the genre paintings include *The Bagpipe Lesson* (1892–93). *Bois d'Amour* (1891) and *Aix-en-Provence* (1894) do suggest that Tanner experimented, however briefly, with French avant-garde styles.

58. Boime, "Henry Ossawa Tanner's Subversion," 438; J. Harper, "The Early Religious Paintings," 70.

59. Tanner, "Introduction," xi–xii.

60. David Levering Lewis, *W. E. B. Dubois: The Fight for Equality and the American Century, 1919–1963* (New York: H. Holt, 2000), 161; Richard Long, "The Genesis of Locke's *The New Negro*," *Black World* 25.4 (1976): 14–20, esp. 16.

61. Marcus Garvey, "Harlem: Mecca of the New Negro," in *The Survey Graphic* (March 1, 1925): quotation on 633.

62. Ibid., quotations on 633.

63. Locke, "Enter the New Negro," 633.

64. For more information about Locke's earlier writings, see Barbara Foley, *Spectres of 1919: Class and Nation in the Making of the New Negro* (Urbana: University of Illinois Press, 2003), 205–17. For the subtext of his editing of *The New Negro*, see ibid., 224–44. I am paraphrasing Locke's line in "The New Negro," the introductory essay in *The New Negro*, that "the mainspring of Negro life" is "radical in tone, but not in purpose" (quoted in ibid., 1).

65. Ibid., 76, 199.

Chapter 4

1. George S. Schuyler, *The Reminiscences of George S. Schuyler* (New York: Columbia University Oral History Collection, 1962), 71.

2. Schuyler traveled from November 1, 1925, until July 4, 1926. "Aframerica Today" appeared in *The Pittsburgh Courier* from December 19, 1925, until April 17, 1926.

3. On June 23, the magazine released "The Negro Artist and the Racial Mountain," which critiques examples of black subjugation of racial pride to an Americanism premised on Anglo-Saxon whiteness.

4. George S. Schuyler, *Black and Conservative: The Autobiography of George S. Schuyler* (New Rochelle, N.Y.: Arlington House, 1966), 157.

5. Schuyler, *Reminiscences*, 75, 78.

6. George S. Schuyler, "The Negro-Art Hokum," *The Nation* 122 (June 16, 1926): 62–63, quotation on 662. *The Nation* hyped up the article by appending to "The Negro-Art Hokum" a note: "An opposing view on the subject of Negro art will be presented by Lanston [*sic*] Hughes in next week's issue."

7. For these and other reviews, see excerpts reprinted in John Earl Bassett, ed., *Harlem in Review: Critical Reactions to Black American Writers, 1917–1939* (Cranbury, N.J.: Susquehanna University Press, 1992), 120–22. For Locke's review, see Stewart, *The Critical Temper*, 212. For *Black No More* as a novel of science fiction, see Jeffrey A. Tucker, "'Can Science Succeed Where the Civil War Failed?' George S. Schuyler and Race," in *Race Consciousness*, ed. Tucker and Judith Jackson Fossett (New York: New York University Press, 1997); and Robert A. Hill and R. Kent Rasmussen, "Afterword," in *Black Empire*, ed. George S. Schuyler (Boston: Northeastern University Press, 1991). See Jeffrey B. Ferguson, *The Sage of Sugar Hill: George S. Schuyler and the Harlem Renaissance* (New Haven, Conn.: Yale University Press, 2005), for Schuyler's allusions to the intelligentsia. See Favor, *Authentic Blackness*, for the subject of passing in *Black No More*.

8. For the reference to Schuyler's "rac(e)ing to the right," see Jeffrey B. Leak, ed., *Rac(e)ing to the Right: Selected Essays of George S. Schuyler* (Knoxville: University of Tennessee Press, 2001). The "urge to whiteness" theory develops in Charles Larson, "Introduction," *Black No More* (New York: Macmillan, 1971).

9. For the minor acknowledgment of Schuyler, see Hazel Arnett Ervin, ed., *African American Literary Criticism: 1773 to 2000* (New York: Twayne, 1999). Schuyler's essay is omitted from Patricia Hill and Bernard W. Bell, eds., *Call and Response: The Riverside Anthology of the African American Literary Tradition* (Boston: Houghton Mifflin, 1998), a more black folk–oriented collection. Hughes's essay is reprinted therein (781–90).

10. *The Crisis* 31.4 (February 1926): quotation on 165. The answers to the questionnaire appeared in *The Crisis* from issue 31.5 (March 1926) until issue 32.5 (September 1926).

11. *The Messenger* 8 (1926): quotation on 361; reprinted in Hutchinson, *The Harlem Renaissance*, 294–95.

12. Locke, "Enter the New Negro," 632; idem, "The New Negro," 10.

13. Napier, "Affirming Critical Conceptualism," 104.

14. George S. Schuyler, "The Negro and Nordic Civilization," *The Messenger* 7.5 (1925): 198–201, 207, quotation on 198.

15. George S. Schuyler, "Thrusts and Lunges," *The Pittsburgh Courier* (August 1, 1925): quotation on 16.

16. George S. Schuyler and Theophilus Lewis, "Shafts and Darts," *Messenger* 7.8 (August 1925): 295, 298, quotation on 298. Although *The Messenger* printed that Schuyler cowrote the column with Theophilus Lewis, a collaboration which ran from issue 6.4 (April 1924) until issue 7.2 (February 1925), the satirical cynicism discernible in Schuyler's independent articles makes an indelible and obvious imprint on "Shafts and Darts."

17. George S. Schuyler, "New York: Utopia Deferred," *The Messenger* 7.10 (1925): 344–49, 370, quotation on 370.

18. The best discussion to date on this subject is Ferguson, *The Sage of Sugar Hill*, which covers Schuyler's essays and short stories between 1925 and 1931.

19. For information about the Irish, see Noel Ignatiev, *How the Irish Became White* (New York: Routledge, 1995). For the Jews, see Karen Brodkin, *How Jews Became White Folks*

and What That Says about Race in America (New Brunswick, N.J.: Rutgers University Press, 1998).

20. For the use of Edward Reuter's *The Mulatto in the United States* (Boston: R. G. Badger, 1918), see E. Franklin Frazier, *The Negro Family in the United States* (Chicago: University of Chicago Press, 1939), esp. chap. 20, "The Brown Middle Class" (317–33).

21. For more information about *The Nation's* racial politics, see Hutchinson, *The Harlem Renaissance*, 209–26.

22. Schuyler, *Black and Conservative*, 157.

23. Robert Bone, *The Negro Novel in America* (New Haven, Conn.: Yale University Press, 1958), calls Schuyler an assimilationist; for the assimilationism of the "lamp-blacked Anglo-Saxon" phrase, see John Cullen Gruesser, *Black on Black: Twentieth-century African American Writing about Africa* (Lexington: University Press of Kentucky, 2000), 680. For "poor choice of words," see Michael W. Peplow and Arthur Paul Davis, *The New Negro Renaissance: An Anthology* (New York: Holt Rinehart and Winston, 1975), 31–39.

24. Schuyler, "The Negro-Art Hokum," 662.

25. Schuyler, "Thrusts and Lunges" (August 1925): 16.

26. Ibid.

27. Schuyler, "The Negro-Art Hokum," 662–63.

28. Locke, "Enter the New Negro," 630.

29. Schuyler, "The Negro-Art Hokum," 662–63.

30. Du Bois, *The Souls of Black Folk*, 5.

31. Rudolph Rocker, *Nationalism and Culture* (Los Angeles: Rocker Publications Committee, 1952), 320.

32. Schuyler, "The Negro-Art Hokum," 663.

33. George S. Schuyler, "Negroes and Artists," *The Nation* 123 (July 14, 1926): quotation on 36.

34. Ibid.

35. All the responses that appeared in *The Nation* 123 (July 14, 1926): 36–37, for the most part, agree with Schuyler and criticize Hughes. These include responses from Schuyler himself, "Negroes and Artists"; Dorothy Fox, "Escaping Seventh Street"; Headley E. Bailey, "Brown-skinned Nordics"; and Michael Gold, "Where the Battle Is Fought." Hughes responded shortly after the publication of the debate to reiterate his point; see "American Art or Negro Art?" in *The Nation* 123 (August 18, 1926): esp. 151. In a review of Hughes's *Fine Clothes to the Jew*, Harry Alan Potamkin, in "Old Clothes," returns to the debate and agrees with the poet about the need for a Negro expression, but criticizes the book for being a poor, unrefined example of such expression (*The Nation* 124 [April 13, 1927]: 403–4). Two writers who lauded Hughes greatly were the poet Fenton Johnson, "Literature Is a Mass Affair" (*New York Amsterdam News* [July 7, 1926]), and the second wife of Marcus Garvey, Amy Jacques Garvey, in "I Am a Negro—and Beautiful," *The Negro World* (Saturday July 10, 1926): 5. The debate continued even into 1931, when Schuyler's *Black No More* was under review. Dorothy Van Doren, in "Black, Alas, No More!" believed that the novelist was "engaged whole-heartedly in an attempt to be as much like the white man as possible. He will be whiter than white; he will, without a thought for the virtues of his own kind, embrace the white man's virtues, although they are foreign to his nature and beyond his comprehension" (*The Nation* 132 [January 25, 1931]: 218–9).

36. See J. A. Rogers, "J. A. Rogers Discusses the Schuyler and Hughes Articles," *New York Amsterdam News* (June 30, 1926): 16; and Gustavus Adolphus Stewart, "The New Negro Hokum," *Social Forces* 6.3 (March 1928): 438–45. Schuyler enjoyed Stewart's article so much that he commented on it in "Views and Reviews," *The Pittsburgh Courier* (Saturday, April 21, 1928): 8.

37. Van Doren, "Black, Alas, No More!" 218–19.

38. Josephine Schuyler, letter to the editor, *The Nation* 132 (April 8, 1931): 382.

39. Favor, *Authentic Blackness*, 112.

40. George S. Schuyler, *Black No More* (New York: Modern Library, 1999). All references to the novel's pages appear parenthetically in the main text.

41. Jones, *Strange Talk*, 104.

42. I borrow from Favor, *Authentic Blackness*, 115, the strategy of alluding to Max Disher's transformation into Matthew Fisher by using the name "Max/Matt."

43. For more information about whom the characters of *Black No More* are spoofing, see Jane Kuenz, "American Racial Discourse, 1900–1930: Schuyler's *Black No More*," *Novel: A Forum on Fiction* 30.2 (Winter 1997): 170–92, on 170.

44. Patricia J. Williams, *The Alchemy of Race and Rights* (Cambridge, Mass.: Harvard University Press, 1991), 44–51.

Chapter 5

1. Richard Wright, letter to Alain Locke, in Manuscript Department, Moorland-Spingarn Research Center, Howard University, Washington, D.C. (July 8, 1937).

2. Foley, *Spectres of 1919*, 5, 7.

3. Smethurst, *The New Red Negro*, 5.

4. Alain Locke, "The Negro: 'New' or Newer: A Retrospective Review of the Literature of the Negro for 1938," in Stewart, *The Critical Temper*, 271–83, quotation on 271.

5. James Baldwin, "Many Thousands Gone," in *Notes of a Native Son* (Boston: Beacon Press, 1955), 24–45, quotation on 32.

6. Richard Wright, "Blueprint for Negro Writing," *New Challenge* 2.2 (Fall 1937): 53–65; Alain Locke, "Spiritual Truancy," *New Challenge* 2.2 (Fall 1937): 63–66. All references to the page numbers of Wright's essay will appear parenthetically in the main text.

7. I focus more on how Locke and Wright considered the Harlem Renaissance a failure than on entering a long-standing debate about whether this was a correct assessment. See Hutchinson, *The Harlem Renaissance*, 14–28, for thorough overviews of the rhetoric of failure.

8. See Brannon Costello, "Richard Wright's *Lawd Today!* and the Political Uses of Modernism," *African American Review* 37.1 (Spring 2003): 39–52, esp. 42 for this discourse. I am disagreeing with Costello's inference that Wright's defense in *Partisan Review* of a writer accused of being "insufficiently radical" indicates his opposition to the field in the mid-to-late 1930s. Wright was quite engaged with radicalism and its protagonists during this period, despite the modernist literatures he might have been attracted to as an artist.

9. See Carla Cappetti, *Writing Chicago: Modernism, Ethnography, and the Novel* (New York: Columbia University Press, 1993), 187–94.

10. For information about the Chicago Renaissance, see Robert Bone, "Richard Wright and the Chicago Renaissance," *Callaloo* 9.28 (Summer 1986): 446–68; Cheryl Lester, "A Response to Lawrence Rodgers," *The Langston Hughes Review* 14.1 & 14.2 (1996): 13–15; Lawrence R. Rodgers, "Richard Wright, Frank Marshall Davis and the Chicago Renaissance," *The Langston Hughes Review* 14.1 & 14.2 (1996): 4–12; Deborah Barnes, "'I'd Rather Be a Lamppost in Chicago': Richard Wright and the Chicago Renaissance of African American Literature," *The Langston Hughes Review* 14.1 & 14.2 (1996): 52–61; Theodore Mason Jr., "A Response to Deborah Barnes' 'I'd Rather Be a Lamppost in Chicago': Richard Wright and the Chicago Renaissance of African Amer-

ican Literature," *The Langston Hughes Review* 14.1 & 14.2 (1996): 62–64; and Cappetti, *Writing Chicago*, 198.

11. Sterling Brown, Arthur Paul Davis, and Ulysses Lee, eds., *The Negro Caravan* (New York: Dryden Press, 1941), 6–7.

12. Bill V. Mullen, *Popular Fronts: Chicago and African-American Cultural Politics, 1935–46* (Urbana: University of Illinois Press, 1999), 4.

13. Michael Denning, *The Cultural Front: The Laboring of American Culture in the Twentieth-Century* (London: Verso, 1996), 38, 62.

14. Wright's most productive year as a published poet was 1935: "Ah Feels It in Mah Bones," *International Literature* 4 (April 1935): 80; "I Am a Red Slogan," *International Literature* 4 (April 1935): 35; "Between the World and Me," *Partisan Review* 2 (July–August 1935): 18–19; "Live and Rise," *Midland Left* 2 (February 1935): 13–14; "Obsession," *Midland Left* 2 (February 1935): 14; "Red Leaves of Red Books," *New Masses* 15.5 (April 30, 1935): 6; "Spread Your Sunrise," *New Masses* 16.1 (July 2, 1935): 26.

15. In 1946, when he first moved to France, Wright redirected many of his efforts into other intellectual and racial political channels. According to Michel Fabre, Wright was involved in "the participation in a third and neutralist force in order to fight against racism more efficiently; the condemnation of totalitarianism in the name of existentialism; the filming of *Native Son*; and his support of the *Présence Africaine* group," which included *Négritude* writers Léopold Sédar Senghor, Aimé Cesaire, and Alioune Diop. Wright became a permanent expatriate in 1947. See Fabre, *The Unfinished Quest of Richard Wright*, 316.

16. Richard Wright, "Negro Writers Launch Literary Quarterly," *Daily Worker* (June 8, 1937): quotation on 7.

17. Richard Wright, "New Negro Pamphlet Stresses Need for U.S. People's Front," *Daily Worker* (October 25, 1937): quotation on 3.

18. For more information about the importance of the radicalism of African American literature published in *Defender* and *Negro Story* to the cultural front, see Mullen, *Popular Fronts*, 44–74, 106–25.

19. Dorothy West, "Dear Reader," *Challenge* (March 1934): 3.

20. According to one of the members of this group, Margaret Walker, in her biography of Wright:

At least five or six members of the South Side Writers' Group contributed to 'Blueprint for Negro Writing': Wright and myself, and possibly Ted Ward, Ed Bland, Russell Marshall, and Frank Marshall Davis. What Wright did was take ideas and suggestions from four or five drafts by others and rewrite them in definite Marxist terms, incorporating strong black nationalist sentiments and some cogent expressions on techniques and the craft of writing. He published it as his own, and I remember my surprise on seeing the printed piece." (Margaret Walker, *Richard Wright: Daemonic Genius* [New York: Amistad, 1988] 355–56n18)

21. Stories were written by Norman Macleod, Benjamin Appel, Valdemar Hill, George B. Linn, and Clarence Hill; poetry by Frank Marshall Davis, Sterling Brown, Owen Dodson, Charles Henri Ford, Robert Davis, Margaret Walker, and Anthony Lespes (translated by Langston Hughes); articles by Wright, Allyn Keith, Eugene Holmes, and Verna Arvey; and reviews by Locke, Marian Minus, Henry Lee Moon, and Ralph Ellison.

22. Alain Locke, "Harlem: Dark Weather-Vane," *The Survey Graphic* (August 1936): 457–62, 493–95, quotation on 457.

23. Dorothy West, letter to Alain Locke, in Manuscript Department, Moorland-Spingarn Research Center, Howard University, Washington, D.C. (September 14, 1937).

24. Alain Locke, "Black Truth and Black Beauty: A Retrospective Review of the Literature of the Negro for 1932," in Stewart, *The Critical Temper*, 215–20, quotation on 217.

25. Locke, "Spiritual Truancy," 63–64.

26. Locke, "Enter the New Negro," 633.

27. Locke, "Spiritual Truancy," 63–66.

28. Ibid.

29. W. E. B. Du Bois, quoted in Cedric J. Robinson, *Black Marxism: The Making of the Black Radical Tradition* (Chapel Hill: University of North Carolina Press, 2000), 237.

30. Smethurst, *The New Red Negro*, 9.

31. Wright, "Negro Writers Launch Literary Quarterly."

32. For more information about Wright's lecture on Hughes (on November 23, 1934), debates with him, and reviews of his plays, see Fabre, *The Unfinished Quest*, 115, 126, 132.

33. Marcus Garvey, quoted in Tony Martin, ed., *African Fundamentalism: A Literary and Cultural Anthology of Garvey's Harlem Renaissance* (Dover, Mass.: Majority Press, 1991), 6.

34. For Wright's discussions of Garveyism, see "How Bigger Was Born," in *Native Son*, ed. Wright (New York: Harper Perennial, 1993), 505–40, esp. 520; and idem, *Black Boy (American Hunger): A Record of Childhood and Youth* (New York: Harper Perennial, 1993), 336–37.

35. Allyn Keith, "A Note on Negro Nationalism," *New Challenge* 2.2 (Fall 1937): 65–69, quotation on 65.

36. See Lewis, *W. E. B. Dubois*, 196; Hill and Rasmussen, "Afterword," 274–77.

37. Wright, "How Bigger Was Born," 327.

38. Richard Wright, "Introduction," in *Black Metropolis: A Study of Negro Life in a Northern City*, ed. St Clair Drake and Horace Cayton (New York: Harcourt Brace, 1945), xvii–xxxiv, quotation on xxix.

39. Certainly, several overviews of the critical reception of *Native Son* and Wright's other works have been done. See John M. Reilly, ed., *Richard Wright: The Critical Reception* (New York: B. Franklin, 1978), xiv–xvii, for *Native Son*, and ix–xli for Wright's entire oeuvre. See Carl Milton Charles, *The Negro Novelist* (Plainview, N.Y.: Books for Libraries Press, 1953), 195–206, for *Native Son*.

40. Most notably, see the review by one of the jurors, Lewis Gannett, *New York Herald Tribune* (March 1, 1940): 17; reprinted in Reilly, *Richard Wright: The Critical Reception* (New York: B. Franklin, 1978), 40.

41. According to Keneth Kinnamon and Michel Fabre, eds., *Conversations with Richard Wright* (Jackson: University Press of Mississippi, 1993), "Sinclair Lewis was the one dissenting judge of the three. He preferred another book. The other two judges, Lewis Gannett and Harry Scherman, threw their hats over the moon in enthusiasm" (5).

42. For a positive assessment, see Samuel Sillen, "The Response to *Native Son*," *New Masses* 35 (April 23, 1940): 25–37; for a negative one, see Burton Rascoe, *American Mercury* 50 (May 1940): 113–16; both reprinted in Reilly, *The Critical Reception*, 77–82, 88–90. By late April, a critical backlash against the overwhelming and immediate praise for *Native Son* is discernible.

43. Sterling Brown, *Opportunity* 18 (June 1940): 185–86; reprinted in Reilly, *The Critical Reception*, 95.

44. The quotations "uncompromisingly realistic" and "fully realized" come, respectively, from Henry Seidel Canby, *Book-of-the-Month Club News* (February 1940): 2–3; "an objectivity which is irresistible," from Jonathan Daniels, *Saturday Review of Literature* 21 (March 2, 1940): 5; Canby and Daniels, respectively reprinted in Reilly, *The Critical Reception*, 40, 51. For the quotation "is a novel only a Negro could have written," Canby,

Book-of-the-Month Club News (February 1940): 2–3; reprinted in Reilly, *The Critical Reception*, 39. For "a performance of great talent," Edward Weeks, *The Atlantic Monthly*, quoted in Charles Poore, *New York Times* (March 1, 1940): 19, reprinted in Reilly, *The Critical Reception*, 43. For "is a Negro and he writes of Negroes," Mary-Carter Roberts, *Washington Star* (March 3, 1940): sec. 5, F–6, reprinted in Reilly, *The Critical Reception*, 55. In sum, as Reilly puts it, "[c]ritics of the book . . . testified to its literary merit mainly by indirection as they remarked upon its power to disturb a reader, measured Bigger by the criterion of plausibility, and compared Wright's story to social reality" (xiv).

45. For the Marxist reviews, see Sillen, "The Response"; idem, *New Masses* 34 (March 5, 1940): 24–25; idem, "The Meaning of Bigger Thomas," *New Masses* 35 (April 30, 1940): 26–28; Ben Davis Jr., (New York) *Sunday Worker* (April 14, 1940): sec. 2, pp. 4, 6; all reviews reprinted in Reilly, *The Critical Reception*, 58–60, 68–76, 77–82, 83–86.

46. Dorothy Canfield Fisher quoted in Peter Monro Jack, "A Tragic Novel of Negro Life in America," *New York Times Book Review* (March 3, 1940): 2, 20; another Fisher citation appears in *Chicago Defender* (March 16, 1940); both reprinted in Reilly, *The Critical Reception*, 53–55, 63–65.

47. For the term "generally Dreiserian," see Poore, *New York Times* (March 1, 1940); for Negro analogy to *An American Tragedy*, see Jack, "A Tragic Novel"; for Steinbeck allusions, see Canby, *Book-of-the-Month Club News* (February 1940); and Malcom Cowley, *New Republic* 102 (March 18, 1940): 382–83.

48. Wright wrote to Locke: "Thanks for allowing me to use your name as a reference on my Guggenheim application." In a letter dated March 27, 1939, he wrote Locke again: "I really got one of the Guggenheim awards, and I want to thank you for recommending me to the Guggenheim people." Richard Wright, letter to Alain Locke, in Manuscript Department, Moorland-Spingarn Research Center, Howard University, Washington, D.C. (September 9, 1938).

49. For information about Ellison's regarding Wright as a mentor, see Ralph Ellison, "That Same Pain, That Same Pleasure: An Interview," in *Shadow and Act* (New York: Vintage International, 1995), 24–44, esp. 15. Ellison discusses *Native Son* in "Recent Negro Fiction," *New Masses* 40 (August 5, 1941): esp. 22–26, and "Richard Wright and Recent Negro Fiction," *Directions* 4 (Summer 1941): esp. 12–13. For Baldwin's description of his relationship with Wright, see "Alas, Poor Richard," in *Nobody Knows My Name* (New York: Vintage, 1993), 181–215, esp. 190.

50. Chester B. Himes, quoted in Michel Fabre and Robert E. Skinner, eds., *Conversations with Chester Himes* (Jackson: University Press of Mississippi, 1995), 49–50.

51. Alain Locke, "Of Native Sons: Real and Otherwise," in Stewart, *The Critical Temper*, 299. For Locke's complete retrospective reviews and contexts of *Uncle Tom's Children* and *Native Son*, see "The Negro: 'New' or Newer" and "Of Native Sons."

52. James Sallis (*Chester Himes: A Life* [New York: Walter and Company, 2001], 88) reprints Constance Webb's impressions of her first encounter with Chester Himes at Richard Wright's home in 1945. She notes that "Wright had read the book [*If He Hollers*] and was enthusiastic."

53. The quotation "wide popular appeal" comes from Stephen F. Milliken, *Chester Himes: A Critical Appraisal* (Columbia: University of Missouri Press, 1976), 74. Hughes went on to say that there were many Negroes "who never murder anyone, or rape or get raped or want to rape, who never lust after white bodies, or cringe before white stupidity, or Uncle Tom, or go crazy with race, or off-balance with frustration" (quoted in Sallis, *Chester Himes*, 68).

54. For reviews of *Their Eyes Were Watching God*, see Locke, *Opportunity* (June 1, 1938); Sterling Brown, *The Nation* (October 16, 1937); Lucille Tompkins, *New York Times Book Review* (September 26, 1937); Sheila Hibben, *New York Herald Tribune Weekly Book Review*

(September 26, 1937). All reviews reprinted in Henry Louis Gates Jr. and Anthony Appiah, eds., *Zora Neale Hurston: Critical Perspectives Past and Present* (New York: Amistad, 1993), 18–22. Indeed, Wright's review came *before* Hurston's review of *Uncle Tom's Children* in "Stories of Conflict," *Saturday Review of Literature* 17 (April 2, 1938): 32.

55. Of Wright's *Uncle Tom's Children*, Hurston remarks that this "is a book about hatreds" and that Wright "does not write [dialect] by ear unless he is tone-deaf" (reprinted in Henry Louis Gates Jr. and Anthony Appiah, eds., *Richard Wright: Critical Perspectives Past and Present* [New York: Amistad, 1993], 3–4).

56. Richard Wright, reprinted in Gates and Appiah, *Zora Neale Hurston*, 16, 17.

57. In 1940, an interviewer summarized Wright's views on this issue: "Probably as interesting as his two works, *Uncle Tom's Children* and *Native Son*, is his reason for writing in the vein that he does. . . . Wright very proudly explained that he is a member of a corps of writers who have for their objective the portrayal of the influence of society on the individual. This school of writers, according to Mr. Wright, includes William Attaway, Arna Bontemps, Langston Hughes, Ralph Ellison, Sterling Brown, Robert Davis, and Eugene Holmes and the movement is growing" (quoted in Kinnamon and Fabre, *Conversations*, 35).

58. Nick Aaron Ford, "A Blueprint for Negro Authors," *Phylon* 11.4 (Fourth Quarter, 1950): 374–77, quotation on 375.

59. Zora Neale Hurston, reprinted in Gates and Appiah, *Richard Wright* 9, 10.

60. Michel Fabre, "From Native Son to Invisible Man: Some Notes on Ralph Ellison's Evolution in the 1950s," in *Speaking for You: The Vision of Ralph Ellison*, ed. Kimberly W. Benston (Washington, D.C.: Howard University Press, 1987), 199–216, quotation on 204. Also see Lawrence P. Jackson Jr., "The Birth of the Critic: The Literary Friendship of Ralph Ellison and Richard Wright," *American Literature* 72.2 (June 2000): 321–55, who has performed a more recent and incisive analysis of the correspondence between Ellison and Wright. Ellison's review of *Black Boy* is entitled "Richard Wright's Blues," *Antioch Review* 5 (June 1945): 198–211. A popular version of the review circulates as a chapter of Ralph Ellison, *Shadow and Act* (New York: Vintage International, 1995), 77–94.

61. Joseph T. Skerrett Jr., "The Wright Interpretation: Ralph Ellison and the Anxiety of Influence," in Benston, *Speaking for You*, 217–30.

62. James Baldwin, "Notes of a Native Son," *Notes of a Native Son* (Boston: Beacon Press, 1965), 13–23.

63. Alain Locke, "Self-Criticism," *Phylon* 11.4 (Fourth Quarter, 1950): 391–92, quotation on 392.

64. Wright, "How Bigger Was Born," 514, 520–21.

65. Thomas D. Jarrett, "Toward Unfettered Creativity: A Note on the Negro Novelist's Coming of Age," *Phylon* 11.4 (Fourth Quarter, 1950): 313–17, quotation on 315.

66. Hugh M. Gloster, "Race and the Negro Writer," *Phylon* 11.4 (Fourth Quarter, 1950): 369–71, quotation on 369–70.

67. A rephrasing of Ellison's prophetic statement to Wright on July 22, 1945, captures this idea. In a letter to Wright, Ellison states that "I'm beginning truly to understand the greatest joke, the most absurd paradox in American history: that simply by striving consciously to become Negroes we are becoming and are destined to become Americans, and the first truly mature Americans at that" (quoted in Fabre, "From Native Son," 207).

68. Albert Halper, quoted in Charles Scruggs, *The Sage in Harlem: H. L. Mencken and the Black Writers of the 1920s* (Baltimore, Md.: Johns Hopkins University Press, 1984), 143.

69. Houston A. Baker Jr., *Blues, Ideology, and Afro-American Literature: A Vernacular Theory* (Chicago: University of Chicago Press, 1984), 69.

70. Era Bell Thompson, "Negro Publications and the Writer," *Phylon* 11.4 (Fourth Quarter, 1950): 304–6, quotation on 306.

71. See Jackson, "The Birth of the Critic," 342, for Hughes; Langston Hughes and Eds., "Some Practical Observations: A Colloquy," *Phylon* 11.4 (Fourth Quarter, 1950): 307–11, on 311, for Petry and West; Ford, "A Blueprint for Negro Authors," 376, for Cullen and Hurston; Locke, "Self-Criticism," 392, for Toomer. Also see Hugh Morris Gloster, *Negro Voices in American Fiction* (Chapel Hill: University of North Carolina Press, 1948), 250, for Attaway; Charles, *The Negro Novelist*, 115, for West, Caldwell, Henderson, Powells, and Bland.

72. Sterling Brown, Arthur P. Davis, and Ulysses Lee, "Introduction," *The Negro Caravan*, vol. 5, quotations in this paragraph on 6–7, 15, 144.

73. Ibid., 6–7.

74. Ibid., 7.

75. "Five American Negro Writers," *Salute* (June 1948): 48–49, quotation on 48.

76. On the topic of sermonizing, see Thomas D. Jarrett, "Sociology and Imagery in a Great American Novel," *The English Journal* 38.8 (October 1949): 518–20, esp. 518. On handicap, see William Gardner Smith, "The Negro Writer: Pitfalls and Compensations," *Phylon* 11.4 (Fourth Quarter, 1950): 297–303, esp. 297; and Gloster, "Race and the Negro Writer," 369. On propaganda, see Smith, "The Negro Writer," 29; and Hughes and Eds., "Some Practical Observations," 209. For one-dimensionality, see Smith, "The Negro Writer," 298. For the Negro Problem as topical and transient, see W. Smith, "The Negro Writer," 299. For the Negro writer's inability to think outside the Negro Problem, see E. Thompson, "Negro Publications," 306. For the Negro writer's hypersensitivity, see Hughes and Eds., "Some Practical Observations," 309; Jarrett, "Toward Unfettered Creativity," 313; Gloster, "Race and the Negro Writer," 369. For Negro writing tending toward didacticism and being fettered to this rhetoric, see Jarrett, "Toward Unfettered Creativity," 313. For the Negro writer's immaturity, see Ford, "A Blueprint," 374; and Locke, "Self-Criticism," 391.

77. E. M. Forster, "[Review of Willard Motley's *Knock on Any Door*]," *New York Times Book Review* (June 19, 1949), quotation on 35.

78. Ellison, "That Same Pain," 16.

79. Lloyd L. Brown, "Which Way for the Negro Writer?" *Masses and Mainstream* 4.3 (March 1951): 53–63, quotations on 60–61.

80. Brown, "Which Way for the Negro Writer? II," *Masses and Mainstream* 4.4 (April 1951): 50–59, quotation on 54.

Chapter 6

1. Yerby was born on September 16, 1915, Wright on September 4, 1908.

2. Richard Wright, quoted in Michel Fabre, ed., *Richard Wright: Books and Writers* (Jackson: University Press of Mississippi, 1990), 177. These words are taken from Wright's unpublished working draft of an introduction to Whit Burnett's compilation of stories about black life, initially entitled *The Violent Conflict* and in 1971 appearing as *Black Hands on a White Face*.

3. Frank Yerby, letter to Michel Fabre, in Richard Wright Collection, Schomburg Center for Research in Black Culture, New York Public Library (April 1, 1963).

4. See Bruce A. Glasrud and Laurie Champion, "'The Fishes and the Poet's Hands': Frank Yerby, a Black Author in White America," *Journal of American and Comparative Cul-*

tures 23.4 (2000): 15–21; and Phyllis Klotman, "A Harrowing Experience: Frank Yerby's First Novel to Film," *CLA Journal* 31.2 (December 1987): 210–22.

5. For noteworthy sustained treatments of Yerby, see Glasrud and Champion, "'The Fishes and the Poet's Hands'"; Darwin Turner, "Frank Yerby: Golden Debunker," *Black Books Bulletin* 1.3 (Spring/Summer 1972): 4–33; Hoyt A. Fuller, "Famous Writer Faces a Challenge," *Ebony* (June 1966): 188–94; Maryemma Graham, "Frank Yerby, King of the Costume Novel," *Essence* 6.6 (1975): 70–71, 88–89, 91–92; Jack B. Moore, "The Guilt of the Victim: Racial Themes in Some Frank Yerby Novels," *Journal of Popular Culture* 8.4 (Spring 1975): 746–66; Klotman, "A Harrowing Experience"; and James L. Hill, "The Anti-Heroic Hero in Frank Yerby's Historical Novels," in *Perspectives of Black Popular Culture*, ed. Harry B. Shaw (Bowling Green, Ohio: Bowling Green State University Popular Press, 1990), 144–54.

6. James Weldon Johnson, letter to Frank Yerby, in James Weldon Johnson Collection, Collection of American Literature, Beinecke Rare Book and Manuscript Library, Yale University, New Haven, Conn. (November 3, 1933).

7. The poems Yerby published include "Miracles," *Challenge* 1.27 (September 1934); "Brevity," *Challenge* 1.27 (September 1934); "To a Seagull," *Challenge* 1.15 (May 1935); "Drought," *Challenge* 1.15 (May 1935); "Three Sonnets: Beginning, Ending, and Afterthought," *Challenge* 1.11 (January 1936); "Weltschmerz," *Shards* 4.20 (Spring 1936); "Calm after Storm," *Shards* 4.20 (Spring 1936); "Wisdom," *Arts Quarterly* 1.34 (July–September 1937); "All I Have Known," *The Fisk Herald* (November 1937); "You Are a Part of Me," *The Fisk Herald* (December 1937); "Bitter Lotus," *The Fisk Herald* (December 1937); "The Fishes and the Poet's Hands," *The Fisk Herald* (January 1938).

8. West, "Dear Reader," 39.

9. James Weldon Johnson, "Foreword," *Challenge* (March 1934): quotation on 2.

10. Charles S. Johnson, Alain Locke, and other black critics had noticed this wave. In *Challenge*'s inaugural issue, Dorothy West excerpted a letter from Charles S. Johnson about this shift: "From Charles S. Johnson at Fisk comes, 'The current here, as generally, seems to be more in the direction of prose than poetry. . . . There will be something that I shall want to say on this when I have gotten farther along'" (Dorothy West, "Dear Reader," 39). Locke noticed this shift as early as 1932. See Alain Locke, "We Turn to Prose: A Retrospective Review of the Literature of the Negro for 1931," in Stewart, *The Critical Temper*, 209–13.

11. Yerby's two stories in *The Fisk Herald* include "Young Man Afraid" (October 1937) and "A Date with Vera" (November 1937).

12. These writers are Elfrieda Babney, Alexander Bergman, John Malcolm Brinnin, Julius Butwin, Alvin Foote, David Greenhood, Richard Greenleaf, Raphael Hayes, Ruth Lechlitner, Leonard McCarthy, Lawrence O'Fallon, and W. C. Williams.

13. Yerby, "The Thunder of God," *The New Anvil* (April–May 1939): quotation on 7.

14. "Notes on the Contributors," *The New Anvil* (April–May 1939): 29.

15. Aside from "Health Card," *Harper's* 188 (May 1944): 548–53, Yerby published "White Magnolias," *Phylon* 5 (Fourth Quarter 1944): 319–26; "Roads Going Down," *Common Ground* 5 (Summer 1945): 67–72; "My Brother Went to College," *Tomorrow* 5 (January 1946): 9–12; and "The Homecoming," *Common Ground* 6 (Spring 1946): 41–47.

16. Yerby, "Health Card," 549.

17. Ibid., 552–53.

18. John S. Cousins, letter to Frank Yerby, in James Weldon Johnson Collection, Collection of American Literature, Beinecke Rare Book and Manuscript Library, Yale University, New Haven, Conn. (May 14, 1944).

19. Frank Yerby, letter to Mr. Cousins, in ibid. (June 11, 1944).

20. Frank Yerby, letter to Mr. Cousins, in James Weldon Johnson Collection, Collection of American Literature, Beinecke Rare Book and Manuscript Library, Yale University, New Haven, Conn. (May 14, 1944).

21. Frank Yerby, letter to Muriel Fuller, in Special Collections, Temple University Library, Philadelphia (July 22, 1943).

22. Muriel Fuller, letter to Mr. Aswell, in ibid. (December 1, 1943).

23. For more information about Moon, see Muriel Fuller, letter to Frank Yerby in Special Collections, Temple University Library, Philadelphia (September 27, 1943); and Yerby, letters to Muriel Fuller in Special Collections, Temple University Library, Philadelphia (October 12, 1943; October 23, 1943; November 25, 1943).

24. For Muriel Fuller's influence, see Muriel Fuller, letters to Frank Yerby, in ibid. (February 27, 1944; March 8, 1944).

25. Edward Aswell, letter to Frank Yerby, in Special Collections, Temple University Library, Philadelphia (December 28, 1943).

26. Muriel Fuller, letter to Frank Yerby, in ibid. (November 29, 1943).

27. Yerby, letter to Fuller (December 1943).

28. Frank Yerby, letter to Muriel Fuller, in ibid. (December 1943).

29. Ibid.

30. Edward Aswell, letter to Frank Yerby, in Special Collections, Temple University Library, Philadelphia (March 23, 1944).

31. Frank Yerby, letter to Muriel Fuller, in ibid. (November 25, 1943).

32. Frank Yerby, letter to Muriel Fuller, in ibid. (March 25, 1944).

33. Yerby took major rejections of his work very personally; at times, he considered giving up literary writing. See Flora Yerby, letter to Muriel Fuller, in ibid. (September 28, 1943).

34. Frank Yerby, *The Foxes of Harrow* (New York: Dial Press, 1946). All references to the page numbers of this novel appear parenthetically in the main text.

35. For more information about these novels, see Earl F. Bargainnier, "Yerby, Frank (Garvin)," in *Twentieth-century Romance and Historical Writers*, ed. Aruna Vasudevan and Lesley Henderson (London: St. James Press, 1994), 741–42, on 742; and Glasrud and Champion, "'The Fishes and the Poet's Hands.'"

36. Jones, *Strange Talk*, 116.

37. For Stephen's interchanging of "Creole" and Frenchman, see Yerby, *The Foxes of Harrow*, 23–24, 68; for "hauteur," see 28; for generational and ideological conflict, see 31; for societal conflict, see 35. For the darkness of Creoles, see 31, 125; for Andre's rebuke of the discourteous stranger, see 140.

38. Jones, *Strange Talk*, 116.

39. The chronology at the outset of *The Foxes of Harrow* is not all that clear. We know that Stephen Fox was born in 1800 and the house on Harrow built by 1827 (Yerby, *The Foxes of Harrow*, 118). I reason that Stephen probably did not begin to build the property until around 1825.

40. For examples of Stephen's ability to distinguish between ethnicities of the African diaspora, see Yerby, *The Foxes of Harrow*, 62–63, 78.

41. For examples of Stephen wrestling with the idea of holding slaves, see ibid., 333–39, 450. Indeed, given that Stephen has already established Harrow and Yerby has not yet deepened the characterization of his family, *The Foxes of Harrow* could very easily have come to a close within the next one hundred pages, before Stephen's son, Etienne, returns from his schooling in France between 1850 and 1853. *The Foxes of Harrow* is thus two novels in one.

42. For examples of Stephen's discussions about slaveholding states, see ibid., 229; slavery, 331; abolitionism, 447; racial-political problems in New Orleans, 340–41; na-

tional racial politics, 490; the Civil War, 486; secession, 492; the impact of the Civil War on New Orleans, 494.

43. See "Masses, not 'Intellectuals,' Support Harlem's Book Stores, Survey Shows," *The Pittsburgh Courier* (April 20, 1946).

44. See "America's Top Negro Authors," *Color* (June 1949): 28–30.

45. C. L. R. James, *American Civilization*, ed. Anna Grimshaw and Keith Hart (Cambridge, Mass.: Blackwell, 1993), 211.

46. Ibid., 118, 129.

47. See Frank Yerby, "How and Why I Write the Costume Novel," *Harper's* 219 (October 1959): 145–50.

48. James, *American Civilization*, 119.

49. For paradigmatic quotations, see the years 1946 (914), 1947 (998), 1948 (950), and 1949 (1018) of the serial reference, *Book Review Digest* (Bronx, N.Y.: H. W. Wilson). However, there also exist reviews stating that Yerby's novels were very good and that *Pride's Castle* was the best one to date.

50. Frank Yerby, quoted in Jeffrey D. Parker, "Frank Yerby," in *Afro-American Writers, 1940–1955*, ed. Trudier Harris and Thadious M. Davis (Detroit, Mich.: Gale Research, 1988), 222–31, quotation on 227.

51. Walter Nash, quoted in Scott McCracken, *Pulp*, 10.

52. Yerby, "How and Why," 145–46.

53. Ibid., 146.

54. Ibid., 148–49.

55. Only two other of his novels treat black-racial themes: his twenty-fourth, *The Dahomean: A Historical Novel* (1971); and his thirtieth, *A Darkness at Ingraham's Crest: A Tale of the Slaveholding South* (1979).

Chapter 7

1. Amiri Baraka (LeRoi Jones), "The Black Aesthetic," *Negro Digest* (June 1969): quotation on 5.

2. Harper, *Are We Not Men?* 49.

3. See Jerry Gafio Watts, *Amiri Baraka: The Politics and Art of a Black Intellectual* (New York: New York University Press, 2001), 57–59, 115–16, 439–41, for Baraka's alterations to his theories of African American literature and culture in general. I say "his" because only Amiri Baraka signed his name to the introduction, presumably claiming it as his own written work, not necessarily the joint expression of him and his wife.

4. The most notable writers in the anthology include Maya Angelou, Toni Cade Bambara, Gwendolyn Brooks, Lucille Clifton, Mari Evans, Gayl Jones, June Jordan, Audre Lorde, Paule Marshall, Toni Morrison, Sonia Sanchez, Alice Walker, Margaret Walker, and Sherley Anne Williams.

5. I would submit that Gates's notion of pretext resembles Gérard Genette's notion of "paratexts," which I discuss in the Introduction. See Genette, *Paratexts*, 1.

6. David L. Smith, "The Black Arts Movement and Its Critics," *American Literary History* 3.1 (Spring 1991): 93–110, quotations on 93, 102.

7. For the best discussion of the role of *Negro Digest* (which later became *Black World*) during the Black Arts Movement, see Julius E. Thompson, "A Literary and Critical Analysis of the Role of Hoyt W. Fuller (1927–1981), *Negro Digest* and *Black World Magazine*, during the Black Arts Movement, 1960–1976," in *African American Sociology: A Social Study of the Pan-African Diaspora*, ed. James L. Conyers and Alva P. Barnett (Chicago: Nelson-Hall, 1999), 240–61; and James C. Hall, "On Sale at Your Favorite Newsstand:

Negro Digest/Black World and the 1960s," in *The Black Press: New Literary and Historical Essays*, ed. Todd Vogel (New Brunswick, N.J.: Rutgers University Press, 2001), 188–206. The other contemporaneous periodicals cited or reprinted from in these edited collections include *African Forum, The Crisis, Freedomways, The Journal of Human Relations, Journal of Negro Education, The Journal of Negro History, Liberator Magazine, Negro History Bulletin, Onyx Magazine, Phylon, Rights and Reviews,* and *Umbra.*

8. For these topics, see essays by Addison Gayle Jr., Julian Mayfield, Hoyt Fuller, and James A. Emanuel in Addison Gayle Jr., ed., *Black Expression* (New York: Weybright and Talley, 1969). Also see essays by Gayle, Emanuel, Ron Karenga, Fuller, and Darwin Turner in Addison Gayle Jr., ed., *The Black Aesthetic* (Garden City, N.Y.: Doubleday, 1971).

9. For the problems with white mainstream publishers and commercialism, see essays by Addison Gayle Jr., Sarah Webster Fabio, Julian Mayfield, LeRoi Jones, and Hoyt Fuller in Gayle, *Black Expression.*

10. Addison Gayle Jr., "Cultural Strangulation: Black Literature and the White Aesthetic," in ibid., 38–45, quotation on 44.

11. Addison Gayle Jr., "The Function of Black Literature at the Present Time," in ibid., 383–94, quotation on 385.

12. Addison Gayle Jr., "Preface," in Gayle, *Black Expression,* xiii.

13. For instance, the poetic language of Melvin Tolson was not "authentically 'Negro.'" Rather, it was a parody of "the pseudo neo-classical Anglo-American diction" (Sarah Webster Fabio, "Who Speaks Negro?," in ibid., 115–19, quotation on 115). "Countless writers foundered and failed in an effort to please the critics—and, of course, the publishers—by shielding their work from the abrasiveness that critics describe as 'protest'" (Hoyt A. Fuller, "The New Black Literature: Protest or Affirmation," in Gayle, *The Black Aesthetic,* 327–48, quotation on 336–37). These writers succumbed to the desire to write about what was "universal" so that (white) readers could identify with the subject matter (John Oliver Killens, "The Black Writer vis-à-vis His Country," in *The Black Aesthetic,* 357–73, quotation on 358). Proponents of the Black Aesthetic warned black critics to avoid perpetuating such truancy in the age of the Black Arts Movement.

14. LeRoi Jones, "The Myth of a 'Negro Literature,'" in *Home: Social Essays* (New York: William Morrow, 1966), 105–15, quotation on 108.

15. Ibid.

16. Ibid., 109, 112.

17. Imamu Amiri Baraka, "Introduction," in *Confirmation: An Anthology of Africanamerican Women,* ed. Imamu Amiri Baraka and Amina Baraka (New York: Morrow, 1983), 15–26, quotation on 21.

18. Ibid., 15.

19. See Robert L. Harris Jr., "The Intellectual and Institutional Development of Africana Studies," in *The Black Studies Reader,* ed. Jacqueline Bobo, Cynthia Hudley, and Claudine Michel (New York: Routledge, 2004), 15–20; and Johnnetta B. Cole, "Black Studies in Liberal Arts Education," in ibid., 21–34.

20. Baraka, "Introduction," 19.

21. Dubey, *Black Women Novelists and the Nationalist Aesthetic* (Bloomington: Indiana University Press, 1994), 13.

22. Ibid., 1–13, 19. Dubey elaborates this point and surveys scholarship that examines the masculinity of the Black Arts Movement.

23. Dubey, *Black Women Novelists,* 13.

24. Henry Louis Gates Jr., "Black Creativity: On the Cutting Edge," *Time Magazine* (October 10, 1994): quotations on 74–75.

25. Tate, *Domestic Allegories*, 8, 234n22.

26. Ibid., 128–34.

27. Ross, *Manning the Race*, 3.

28. Henry Louis Gates Jr., "Preface to Blackness: Text and Pretext," in *Afro-American Literature: The Reconstruction of Instruction*, ed. Dexter Fisher and Robert B. Stepto (New York: Modern Language Association, 1979), 47–48, 49, 50, 54, 66.

29. Harriet E. Wilson, *Our Nig, or, Sketches from the Life of a Free Black, in a Two-Story White House, North, Showing That Slavery's Shadows Fall Even There*, 2nd ed. (New York: Vintage Books, 1983); Hannah Crafts, *The Bondwoman's Narrative* (New York: Warner Books, 2002); Henry Louis Gates Jr., "Phillis Wheatley on Trial," *The New Yorker* (January 30, 2003), appears in expanded form as *The Trials of Phillis Wheatley: America's First Black Poet and Her Encounters with the Founding Fathers* (New York: Civitas, 2003).

30. Friedrich Schleiermacher, "Hermeneutics," *The Norton Anthology of Theory and Criticism*, ed. Vincent B. Leitch (New York: Norton, 2001), 613–25, on 623.

31. Ibid., 622.

32. Wallace Martin, "The Hermeneutic Circle and the Art of Interpretation," *Comparative Literature* 24.2 (Spring 1972): 97–117, quotation on 97.

33. Ibid., 114, 115.

34. Dubey, *Black Women Novelists*, 7, 55.

35. Dubey, *Signs and Cities*, 47.

36. Toni Morrison, "Recitatif," in Baraka and Baraka, *Confirmation*, 243–61. All references to this story's page numbers will appear in parenthesis in the main text.

37. For an exploration of the racial possibilities, see Elizabeth Abel, "Black Writing, White Reading: Race and the Politics of Feminist Interpretation," *Critical Inquiry* 19 (Spring 1993): 470–98, quotations on 472–75.

38. Ibid., 476.

39. Kathryn Nicol, "Visible Differences: Viewing Racial Identity in Toni Morrison's *Paradise* and 'Recitatif'," in *Literature and Racial Ambiguity*, ed. Teresa Hubel and Neil Brooks (Amsterdam, Netherlands: Rodopi, 2002), 209–31, quotation on 222.

40. Toni Morrison, *Playing in the Dark: Whiteness and the Literary Imagination* (Cambridge, Mass.: Harvard University Press, 1992), xi.

41. Nina Baym, ed., *The Norton Anthology of American Literature* (New York: W. W. Norton, 2003), xxi.

42. Morrison, "Unspeakable Things Unspoken," 19.

43. Toni Morrison, "Home," in *The House That Race Built: Black Americans, U.S. Terrain*, ed. Wahneema H. Lubiano (New York: Pantheon Books, 1997), 3–12, quotation on 3.

Index

academy: black and white scholars in, 170; Tanner and black painters in, 86–87. *See also* Locke, Alain; Tanner, Henry Ossawa

aesthetics: and anomalies, 21; and literary realism, 33, 36, 44, 62; and literary value, 2, 23, 48, 168; and racial realism, 7–8, 23, 82, 102, 117, 122, 140, 171, 175–76

African American literature: anomalies of, 10–14; and classification of, 2–7; and definition of, 1; and racial realism of, 1–2, 7–10; and theoretical history of, 14–17

African American studies, 5–6

African diaspora, Alain Locke on, 76–77, 80–82

Americanism, 24, 96, 98–99, 105, 107, 135–36, 170, 186

Anglo-American literature: black characters in, 9–10; and the Harlem Renaissance, 77–80; and the plantation tradition of, 36–37, 51; and the racial characterology of, 16

anomalies: in African American literature, 10–14; in taxonomy, 10–11, 16–17. *See also* aesthetics

anthology, and canon formation, 6–7, 173–74, 185–86

assimilation: and racial uplift, 53, 56–58; George Schuyler on, 96–97, 114

authenticity, racial, 11. *See also* African American literature; Dunbar, Paul Laurence

Azoulay, Katya Gibel, 4, 17

Baldwin, James, 117, 133, 135–36, 172; and *Giovanni's Room*, 26–27

Baraka, Amiri, 14, 17, 24, 167–74; and the Black Aesthetic, 1–2, 167–74; and *Confirmation*, 23–24

Black Aesthetic, 1, 167, 169–74, 177, 185. *See also* Black Arts Movement

Black Arts Movement: and the Black Aesthetic, 169–72; gender politics of, 25, 173–74; racial nationalism in, 76. *See also* Black Aesthetic

Braithwaite, William Stanley, 50, 80

Brown, Sterling, 72, 75–76, 119, 126, 135

Burns, Robert, 45, 47. *See also* Dunbar, Paul Laurence

Cable, George Washington, 29, 57, 69, 80

canon: African American, 2, 6, 13, 40, 115, 145, 172; ethnic expansion of, 5; Howells's racial imagination of, 25, 38, 47; and Schuyler's lampblacked Anglo-Saxons, 93, 104–6; and tradition, 15–16. *See also* anthology

Carby, Hazel, 26, 173

Chesnutt, Charles W., 33, 36, 38, 49–50, 104, 172; William Howells's influence over, 18; racial inauthenticity of, 39–40, 47. *See also* Howells, William

color: as the basis for human classification, 76, 80, 96–97, 99–101, 107–15; as the basis for judging books, 2–5, 30–32, 38–42, 44, 141, 152; and its significance to Creoles, 153–55. *See also* authenticity

Connerly, Ward, literary-racial profiling, 2–3. *See also* color

Crane, Stephen, 33, 36, 62; and *Maggie*, 32, 64; and *The Red Badge of Courage*, 32

creole, 153–55

Cullen, Countée, 87, 121, 140, 146

dialect: in African American literature, 38–39, 56–57; in Anglo-American literature, 44–45; in Paul Laurence Dunbar's poetry, 17–18, 31–32, 40, 44–48, 75–76; in Dunbar's *The Uncalled*, 59–60; and

Acknowledgments

Of course, more people than those I mention below inspired me as I wrote this book. To anyone I may have forgotten, please accept my apology and my sincere thanks for your help.

While conceiving this book, I sought the opinion and advice of Claudia Tate. She advised me to "historicize the anomaly" in order to answer some of the questions about African American literary theory, history, canons, and traditions that vexed me. Her advice arrived right on time, along with her wonderful book, *Psychoanalysis and Black Novels: Desire and the Protocols of Race* (1998). Needless to say, the rest is history. Her passing away before I completed this book, could show it to her, and could thank her personally saddens me no end. Thus, I partially dedicate this book to the memory of Claudia Tate, an excellent scholar of African American literature.

The intelligence, tact, and faith of Jerry Singerman, humanities editor at the University of Pennsylvania Press, guided me and this book along the bumpy road toward publication. The leadership and vision of Henry Louis "Skip" Gates Jr. have influenced me beyond words. Indeed, I cannot imagine what this book and my other scholarly work would have looked like if Skip and I had never begun working together on an anthology of New Negro criticism, and if I had never witnessed firsthand his sagacity, talent, and work ethic.

I thank the following people for commenting on, or helping me with the revision of, earlier drafts: Nancy Armstrong, Rene Ater, Jonathan Auerbach, Jackson Bryer, James T. Campbell, Kandice Chuh, Madhu Dubey, Michele Elam, Verlyn Flieger, Philip Gould, Meta Jones, Eileen Julien, Daniel Kim, Ronald Lear, Robert S. Levine, Carla L. Peterson, Sangeeta Ray, Werner Sollors, James Smethurst, Leonard Tennenhouse, Jeffrey Allen Tucker, Mary Helen Washington, Daryle Williams, and Thomas Wortham.

A fellowship at the David C. Driskell Center for the Study of the African Diaspora at the University of Maryland, College Park, and a Career Enhancement fellowship awarded by the Woodrow Wilson Foundation enabled me to write sections of this book at crucial junctures. The librarians and resources at Brown University, Columbia University, Harvard University, Howard University, the Library of Congress, Princeton University, Temple University, the University of Maryland, and Yale University assisted me at important stages of my research.

Finally, I must thank my dearest friends and family for their love and support outside of the academy. Jerry and Celeste Bloomfield, Joseph and Onyi Freeman, and Matthew and Liza Jones always remind me about the fun things in life. The Jarrett and Boynton families always replenish me whenever I find academic work draining. The wisdom of my father, Eustace Jarrett, has almost always alerted me to potential pitfalls in my life and work. I thank him for always having faith in me.

Last but not least, I must thank my immediate family, to whom I also partially dedicate this book. Even more than I did, my wife, Renée, always believed that somebody would publish this book someday, somewhere. I am forever grateful for the support, care, and understanding she showed when I needed them most. And my toddling daughter, Nyla, is the perfect blend of joviality and unpredictability to keep me looking forward to what tomorrow brings.

Sections of some of the chapters have previously appeared in slightly revised form.

Part of the Introduction appeared in "Introduction: African American Noms de Plume," in the January 2006 issue of *PMLA*. Reprinted by permission of the copyright owner, The Modern Language Association of America.

Another part of the Introduction appeared in "Introduction: 'Not Necessarily Race Matter,'" in *African American Literature beyond Race* (New York University Press, 2006). Reprinted by permission of the copyright owner, New York University Press.

Sections of Chapter 1 appeared in "'Entirely *Black* Verse from Him Would Succeed': Minstrel Realism and William Dean Howells," in the March 2005 issue of *Nineteenth-Century Literature*. Reprinted by permission of the copyright owner, the University of California Press.

Sections of Chapter 2 appeared in "'We Must Write Like the White Men': Race, Realism, and Dunbar's Anomalous First Novel," in the summer 2004 issue of *Novel: A Forum on Fiction*. Reprinted by permission of the copyright owner, the Novel Corporation of Brown University.

Part of Chapter 6 appeared in "'For Endless Generations': Myth, Dynasty, and Frank Yerby's *The Foxes of Harrow*," in the December 2006 issue of *Southern Literary Journal*. Reprinted by permission of the copyright owner, the *Southern Literary Journal* and the University of North Carolina at Chapel Hill Department of English.

Part of Chapter 7 appeared in "The Black Arts Movement and Its Scholars," in the December 2005 issue of *American Quarterly*. Reprinted by permission of the copyright owner, the Johns Hopkins University Press.